On June 15, 1938, Lawry's, The Prime Rib, opened its doors and simultaneously created a sensation in restaurant circles. The idea of serving only one entree was unheard-of. While bold and original, the idea was sound — as the intervening years have shown. Along with the tradition-shattering concept of highest-possible specialization, other factors contributed to Lawry's renown. Lawry's was first to feature a green salad as an integral part of every meal—now an accepted service among better restaurants comparable to serving potatoes with meat. The spinning salad bowl, an innovation, has been copied widely. Lawry's Seasoned Salt was introduced here to be served with prime ribs, and the acclaim it received swept it to use in homes all over America. Other Lawry products followed, making Lawry's a household word indicative of fine quality foods. In a comprehensive survey of restaurant popularity conducted by a magazine, Lawry's ranked first in the West, seventh in the United States. Lawry's received the honored "Top Award of Merit" at a national restaurant convention, and other honors have come to Lawry's in recognition of superlative quality, excellent service, and highest standards of sanitation. Lawry's are especially proud of their personnel whose gracious smiling service has been widely acclaimed.

OLD ENGLISH COOKERY Following an old Yorkshire method, the prime ribs are placed in huge pans, then covered with a thick layer of highly refined rock salt. The heat, passing through the crystals, diffuses and is distributed evenly and thoroughly through the prime ribs. By this method, the rich beef juices are retained.

COFFEE, FRESHLY GROUND By brewing immediately after grinding, the coffee's natural oils are retained, assuring a beverage with a delicious mellow flavor. Fresh coffee is brewed every 30 minutes. The blend, created especially to conform to the Lawry meal, achieves a marked degree of smoothness. Sounding of a gong, denotes completion of fresh coffee.

KOWLOON has bee... on the mainland, across from the British island of Hong Kong, streamed the masses of... did the hard work at the gold mines, who later worked on the first transcontinental railroad, who founded San Francisco's famous Chinatown over a hundred years ago. They brought with them their arts, their customs, their food, all the paraphernalia of their ancient culture.

NEVER did they forget the wonderful food of Canton, north of Kowloon. Cantonese food, in China, is the fare of the gourmet, the food for celebrations. As an Occidental looks to Paris for fine foods, fine living, so does the Oriental look to Canton. Cooks have been ennobled for the invention of a single dish. Treasured recipes have been the foundations of family fortunes through generations. The Mings, the Mongols, the Manchus may have conquered the South Chinese, but each of them in turn was conquered by their cookery, and adopted it as his own.

MARCO POLO encountered noodles, macaroni, raviolis at the Court of Kublai Khan. He brought them back to Italy and changed the eating tastes of the whole Western World. Catherine De Medici went from Florence to become Queen of France, and started the Frenchmen on the road to proper cookery. China began it all. Columbus found a new world in a search for the Spices of the East. The Suez Canal was built to aid the spice trade. Small wonder that the food of Canton became one of the marvels of mankind.

WHEN your host, George Lim, came to the United States from Kowloon, his cherished memories were of the magnificent foods served on great family occasions. He resolved to become a cook himself. He worked in every sort of restaurant, American, Chinese, French. He became adept at a dozen different forms of cooking, but always, his ideal remained unattained.

IN 1946, he was operating, of all things, a successful French restaurant in downtown Los Angeles, when suddenly, one day, he found everything around him inadequate. He sold the place abruptly, and sailed, alone, for China. He found the city of Canton strangely changed. Unrest in China, the war, had driven its wealthy folk away. Its world famous restaurants were closed. But the gourmets, and the chefs who served them, had not gone far. He found them in his native city of Kowloon, and on Hong Kong Island, living sumptuously under the protection of the British flag.

FOR months, he sought the greatest chef in Kowloon, who ranked as the finest in all South China. Then he made him a proposition. He offered him $800, U. S., for the privilege of becoming his apprentice, of working with him and learning all the secrets of his culinary arts, of all his sauces, for two whole years.

THE CHEF thought him mad, but he knew a good offer when he heard one. He took him on. Old Mme. Lim found George a wife, to keep him busy and contented, and he went to work. By 1949, the chef admitted George was now his equal, and would he please pay up? He did. The chef immediately retired. $1, U. S., is worth $5, Hong Kong. The chef was now a tycoon, and he never cooked again. Kowloon still holds a grudge against George Lim for losing them their greatest cook!

LIM left his family in China, and came back to Los Angeles. In partnership with genial Joe Ho, who himself looks much like the Chinese Kitchen God, smiling and round and amiable, he started a little Chinese restaurant, the KOWLOON. George built the rock work in the bar with his own hands, installed the fountains, planted the gardens. Together, they hammered and painted and sawed. Then, when the doors were open, Lim sent for his family, and went to work to cook.

NEWSPAPERMEN found the KOWLOON first. Gourmets who had eaten everywhere on earth, they flocked to revel in the perfect Cantonese cuisine. Words being their stock in trade, they talked, they wrote, and others came in droves.

Once upon a time ....

CAROLINA PINES was but a quaint and tiny mite of the Deep South transplanted, when first it came to Los Angeles in 1923 with its darky help and Southern Cookery. Today in its own spacious Colonial home, Carolina Pines endeavors always to welcome as warmly as ever its many friends and guests with the same sincere hospitality for which the South is famed—and to serve graciously a Cuisine unexcelled in deliciousness and abundance.

MANY a true lover of fine food has brought parties of friends to Carolina Pines because, they say, "There's something about real Southern cookery that makes you want to eat!" Would you like to share with us just a few of our treasured secrets for the appetizing savoriness of our food . . . .

DO you know that our Southern-Baked ham is especially cured for us—to protect its juicy tenderness?

AND that the tasty crispness and rich tantalizing flavor of our tender fried chicken is due in part to the special feeding of our fowl?

AND that Carolina Pines' Prime Ribs come from the choicest quality of Eastern steer beef?

AND that only creamy pure butter and whole pasteurized milk are used in any of Carolina Pines' food?

AND that a special broiler cooks your steaks and chops to the point of perfection because flames at top and bottom are lighted at the same time to prevent parching and to preserve the luscious juicyness?

AND that, last but not least—the delectable desserts for which we've earned repute are skillfully concocted in our own pastry room by the same two bakers who created these recipes for us when Carolina Pines opened years ago! Three especially popular favorites are their Butterscotch Tarts, Apricot Fluff, and their French Crumb Apple Pie topped with a lush scoop of whipped cream.

THOSE who serve you at Carolina Pines have been here for many years and feel a personal interest in seeing that your appetites are completely gratified and that you enjoy to the full the leisurely, friendly atmosphere of the Old South. We hope to see you here at Carolina Pines very soon again.

San Diego, California's magnificent 1,400 acre Balboa Park.

California Poppy
(Eschscholtzia californica)
State flower and best known of all California wild flowers. Blossoms are two to three inches in diameter, deep golden yellow. Plants grow about a foot high. Blooms February to June.

THE name "California" was taken from Ordonez de Montalvo's romance of chivalry, *Las Sergas de Esplandian* (Madrid, 1510), in which is told of black Amazons ruling an island of this name "to the right of the Indies, very near the quarter of the terrestrial paradise."

Perhaps the charm of our California lies in the fact that it means many things to many people. Here are orange groves and mountains; flowered valleys and desert lands; historic missions and Movieland; the sparkling waters of a great sea and virgin forests with mighty trees older than any other living thing; then of course there is metropolitan city life for those who prefer that.

Contrasts? Yes, fascinating, never ending contrasts. There are even places where one may actually look from sea to desert and from snow to orange groves simply by turning his head!

The Los Angeles Limited, with the California Poppy (state flower) as its motif, gives the traveler a *foretaste* and *aftertaste* of the atmosphere and charm of California. It, too, means many things to many people, and not the least of these is COMFORT.

WE BOAST OF THE FINEST COLLECTION OF CHINESE CARVINGS IN THE UNITED STATES

ENTRANCE
Many of the carvings on the front of our building are real museum pieces.

THE BUDDHA SHRINE
One of the very few teakwood, gold covered, hand carved pieces of the fourteenth century in perfect condition, this shrine is a work of grace and beauty. Reflecting through the hundreds of years of its existence, is there any wonder why it is a favorite place of worship?

RARE OLD CHINESE CABINET
This rare old Chinese cabinet is the source of much comment and expression of enjoyment, as there is not another one like it in the whole world. It is finished in pure gold and red lacquer.

VIEW OF DINING ROOM
This room contains many fine examples of Chinese carvings and other art. The screen in the center is beautifully carved teakwood, ivory and pearl. The cabinet on the right is also of teakwood in an elaborate arrangement of intertwined dragons with insets of ivory. In the left foreground is a twelfth century teakwood and gold leaf statue of the goddess Quan Yin in a devotional attitude. This is the goddess who brings eternal good fortune to all who pay homage.

CHINESE GRIFFON
This centuries old teakwood dragon was also owned by Mary Pickford and is one of the very few teakwood carvings of this fabulous creature in the world. The framed archway surrounding the Griffon is of a very rare design in Chinese art carving.

THE BUDDHA THRONE HEAD PIECE
Here is an excellent example of the patience and dexterity of the Chinese Wood Carvers of the sixteenth century. This altar piece is carved of teakwood and inlaid with twenty four carat gold. It is seven feet tall and eight feet wide, weight approximately two hundred pounds.

MAIN BAR
The finest carved Chinese backbar in the United States is hardly sufficient in describing the splendor and exquisite detail of this masterpiece of the thirteenth century. It was originally a devotional shrine and a familiar and sacred figure in the ancient times.

COCKTAIL LOUNGE BACKBAR
Here is the largest piece of teakwood furniture in the United States. Exquisitely carved by one of the foremost artists of China and formerly owned by Mary Pickford, we are most fortunate to possess this fine piece.

Inglewood . . .
"THE HARBOR OF THE AIR"

Inglewood, Harbor of the Air is a progressive, growing city, about seven miles southwest of Los Angeles. During the war it became one of the most important aircraft centers in the west. Today it is a city of small, clean industries having within its city limits more than 112 industrial plants.

But Inglewood is first of all a city of home owners. It is estimated that seventy per cent of its residents own their own homes. It is an ideal place in which to live as the winter climate is mild and temperate and being only six miles from the Pacific Ocean the summers are several degrees cooler than inland cities.

Inglewood has seven elementary schools and one intermediate school. In 1945-46, 3930 pupils were enrolled and there were 128 teachers. There are two private nursery schools, one private school and six church schools.

The Centinela Valley Union High School District has an estimated population of 65,000 people with an area of 21.75 square miles and serves the Hawthorne, Inglewood, Lennox, Lawndale and Wiseburn elementary school districts.

El Camino Junior College, to be located at Alondra Park, is already teaching 500 students. Classes are being held in three of the high schools in the district.

Hollywood Park Turf Club is located in Inglewood at Prairie Avenue and Century Boulevard. The 320 acre plant which represents an investment of $3,500,000.00 attracted a total attendance of 1,572,005 people in 1946. Stable accomodations are provided for 1600 horses. The infield is the most beautiful in the country with its landscaped acres, including 6 lakes, a wide water course and many thousands of flowers and semi-tropical shrubs. Grandstand, Clubhouse and Turf Club will accommodate approximately 15,000 persons, while wide ramps provide comfortable spectator space for another 50,000. Parking space is available for 22,000 automobiles.

Centinela Park, covering 60 acres, is an ideal recreation center with its beautiful grounds, outdoor amphitheatre, tennis courts and swimming pool.

Los Angeles Airport is located just southwest of Inglewood. It is now operating on limited facilities, but when completed, it is estimated a plane will take off or land every thirty seconds. Plans are now being completed for a freeway from downtown Los Angeles to the Airport.

Inglewood Chamber of Commerce is celebrating its Silver Anniversary in 1947; its slogan "A Quarter-Century of Civic Service." Its officers and directors have dedicated themselves to carry on the aggressive campaign started 25 years ago to continue to build a better Inglewood.

LORD PRINTING CO., L.A.

---

yes . . . we're very happy you came!

We're also gratified . . . and complimented. Happy, because preparing the very finest food for you and serving it with thoughtfulness and good cheer is what we most like to do. Gratified, yes, because you are giving us the opportunity to serve you and prove our philosophy that good food, cleanliness and friendly hospitality can travel hand in hand. Complimented, because you have chosen Bob's in your quest for good things to eat. Fulfilling this quest is our purpose and our opportunity to contribute to this part of our great American standard of living. May I assure you that we will do everything possible, as we have since the opening of our first place in 1936, to make you feel "glad that you came to Bob's."

Cordially yours,

Bob Wian

Robert C. "Bob" Wian

IN ADDITION . . .
You may enjoy these specialties at home, made from Bob's own recipes.

Bob's Frozen Chili & Beans
(2 Boil-In-Pouches) 69
Bob's Yummy Boy Doughnuts
(1 doz.) 70

Bob's Famous Salad Dressings and Sauces

Tomato 'N Spice Cream French 39
Shrimp & Cocktail Sauce 39
Tartar Sauce 39
Garlic-'N-Oil Italian Style 39
1000 Island 39
Hamburger & Steak Relish ... 39
Bleu Cheese 49
Seasoning Salt 29

You may purchase these quality foods at good grocers everywhere.

"Hall Of Fame" Plaque Awarded Us By American Restaurant Magazine

IN CALIFORNIA . . .

GLENDALE
BURBANK
PASADENA
VAN NUYS
MISSION HILLS
NO. HOLLYWOOD
EAGLE ROCK
WHITTIER
GARDEN GROVE
WEST COVINA
COSTA MESA
LAKEWOOD
LONG BEACH

TORRANCE
CANOGA PARK
INGLEWOOD
ALHAMBRA
FRESNO
SAN JOSE
CULVER CITY
BUENA PARK
DOWNEY
PANORAMA CITY
CHULA VISTA
SANTA CLARA
ANAHEIM
SAN DIEGO

IN ARIZONA

PHOENIX
MESA
TUCSON
SCOTTSDALE
CHANDLER

IN NEVADA

LAS VEGAS
RENO

BOB'S BIG BOY INC., A DIVISION OF MARRIOTT CORPORATION
ENTIRE MENU COPYRIGHT 1965

TO
LIVE AND DINE
IN L.A.

MENUS AND THE MAKING
OF THE MODERN CITY

Ambassador Hotel / Afternoon Tea • 3400 Wilshire Blvd., Los Angeles • 1940s

TO LIVE AND DINE IN L.A.

MENUS AND THE MAKING OF THE MODERN CITY

JOSH KUN

FOREWORD BY
ROY CHOI

FROM THE COLLECTION OF THE
LOS ANGELES PUBLIC LIBRARY

It is with great pleasure that the Library Foundation of Los Angeles
recognizes the generosity of the supporters who helped make
the To Live and Dine in L.A. project possible:

Principal Funders:
Dwight and Julie Anderson
Annenberg Foundation
Judith Krantz

Benefactors:
Donna Schweers and Tom Geiser
Judith Selbst Kamins and Kenneth Kamins

Patrons:
Sharon and Michael Kelley/Sidley Austin LLP
Gwen T. Miller

Special Thanks to Michael K. Lindsey

For Yamila,
who became an eater over the course of this book,
and helped me understand just how important the right menu can be

TABLE OF CONTENTS

Home of the nationally famous original doubledeck hamburger

the **BIG BOY**

We are proud of these quality breakfasts • serving ranch-fresh eggs • choice corn fed ham & bacon • golden pancakes made from our own recipe, served with plenty of butter & syrup

FOR YO

Bob's Big Boy blank menu template • 1950s

*Good
Morning*

A LETTER FROM THE CITY LIBRARIAN

Menus are like libraries. They serve as windows to the world and take you places. Every day, over 42,000 people come through the doors of our Central Library and seventy-two branches. They enter looking for books, help with a job search, Internet access, or even assistance in taking the first step on the path to citizenship. And there are some who come simply for the respect they might not receive elsewhere.

In addition to being trusted places of information and learning, our libraries are also engines of economic development, helping people achieve their career goals, start a business, learn a new language, or receive their high school diploma.

One of the many important roles we play is celebrating Los Angeles, its history, the fabulous and complex diversity of its residents, and L.A.'s tremendous contributions to the arts, technology, and culture. With over four million items in our special collections, our Central Library is a nationally recognized research institution. There are photographs, maps, autographs, rare books, movie posters and lobby cards, scripts, sheet music, and even citrus crate labels. Perhaps no collection, though, captures the wonder, whimsy and eclectic spirit of this amazing city more than our menus. This book and the public programs that blossom from it showcase a stunning and historically significant collection that is as notable for its art and interesting dishes as it is for what it reveals about Angelenos and their City.

More than books, our libraries are about empowerment, equity, service, and access. *To Live and Dine in L.A.* is certainly about greater access to an impressive menu collection and the celebration of food and dining in L.A., but it is also about the health of our City—health equity and access to quality, nutritious food. This effort, using our menus as a launching point, also beautifully connects with the work our libraries do to address the biggest issues facing Los Angeles. I hope it will serve as an inspiration for our work with urban gardens, health disparities, nutrition issues that result in many students' "summer slide," and linking L.A.'s marvelously diverse communities together through food.

The menu collection, along with other culinary arts ephemera, was started in the 1980s by librarians Billie Connor-Dominguez and Dan Strehl. My sincerest appreciation and admiration goes to them and our Central Library staff, past and present, as well as the Culinary Historians of Southern California, who have cared for and cultivated this rich collection for decades.

The Library Foundation of Los Angeles and its loyal and generous supporters enthusiastically invest in our innovative programs and have made this project possible. Thank you to Ken Brecher and his talented staff for their strong support and leadership on this effort. And, of course, to Josh Kun who brings this collection to life not only through his words and wisdom, but with his passion for the library's mission.

John F. Szabo
City Librarian
Los Angeles Public Library

PREFACE

It is nearly midnight in Los Angeles, and I am hungry. I know that I have nothing to eat in my little apartment at the top of Douglas Street, just west of downtown. I have been working late, very late, and I feel tired but satisfied. The job is going well, but I have to admit that my social life could improve. I am tired of eating alone, but know I will feel better if I make a hard right at the corner of Beverly and Rampart and pull into Original Tommy's for a chili cheeseburger.

That was me, just out of graduate school and finding my way in a new city. I was living in my first apartment and had a job I loved, but it required a lot of late nights. The stove my parents bought as a housewarming gift sat inert and unused. It comforted my mom to envision me making myself a cup of tea, or hosting friends for brunch on Sunday. Those brunches never happened. Eventually I had to come clean and tell her that "I have been way too busy at work, and anyway this is L.A.—young people eat out. But don't worry because I am discovering all these great little neighborhood restaurants. They are not expensive, and the food comes from all over the world."

As each weekend approached there would be an exchange of messages with new friends: "How about trying this great little dim sum place I heard about?" or "There is an amazing Armenian restaurant in Glendale—you have to taste the stuff they make with quince," or "I know these people who live in Venice, and they took me to a new restaurant where the food is incredible, plus you won't believe who I saw there last week."

As time went on, I began to brave the freeways and could be found in Artesia having my first southern Indian food or in Monterey Park having dishes that were Islamic Chinese and what one might eat along the Silk Road.

As a cultural anthropologist by training, I discovered that going to an Ethiopian restaurant or having a traditional Korean breakfast *juk* (porridge made with rice, pine nuts, sesame, pumpkin, beans, and abalone) in an L.A. strip mall, provided me with an entry point to experiences I had previously associated with international "field work." Restaurants became a part of my journey to understanding the advantages of living in a city like Los Angeles. Just as every culture has its own recipes and rituals associated with food, this city contains many diverse responses to our common search for what feels, looks, and tastes like "home."

To Live and Dine in L.A. is the second in a series of books commissioned by the Library Foundation of Los Angeles and curated by Josh Kun. It may be the first book to explore the long history of restaurants in Los Angeles, and at its heart is a celebration of how a fundamental human need both inspires creativity and defines a city.

Ken Brecher
President
Library Foundation of Los Angeles

FOREWORD

I never really thought about history too much when I was growing up in and around Los Angeles. Life was always in the moment. The town seemed to exude and reinforce that state of being in everything that we did. We moved a lot and even when we weren't moving, I was moving a lot through my car or cruising the streets. It was a city filled with people coming for all kinds of different reasons, whether immigrant dreams or dreams of playing an immigrant in a Hollywood movie. The weather made it only worse, in a good way. Blue skies and warm air would act as cleansers. Each day was a new day, no matter what the day before was like or what would come after. L.A. shit.

We never talk about the good ol' days. We talk about the days to come. We never say that can't be done, we say let's get it done—it's a constant phoenix of a city built on the ashes of people's pasts. A city in the moment, always figuring itself out.

This even guided the way I experienced menus as I ate growing up in this vast wonderland. Menus were never that important—they just belonged to the moment. Many of the meals I ate then, and even today, involve no menu or a very simplified one. I grew up eating at home or in Korean restaurants, taco trucks, burger stands, convenience stores, Chinese and Vietnamese cafés, delis, and coffee shops. The menus were either non-existent, handwritten on cardboard, in pictures, on a small plastic table tent, mutually understood, or sometimes if there was one at all, it never changed.

I remember the times I encountered "real" menus in fancy restaurants and even then, those big sheets of embalmed paper nestled in a heavy book felt more like a museum piece to me. It didn't feel like the city I knew or the life I led. It felt like a relic from a place I never understood, a play in a town of entertainers putting on a show. It felt unreal.

Then I became a chef and started to write my own menus. How I write them comes from my upbringing. I don't challenge conventional wisdom just for the sake of ruffling feathers, but I do write some weird-ass menus. Some of my menus don't even have words, and some are just pictures, and the truck that gave me a second life started with no menu, just tacos and burritos. I just wrote them in the rhythm of how life was being led and what I was feeling, and I trusted if you are here in L.A., you get it. Because we all get it. Because we live it.

When I was first approached about this project, it got me thinking about our city again, but this time, for the first time, in a historical sense. It got me thinking about where I am and what my place is in the context of L.A. food and menus. And it got me thinking about where we are in our city and its opportunities and its disparities with regard to food. It got me thinking about what people were eating and what that said about the times. Were there problems with accessibility and affordability? Were there chefs? What were those chefs saying? Who was eating food in Los Angeles at the turn of the last century and as the century grew?

Then I felt like Christopher Reeve in *Somewhere in Time* (1980) when he touches the pocket watch and goes back to the past. I walked into the rare book vault in the halls of the Los Angeles Central Library, and librarians brought out the menus, and time became an illusion. Los

Angeles had forever changed for me. I finally started to feel the history of our city, but not from an intellectual standpoint—from a visceral one. Every menu I touched brought me to that place. Not only those who ate the food, but those who wrote each menu, their lives, what they were thinking, the printer who printed it, how long it took to deliver it by carriage or foot, the special parties they were written for—especially one that was a special dinner for Albert Einstein.

The more I looked at the menus, the more they told me about the city and how neighborhoods developed. But it was the menus that I couldn't find that started to force me to ask questions about how life really was. I started to think about how the city is now and if those missing menus were a reflection of life just as it is now. Were these menus of the affluent and middle-class? Were the working classes even eating with menus, or were they mostly eating at stands and carts? Were there disparities and access problems just like today? And especially in the early days when many of the menus were from Pasadena and mid-Wilshire, how were the restaurants getting the food? There weren't big stores and delivery trucks and refrigeration—how was the food distributed?

My menus are a story I write every day, and the story is a reflection of my past, but also a keyhole into what I'm going through. For many of us who have a hard time with grammar and structure—like me, a menu is a way to tell you something in our own way, like a song.

So this is our song to you. A book filled with other songs, stories written in menus from the people who built this city in the moment.

I hope you enjoy the pages of this book and find a little bit of yourself and the identity of a city through these guides to what people ate and cooked. I hope you realize that a menu can be a gateway into someone's soul, even if there is no menu at all.

Bon appétit.

Roy Choi aka Papi
Taquero

INTRODUCTION

The first restaurant menus in Los Angeles appear in the 1850s during the city's earliest years as U.S. territory. From then on, nearly every phase of L.A.'s growth has had a menu to go with it: the arrival of the transcontinental railroad, the zeal of booster tourism, the automobile craze, the tag team of Prohibition and the Great Depression, the economic boom of World War II, the social movements and rebellions of the 1960s, the economic chasms of the 1980s. Take your pick, there's a menu out there that captures the spirit of the day and filters the city through the lens of dishes and courses, steaks and salads, illustrations and typefaces, prices and wine lists. As the city has changed, so has both the way we eat and the way we talk about what we eat. Menus and restaurants can help shape our lives—they are mirrors and mementos both. This is the premise of the book that you hold in your hands: menus are keys to understanding a city and its people.

In 1949, the historian Arthur M. Schlesinger explored "food in the making of America," a topic that in decades since has received a bounty of attention from journalists, chefs, and scholars alike, but where do we start with food in the making of Los Angeles, a topic that has yet to inspire a single book of its own? Most national anthologies of food writing and studies of food history barely mention Los Angeles, and for a place that, at least since the 1940s, has been restaurant obsessed, there has yet to be a one-stop volume dedicated to the long, and complicated, historical arc of dining out. As I write, Los Angeles is rightly considered one of the great food capitals of the world, yet we know little, to paraphrase Georg Simmel, of the sociology of the L.A. meal—served everywhere from car wash taquerias (windows tinted while you eat) to five-star outposts of French technique—and even less about how those meals have helped make what we know of as the modern city. The one great exception to this deficit is the extraordinary work of the Southern California Culinary Historians, whose archived lectures are crucial guides to the L.A. food past.

To Live and Dine in L.A. attempts to mend this gap by diving into one of the most valuable and vast pools of local and regional food history that exists: the menu collection of the Los Angeles Public Library. Founded by librarians and maintained by librarians, the menu collection— which features Southern California amidst its nearly nine thousand holdings—begins in 1875 and continues to grow to this day. In fact, in the middle of this project, a significant donation came in: a collection of menus, design templates, business ephemera, and printing hardware from the twentieth century's leading L.A. menu manufacturer, Lord Printing Company (courtesy of Paul Abram, son of Lord lithographer and manufacturing manager Albert Abram). It joins a massive physical and digital archive that includes menus of all stripes: priced restaurant meals, private banquets, Thanksgiving, Christmas, and New Year's Eve specials, newspaper advertisements, and since the 1980s, take-out menus designed to fit around any urban door handle.

There's only a century's slice of this immensity in these pages, focusing primarily on menus from 1875 through the 1980s. A year that looms particularly large over the stories these menus tell is 1965, when new immigrants from Asia, Africa, and the Middle East made L.A. home (riding

Eater's Digest

FAMOUS FROM HOST TO HOST

I Pledge Allegiance to the Fact — That When Better Food Can be Served — That I Will Serve It — and That if It Can be Served for Less, I Will Do So.

EDITOR'S NOTE

This, the Second Edition of the Eater's Digest (the First One Born in 1941) is Published By-What-For and Why, We Don't Know, Except that it Contains some Dog Gone Good Suggestions for Jaded Appetites, and then again maybe I am just a Frustrated Copy Writer.

I have had the Pleasure of Serving Los Angeles Patrons Since 1936 and am Happy to Say, the Wife and I have made a Host of Friends.

If by any Chance there Should Arise any Cause for Complaint as to Food, Service or Price (or Something Else as Trivial) Contact me at once, I will be Found around the Corner at Berliner's or the Downtowner having a Sandwich.

Have you Noticed All those Pastrami Dip Stands that have Sprung up All Around Town, Since 1946.

It may Interest Many of You that the Pastrami Dip Sandwich on French Roll was a Featured Item on My Menu at 8th St. and Hill in 1941 at 20c. (Proof on Request), Also Roast Beef and Roast Tongue Sandwich at 15c — Corned Beef and Cabbage 35c — Pot Roast with Noodles 35c — Ham and Eggs 35c Those were the Good Old Days — or were They?

START THE DAY "BRIGHT"
BREAK YOUR FAST
WITH
BREAKFAST at Nate's

CLUB SPECIALS — 7 A. M. TO 11 A. M.

"EARLY BIRD SPECIAL": Lox and Cheese Spread
Open-Face on Bagel, with Coffee 35

Nate's • downtown Los Angeles • 1953

the wave of the Hart-Cellar Immigration Act), when the Watts uprising woke up the city to its deeply entrenched economic and racial inequalities, and when the whole region subsequently underwent a series of rapid economic and spatial changes that, as UCLA urban geographer Edward Soja has long argued, would forever change the character of the city. These menus are both prophecy and product of that key moment in L.A. history.

America is a dining-out nation, and our research indicates that L.A. has long been one of its top dining-out towns. The Library's collection is a living repository of meals past, an archive of urban eating that tells us about the changing historical role of food in the city, which is to say it tells us about just about everything that food touches: economics, culture, taste, race, politics, architecture, class, design, industry, gender, to name just some of the themes that recur on the pages that follow.

Café Vendome • 6666 Sunset Blvd., Hollywood • 1930s

How do menus express a sense of collective identity—the urban we, the ethnic us, the familiar, the foreign—in an immigrant networked, multi-diaspora city where home-cooking can refer to thousands of different homelands?

In his introduction to the 2012 anthology *The Oxford Companion to Food History*, food historian Jeffrey Pilcher makes a strong case for five themes that should be central to any project dedicated to the complexities and pleasures of food history. Here's his menu: as starters, political history and food policy history plus cultural and culinary change over time; as main courses, food and the shaping of identity and the increasing industrialization of the food system; and for dessert, food's role in determining nutritional health trends and issues. My hope with this project is that all of these themes find their voice in these pages and in the public programming around hunger, food history, and food justice that the book inspires. Less signposts, these are our goal posts, the horizons we've kept aiming toward every step of the way—history, identity, economics, social change, and health—goals that linked my own desires with those of Library Foundation of Los Angeles President Ken Brecher and City Librarian John Szabo, who together have been working to increase the Library's role in raising awareness about health and food issues throughout the city.

When I was first asked to take a look at the Library's extraordinary menu collection, my impulse

The Biltmore Coffee Shop · 515 S. Olive St., Los Angeles · 1960s

was to bring a chef with me. I had just seen Roy Choi deliver a moving lecture at the MAD3 conference where he expressed frustration with the gap between his successes as a chef and his failure to feed enough people in the city that he loves. He made a call for all celebrity chefs to create new entrepreneurial schemes that can turn our increasing passion for food and restaurant culture into food justice. I had eaten from Roy's menus, and I had been impressed by the way he and his graphic designers used menus to tell his story of Los Angeles with a sophisticated, open, and warm swagger that I'd never seen before. As Roy and I began looking through the collection, we immediately realized the crossroads where this project would live: a historical book of menus and L.A. restaurant history in an age of intense urban hunger.

To embed this crossroads in our consciousness, the first meetings with my student researchers at USC were held at 3 Worlds Café on Central Avenue, a student-run, food-meets-food-justice venture that Roy opened in 2013 in partnership with Roosevelt High School, Dole Foods, and the Coalition for Responsible Community Development. Named for the Black, Latino, and Asian cultural mix of its Central-Vernon neighborhood and serving fresh and nutritious ingredients, 3 Worlds was created as a social experiment: a menu with a socially and locally conscious mission in the heart of an area that's often diagnosed as a "food swamp" or "food desert."

Our first conversations there orbited around the contemporary food challenges facing the city that the Library's menu collection puts into historical context. As the USDA has declared, Los Angeles is the nation's "epicenter of hunger," where the phrase "food insecurity"—lacking reliable access to nutritious and safe food—has become as much a part of the local culture as sunshine and traffic. The statistics may be well known by activists and organizers, but they bear repeating here. For young people, Los Angeles County is the most insecure county in the nation, with nearly 85% of all Los Angeles Unified School District students coming from food-insecure homes. One in ten families, four in ten low-income adults, and five in ten seniors are all food insecure. Our 1950s heyday as the top agriculture producing county in the nation has been reversed: we are now agricultural underdogs, with food swamps and fast

LUCCA
IN LOS ANGELES
FIFTH and WESTERN AVE.

The Restaurant that captivated Southern California in 13 months with a record attendance of 1,678,000 Satisfied Patrons

Lucca • W. 5th Street and S. Western Avenue, Los Angeles • 1930s

food retailers leaving small farms in the dust of industrialized food production. To borrow a phrase from chef and critic Evan Kleiman, Los Angeles is the poster child of what she calls "the schizophrenia of food culture." The food scene is as trendy, tweeted, pop-upped, and profit-busting as it's ever been, and more people are going hungry at a greater rate than perhaps any other in the city's history.

How did we get to this place? This book will not sufficiently answer that question, but our hope is that it opens up invaluable historical vaults that allow us to begin thinking about the past that has produced our present. Its contents will also serve as the springboard for a series of public programs that the Library Foundation of Los Angeles is sponsoring that aim to raise awareness of food history, food culture, and contemporary food crisis. Throughout the year, these menus will be used not just as windows into urban history, but as sparks for the urban now, each of them a singular opportunity to re-think our culinary and dietary relationships to place, community, and culture, and to jump-start new conversations about the future of eating in Los Angeles.

Tupac Shakur wrote the song "To Live and Die in L.A.," which, along with a little help from William Friedkin and Wang Chung, inspired the name of Chef Micah Wexler's 2013 culinary series dedicated to L.A. geography (menus born of Pico Boulevard, Koreatown, Boyle Heights, The Beach, & more). Micah then generously allowed us to take the title "To Live and Dine in L.A." and run with it for this project.

Lastly, my gratitude goes out to all of the other contemporary chefs featured on these pages who generously donated their time and creativity to answering a left-field question in their own singular way: if you were to cook a vintage L.A. menu in your restaurant, how would it need to be changed? All of them found a way to do what *To Live and Dine in L.A.* is all about: re-thinking the modern city through the menus of its past.

That past, I quickly learned in writing this book, is a vast landscape, impossible to fully represent in a single volume. That means that undoubtedly, you might not find the restaurant you are looking for on these pages (What? No Madame Wu's Garden??). Some didn't make it in, and some aren't included in the Library's collection. This is the challenge that all archives hold out: they represent what's there as much as what's missing. If you have menus you wish to donate to the Library to help complete this picture, please visit us at LFLA.org, where you will also find additional resources and essays (by food historian Charles Perry and food policy expert Alexa Delwiche), rare restaurant ephemera, and updates on the To Live and Dine in L.A. project. We look forward to broadening the story with you all.

Josh Kun

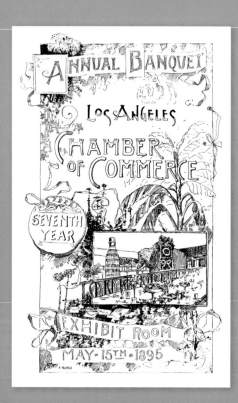

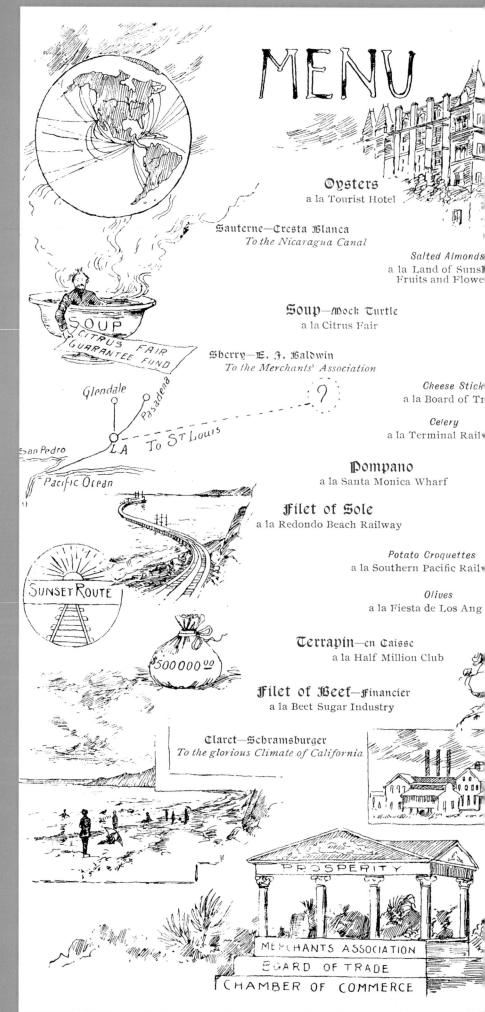

Los Angeles Chamber of Commerce Banquet Menu • 1895

Lime Frappe
a la Mount Lowe Railway

Russian Salad
a la Our Electric Railways

Roast Lamb with Mint Sauce
a la Harbor at San Pedro

Port—Sunny Slope
To 100,000 Population

Green Peas
a la Santa Fe Railway

Chicken—a la Maryland
a la Boom of 1887.

Champagne—Mumm
To the Chamber of Commerce

Ice Cream and Cake
a la Wilmington Transportation Co.

Figs, Nuts and Raisins
a la Good Roads

Strawberries
a la Irrigation

Crackers and Cheese
a la Los Angeles Press

Oranges
a la Southern California
Fruit Exchanges

Coffee and Cigars
a la Salt Lake Railway

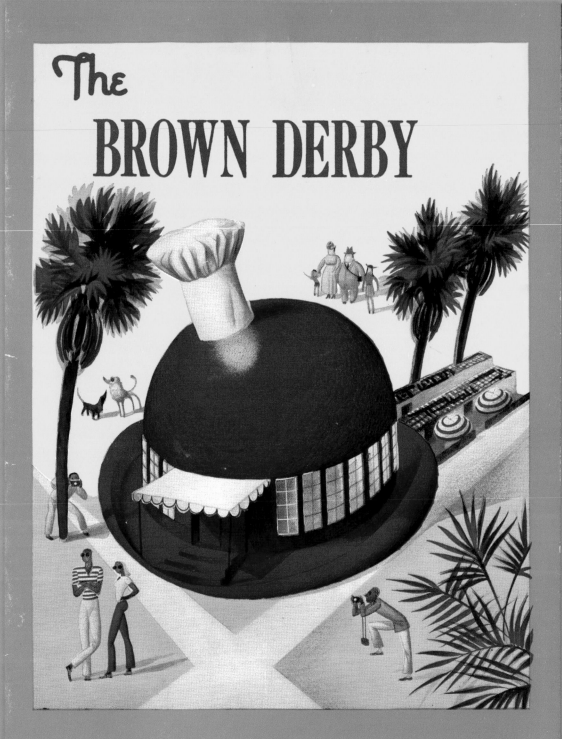

The Brown Derby • Wilshire Boulevard at Alexandria Avenue, Los Angeles • 1952

Cocktails

Seafood Cocktail 1.75   Dungeness Crablegs 1.75

Baja California Jumbo Shrimps 1.50

Derby Cocktail (Crablegs, Celery, Avocado, Strained 1000 Island Dressing) 1.75

Appetizers

Smoked Nova Scotia Salmon 1.40   Half Order 90

Chopped Chicken Livers 1.00   Half Order 60

Marinated Herring 1.10; Half Order 65   Hearts of Pascal Celery 75

Assorted Hors d'Oeuvres 1.75; with Caviar 2.25

Entrees

For our main course this evening,
To Live and Dine in L.A.,
we offer an essay on menus past and present,
restaurants lost to time and some to
good fortune, and the changing habits,
economics, demographics, dreams,
and tastes of L.A. diners

Vegetables and Potatoes

Corn Saute 50; O'Brien 60   Casserolette of Fresh Frozen Corn with Cream and Tomatoes 75

Fresh Broccoli, Hollandaise 60   Baby Lima Beans 50   Green Peas and Carrots 50

Julienne String Beans 50   Creamed Spinach 60   Zucchini Florentine 50

Cottage Fried Potatoes 50   Hashed Brown Potatoes 50   Giant Idaho Baked Potato (5:30-9:30) 50

Whole Artichoke, Sauce Hollandaise 75

Desserts

Charlotte Russe 60   Frozen Eclair 60

Cherry Flambe or Crepe Suzette 2.50   Parfaits 60

Sherbet 50   Fresh Fruit Compote 75

Ice Creams: Vanilla, Fudge and Vanilla, Chocolate or Mocha 50

Beverages

Coffee: Cup 15; Mug 15; Pot 25

Tea, Pot 25   Hot Chocolate 25   Ovaltine 25   Milk 25

Iced Tea 25   Iced Coffee 25   Sanka 25   Postum 25

We are entangled in our meals.

—GARY ALAN FINE, *Kitchens*, 2008

My grandfather fled the Nazi takeover of Hungary for a life in L.A. restaurants. His first local job, in 1951, was waiting tables at the Brown Derby on Wilshire. He served Cracked Alaska King Crab, Chicken à la King, and Cobb Salad for two dollars each, Crabmeat Louie for twenty-five cents more, and for the high rollers willing to part with $2.85, the all white meat Creamed Turkey Derby topped with cranberry jelly. He left the Derby for another Wilshire mainstay, Ollie Hammond's Steak House, where he took orders from red leather booths for both the World's Finest Small Steak and the World's Thickest Small Steak (the thickness was worth seventy-five cents), alongside Chateaubriand for Two, and a Steak n' Eggs that was being modest—really filet mignon, eggs, hotcakes, bacon, and coffee. The wordy menu made his job easier. "Please realize that this is not the normal manner in which we serve our steaks," it told anyone eyeing the Steak and Spaghetti Platter, and its desserts came with a confession: "We do not bake our own desserts or freeze our own ice cream. We can buy better ones."

My grandfather's Old World accent was still fresh in those days and he fit right in at Little Gypsy, a Hungarian restaurant up on Sunset. He kept his black bow-tie straight, his white shirt pressed, and his white jacket as spotless as one can when balancing plates of *Magyar Fasirozott*, *Kolozsvari*, stuffed cabbage, and Szegediner Paprika Chicken. If you didn't want a trip back to the old country, he also served assimilation on a plate: hamburger steaks, New York cuts, top sirloin, and other "welcome to America" dishes cordoned off from the goulash and schnitzel on the menu's left page. Little Gypsy wasn't the only Hungarian place in town and soon my grandfather's waiter wages were enough to earn him an ownership piece of Budapest Hungarian Restaurant on Fairfax, where

Little Gypsy • 8917 Sunset Blvd., West Hollywood • 1940s

Budapest • 432 N. Fairfax Ave., Los Angeles • 1960s

Stern's Famous Barbecue • 12658 W. Washington Blvd., Culver City • 1965

my father dispatched meal tickets after his junior year classes at Hamilton High (if you ever listened to music in the old Largo, you've sat amongst the Budapest's bones). Its menu was pure national fantasy. With an aerial shot of the Danube and the Hungarian parliament on its cover and a shot of an elegant outdoor restaurant in Budapest on the back, it did far more than describe what you could order. It was time travel, an exile's return ticket home with imported Hungarian wine, Chicken Paprikash, and nockerl as an in-flight meal (though you were probably wise to avoid its roast goose which was once described by Paul Wallach as tasting like "it had been cooking since last Yom Kippur").

After selling his share of the Budapest, my grandfather went back to waiting tables at the steakhouse at the downtown Hilton where he worked for over two decades. The only possession of his that I still have is a gift given to him by the Hilton when he left to take yet another job waiting tables at the Ramada. They spelled his name the old Hungarian way—Nicholaz—and thanked him for twenty-three years of service on the back of a gold-plated pocket watch.

My mother's father ran a men's clothing store in the Ladera Center and his favorite restaurant was wherever somebody else was paying. He wasn't much for menus. He'd start by asking for what he was in the mood for and then negotiate his way into a version of something actually being offered. Luckily his choices rarely veered too far from a flank steak and grilled onions which meant that on the rare occasions he was picking up the check, he was at Scotch and Sirloin, Stern's, Love's, and Lawry's. At our Sunday night family dinners at the Hamburger Hamlet (the one that was tucked under the 10 on Sepulveda), he always ordered the Plank Hamburger Steak and tried to shuffle us out before anybody ordered coffee or dessert. Yet the longest conversations I ever had with him were across the table at Nate 'n Al's, where he ate bagel crusts while delivering soliloquies on the Mills Brothers and Shecky Greene. My grandmother preferred menus that looked like Du-par's and Bit of Scotland. She was a woman of crisp bacon and short stacks of pancakes, of chicken and chips, of shortbread packed in a pink box to go.

My parents inherited different strands of their respective restaurant DNA—class conscious, frugal and at home with Formica

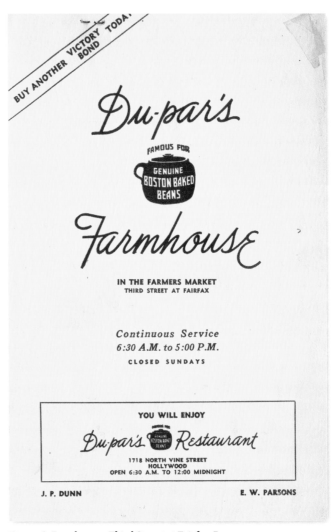

Du-par's Farmhouse • Third Street at Fairfax Avenue, at Farmer's Market • 2007 (Souvenir Menu of 1938)

counters on the one hand, but on the other, equally happy with white tablecloths, prix fixe elegance, and menus that change daily. Neither of them can talk about growing up here without a reference to the Apple Pan, and they celebrate the occasional anniversary eating Pink's in their car, but there was never a new buzz-worthy restaurant they couldn't find time to try. I remember us always eating out, sitting down at restaurant tables, parsing menus like lit majors, and figuring out who would split what with my mother. When we weren't eating together, you could find me on a stool at Marty's, the burger stand on Pico Boulevard, squeezed into a cement strip between a fire station and a gas station. There were baseball card trades in the back, but up front it was all about that distinctly L.A. phenomenon, the combo: burger patty, chili, cheese, hot dog, lettuce, and tomato, piled between two grill-shined buns and wrapped in paper (come early enough and they throw on an egg).

One of our family favorites was Fratello's, an all-burgundy Italian dining room lit by candles and decorated with hanging wine jugs. It was the first time I had ever seen a dish prepared tableside and I never ceased to be awed by the flaming theater of their Fettuccine Fantastica that tossed noodles, peas, ham, and mushrooms into molten pools of smoking white cream sauce.

The owners were Mexican, not Italian, and they'd always prepare it themselves, with great pride and smooth pomp, as if it was a family recipe from back home.

That cultural mash up—which they celebrated as openly as their deals on Chianti carafes—and the fact that it was crammed into a car-choked mini-mall and was about ten cottage-cheese-ceilinged apartment complexes down from a freeway off-ramp, made Fratello's a perfect early introduction to the character, and possibility, of the L.A. restaurant. When I read its menu now—one of the thousands in the collection of the Los Angeles Public Library—I see my family staring back at me, a history of eaters and servers, immigrants and natives, talkers and sharers and side-order experts. But I also see the city itself and read that menu as a humble urban fossil, one of so many unexpected and informal metropolitan texts just waiting to tell us something about who we are and this place we all call home.

Fratello's • 10433 National Blvd., West Los Angeles • 1983

**When it comes to a variety of eating places, I have never seen a city in the
United States that can produce more types of restaurants than Los Angeles.**

—C.O. Patterson, *American Restaurant* Conference, 1923

Before Los Angeles became a city of restaurants it was a city of food. The City of Angels began as a Pueblo of Dandelion and Prickly Pear, of Acorns and Amaranth, Pigweed and Pine Nuts. It only exists because of its food: Spanish troops needed something to eat. As it grew it became a City of Oranges, Limes, Grapes, Oysters, Cattle, Potatoes, Pan Dulce, and Tamales. "Here, on the western sun-kissed Pacific," Ana Bégué de Packman wrote in *Early California Hospitality*, "The earth gave forth bountifully of her store—green garlands of cress and pigweed, festooned garlic heads, strings of red chile peppers, pearly corn, and pink beans."

In the eighteenth century, local missions flourished on homegrown crops of quince, pigweed, and berries and imported all of the oranges, grapes, and figs that would quickly be seen as native like that other iconic imposter, the palm tree. "It has good land for planting all kinds of grains and seeds," wrote the Franciscan Father Juan Crespi of the Los Angeles basin, "and is the most suitable site of all that we have seen for a mission, for it has all the requisites for a large settlement."

It was also good land for planting grapes. Starting in 1832 with Jean-Louis Vignes's El Aliso vineyard—a quarter mile of grapes along the L.A. River—Los Angeles was a vintner's paradise and quickly emerged as the nation's top profit-turning wine center (by 1850 there were one hundred vineyards in L.A. County, more than anywhere else in the nation). There are still grapes in the city's official crest. In the nineteenth century, Chinese farmers worked the fields that are now the L.A. Live entertainment megaplex, ran a booming abalone trade, and grew daikon and gobo with Japanese farmers up and down the L.A. River. By 1903, the City Market was up and running in Chinatown. Cows and sheep roamed free on the old ranchos, wheat grew in the San Fernando Valley, corn sprouted in El Monte, and seafood was bountiful at the beaches.

In 1903, the city's most zealous Old California booster Charles Lummis used regionally proud recipes to remind newcomers of the cultural worlds already here. *The Landmarks Club Cookbook* gathered hundreds of recipes—from chile sauce to stewed jackrabbits—to argue for the supremacy of the Southwestern diet. The book also included an entire chapter of menus, perhaps the very first attempt to collect and curate menus as artifacts of L.A. history and identity. Next time you throw a "Midwinter Luncheon in Southern California" you might consider Lummis suggestions like mushrooms on toast with a brown sauce and a chestnut salad served with pimiento sandwiches.

You moved here for the climate and stayed for the agriculture. Eating well was part of the pre-urban draw, a theme that left a strong mark on early L.A. publishing. There were menus printed here before there were books, and of the first two hardcover books ever published in Los Angeles, one of them was a cookbook, *Los Angeles Cookery*. Debuting in 1881, the same year as Horace Bell's *Reminiscences of a Ranger* and with the same publisher (the Mirror Printing and Binding House that would later become Times-Mirror), the fund-raising collection from the Ladies' Aid Society of Fort Street Methodist Episcopal Church gathered local family-friendly recipes from Madame Chevallier's cabbage soup and Mrs. Hazeltine's fishballs to Mrs. M.G. Moore's katydid pudding that were all "scrupulously temperate." *The Plymouth Union Cookbook* and *How We Cook in Los Angeles* both followed in 1894, setting the stage for the popular *Los Angeles Times* cookbook series that debuted in 1902.

In her 1925 memoir *Adobe Days*, Sarah Bixby Smith offered glimpses of food production on the ranchos and its distribution to markets and restaurants in the city. When her family sat down for a meal at Rancho Los Alamitos, the meat was sourced from outside the kitchen window, sugar and flour came in barrels from Los Angeles, veggies came from a "Chinese peddler," and all the cooks were "Chinamen." "Salads were unknown," she wrote, "but we sometimes had lettuce leaves, dressed with vinegar and sugar." Creamed toast was a main dish, and doughnuts were a staple. By the time her family moved to L.A. in the 1870s, there were fruits, jellies, and cakes all for sale at Hazard's Pavillion, where you could also enjoy a "New England dinner." In the old Plaza, there was the first L.A. ice cream man, the "white-clad Mexican" selling treats from a freezer on his head. And out in El Monte, the corn, melon, pumpkins, and hogs were all bountiful.

The abundance of vegetables, fruit, fish, and cattle helped keep the city's cost of living down. An 1895 article in the *Los Angeles Times* proclaimed L.A. the most affordable big city in the country because everything from its mutton, tomatoes, and potatoes to its flour and butter was cheaper here than anywhere else. By the turn of the century, food—as cheap as it was healthy—became an official real estate lure. Citrus, avocados, and walnuts all played a starring role in the civic booster campaigns that helped sell the place to the sickly and to all those sun-deprived Midwesterners dreaming of a new life among the orange groves. At the 1893 Chicago World's Fair, Los Angeles represented itself as an elephant covered in 850 pounds of walnuts, wearing a belt of lemons and touting a basket full of corn, wheat, and barley.

Scenic food tours regularly left downtown for nearby farms and ranches like they were amusement parks. In the 1920s, the Cudahy Ranch tours departed from downtown's Savoy Hotel and included a "real ranch dinner" of hot roast beef, mashed potatoes with gravy, and homemade pie cooked by "Sam, the famous cook" (ads for the tours included a photo of him posing in his kitchen whites). Tours of orange groves were the most common; it was the orange that was the city's true food icon. It became hard to separate Los Angeles from a postcard image of a giant orange and the constantly reproduced taunt: "I'll eat oranges for you. You throw snowballs for me." You have winter. We have fresh fruit.

For those who took the bait, food remained central to their identity once they got here. L.A. was the capital of "the greatest of all Western lures—the Southern California picnic," as one writer with the Works Progress Administration's America Eats program noted in the late 1930s. In the early 1900s, Greeks, Japanese, Koreans, Armenians, all gathered in parks for formal community picnics, sharing dishes and recipes that bridged one home to another. Most famous of all were the Iowan picnics of Long Beach, elaborate public spectacles of Midwestern nostalgia that helped give "Iowa by the Sea" its nickname.

The jury is still out on the name of the very first L.A. restaurant. There undoubtedly was more than one Mexican eatery on the original Plaza in the 1840s, but judging by ad-

"*Here I am Folks*"—
Good ol' Sam the famous
Cook of the Old Cudahy Ranch
*Come down and eat one
of my real Ranch Dinners*
ABSOLUTELY FREE

MENU	Points of Interest on Trip
Hot Roast Beef	Westlake Park
Mashed Potato	Wilshire Residence Dist.
Brown Gravy	Gen. Otis' Home.
Bread and Butter	West Adams
Home-made Pie	Homes of
Coffee Ice Tea	E. L. Doheny
	Clara Kimball Young
	Roscoe "Fatty" Arbuckle
	Exposition Park
	and Buildings
	Model Dahlia Farm
You are assured	Vernon and
Courteous Treat-	Manufacturing District
ment and suffer no	Huntington Park
Obligation whatsoever	thence via Long Beach
	Boulevard to
	SOUTHGATE GARDENS

AUTOMOBILES LEAVE
Every Tues., Thurs. and Saturday
FROM
728 West Sixth St.
OR SAVOY HOTEL CORNER
at   10:45   A. M.
This is your Ticket—Be sure to bring it with you.

Cudahy Ranch • Cudahy, California • 1910s

vertisements in various local papers of the time, it wasn't until 1849 with the opening of the Bella Union hotel that nineteenth century Los Angeles had its first sit-down restaurant on record. As with most formal U.S. restaurants of the period, its menu was French.

Restaurants in hotels and boarding houses would quickly become commonplace throughout downtown. In his memoir *Sixty Years in Southern California*, businessman Harris Newmark was a regular diner at the Bella Union until a price hike convinced him to start eating his steaks, mutton, vegetables, and pork chops at the more humble La Rue's, a French restaurant with flatware "of the homeliest kind," dirty tablecloths, a mud floor, and flies. "Nothing in Los Angeles, perhaps, has ever been cruder than this popular eating-place," Newmark wrote. "I paid him nine dollars a week for three more-or-less hearty meals a day, not including eggs, unless I provided them." Though many have claimed LaRue's, which opened in 1852, as the city's first stand-alone restaurant outside of a hotel, the Old American restaurant on Commercial Street, also known as American House, might actually hold the honor. It appears to have been doing business since at least 1850.

From then on, every year brought more restaurants. They grew and evolved alongside the evolution of L.A. urbanism, from rural Mexican pueblo to small American town, from the breakup of the rancho system to an automobile-designed modern city that, by 1930, was the fourth largest in the nation. As Los Angeles began its journey from a village twenty-eight square miles small, built around a single plaza, to a city that stretched out for miles in every direction down boulevards and freeways, its restaurants grew right along with it.

A timeline of pre-1900s L.A. restaurant growth might look something like this:

- **1849:** The French restaurant of the Bella Union hotel opens.
- **1850:** Both the Old American and the Franklin restaurant open.
- **Early 1850s:** Nelson's Opera Restaurant opens on Calle de Los Negros.
- **1852:** John La Rue opens La Rue's restaurant. "The food made up in portions what it lacked in quality," was Harris Newmark's review.
- **1855:** Restaurant Francais opens; Lafayette Restaurant on Commercial serves partridge, rabbit, and chicken pies; Captain Weiner's in San Bernardino offers steaks and chops.
- **Late-1850s:** Bartolo Ballerino opens his Italian restaurant on Calle de los Negros.
- **1856:** Restaurant du Commerce opens.
- **1860:** Emile Bordenave opens the Louisiana Coffee Saloon with a French menu that included roast duck and oysters.
- **Early 1860s:** The city's first Chinese restaurant opens on Calle de Los Negros.
- **1870:** Three-story luxury hotel Pico House opens on Main Street, also with a French menu.
- **1873:** A series of restaurants announce their business in local papers: the Delmonico; the National; Solomon's; and Johnny Moore's the San Francisco, a reliable spot for meats and vegetables.
- **1874:** The Star restaurant opens, as do a string of boarding house eateries like Brown's, Soulen's, John McDonald's, and Otto Evers'.
- **1875:** The St. Charles restaurant boasts of a "dining-room floor covered with a fine Brussels carpet; the Barnum is known for its enchilada Sunday dinners and its "delicacies of the season" served "metropolitan style"; and the Occidental promised "poultry, fish, and game, washed down with the richest vintage of France and Los Angeles."
- **1876:** Victor Dol opens his first French restaurant, the Commercial, on Spring near Temple. It had an elegant dining room set back from the street with a fountain courtyard, where what one diner called "an excellent French dinner" could be had for fifty cents. That same year, opposite the Pico House, another French restaurant advertises food "in European style" (but calls itself the Oriental) and opens opposite Pico House; Brown's serves four hundred meals on a single Sunday.
- **1877:** Montgomery House opens.
- **1878:** Restaurant de Paris opens.
- **Late-1800s:** The beloved Italian restaurant of the Italia Unita Hotel starts serving meals inside the old Avila Adobe.
- **1881:** Hilario Preciado opens the simply titled Mexican Restaurant with a menu that was also Spanish, French, and American.
- **1885:** The United States Restaurant opens.
- **1886:** Campi's Italian Restaurant on 309 N. Main, advertises tagliarini, macaroni, spaghetti, ravioli, *risotto alla milanese*.

- **1887:** The restaurants of Hotel Arcadia in Santa Monica and Hotel Metropole on Catalina Island open their doors.
- **1886:** Hamanosuke "Charles Hama" Shigeta opens the city's first Japanese restaurant on E. First Street.
- **1888:** Frank Blackburn opens what was perhaps the city's first black-owned "race" restaurant, a "coffee and chop house," at First and Los Angeles Streets.
- **1889:** J.R. Walker opens the second "race" restaurant on San Pedro and First.
- **1889:** The Maison Doree, Hollenbeck, and Ebinger's restaurants all open.
- **1890:** Man Jen Low opens in Chinatown and Zuccha's Restaurant opens downtown.
- **1897:** Al Levy, L.A.'s most successful early restaurant entrepreneur parlays his popular sidewalk oyster cart into a sit-down restaurant, Al Levy's Oyster House. The pushcart ends up immortalized on the roof. The same year, the Belmont Café on Fifth and Main, with its lush canopy of pomegranate, orange, and magnolia trees, is "the scene of many a gastronomic event these nights when the mercury has coquetted among the eighties elsewhere." They offered a strictly Mexican menu of *carne seca con arroz* and *gallina con chile y frijol* in rare downtown shade.

Between the industrializing years of 1880 to 1930, the national restaurant population increased by four hundred percent. Across the country, more people were eating out than ever before, in part because of a growing lunch-eating workforce with fixed hours and longer commutes between work and home. L.A. was no different. In the downtown of the early 1900s, there were plenty of restaurants to choose from, and a few of them live on in names still hovering over contemporary downtown on ghostly marquees: Barclay, Stillwell, Alexandria, Rosslyn. The marble elegance of the Mission Indian Grill at the Alexandria Hotel attracted well-off business travelers and the local luxury set, and the "fancy sundaes" of the "aristocratic" Pig'n Whistle, with its elaborately illustrated gold leaf menus of dancing pigs and woodland faeries, aimed its sites at the growing Broadway district's theatergoers, advertising in show programs and entertainment trade magazines.

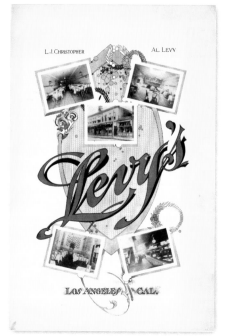

Levy's • **Third and Main Streets, Los Angeles ca. 1910**

The bulk of downtown eating was less regally inclined. There was the Imperial Café on Broadway, a "popular headquarters in Los Angeles for miners and business men" as the *Los Angeles Herald* described it in 1907. You served yourself roast beef sandwiches, coffee, and pie at Cole's and Philippe's which both opened a year later (and are the two lone survivors of downtown's original restaurant boom). At Third and Traction, Biscuit Jones catered to African-American diners and restaurants abounded in Little Tokyo, from lunch counters to the city's earliest *sushi-ya* (sushi bars). The Royal, the Bristol, the Pacif-

See the cunning little pig—
  Hear him sweetly play;
We could follow where he leads
  All the livelong day.
He will take us where he lives,
  In a lovely store
Full of candies, cakes and sweets,
  And good things galore.

Ye Pig'n Whistle Candies

LOS ANGELES
SAN FRANCISCO - OAKLAND
PASADENA

Printed by Taylor & Taylor, San Francisco

Pig 'n Whistle • (various locations) • 1919

ic Electric Grill, McKee's, Child's lunchroom and the restaurant of the Rosslyn Hotel were all favorites of the city's emerging middle and "bohemian" classes for whom "quick service, good food, low prices" was the only meal mantra that mattered. Godfrey's on Broadway advertised itself on a 1910 souvenir postcard as "the largest popular-priced restaurant in the city." The key to success was a flexible menu, like the one at Tait's Coffee Shop where, as the *Pacific Coast Record* reported, "one can order anything from 'coffee and' to a full-sized dinner."

By 1910, Los Angeles was being declared the number three "Top Restaurant City" in the country. Restaurants were still mostly centered downtown in the heart of the city's commercial and financial district, but that was beginning to change as well. Early Santa Monica hotels like the Sunset Inn and the Hotel Arcadia had dining rooms and cafés of local renown since the 1880s, and restaurants were turn-of-the-century hallmarks of both the Santa Monica Pier (Nat Goodwin Café) and the Venice Pier (the Ship Café). The latter was the creation of boxing promoter Baron Long who in 1912 also opened his Vernon Country Club southeast of downtown.

MENU

Thanksgiving

Hotel Rosslyn

LOS ANGELES, CAL.

1904

HART BROTHERS
Proprietors

HOTEL ✦ ARCADIA.

Santa Monica, Cal.

LUNCH.

Spaghetti.

Fried Surf-fish, Tartare Sauce.

Ragout of Veal, French Peas.

Sautee of Lamb, Spanish Style.

Braized Beef au Madre.   Fricasee of Chicken a la Romaine

COLD MEATS

Roast Beef.   Roast Lamb.   Corned Beef.   Ham.
English Brawn.

POTATOES.

Baked Potatoes.   Boiled Potatoes.
Sweet Potatoes.   Stewed.   Sautee.
String Beans.   Tomatoes.

Lobster Salad.

Vanilla Ice Cream.
Apple Pie.   Cocoanut Custard.
Tapioca Pudding, Cream Sauce.
Fruit Cake.   Assorted Cake.

BREAD
Plain Bread.   French Bread.
Graham Bread.   Dry Toast.   Cream Toast.
Tea.   Coffee.   Chocolate.   Milk.
Sonoma Riesling and Zinfandel, half pints, 25 cents.
SUNDAY, October 16, 1887.

Hotel Rosslyn • 112 W. 5th St., Los Angeles • 1904

Hotel Arcadia • Ocean Avenue, Santa Monica • 1887
Anonymous Donor

There were two hotels in an otherwise empty Laurel Canyon, each with their own restaurant. But one of the biggest signs of pending change was the opening of Frank's Café—soon better known as Musso & Frank's Grill—in 1919, on Hollywood Boulevard. The first restaurant in Hollywood, Frank's opened its doors with a "special French dinner" for one dollar (a "French chicken dinner" was offered only on Sundays), and it quickly became the unofficial commissary and industry watering hole for Hollywood stars and scribes like Charlie Chaplin, Rudolph Valentino, Greta Garbo and Orson Welles (who famously said that eating at Musso's "is like being in the womb"). Its menu set an early L.A. standard of leather-booth dining and mahogany-bar drinking: tongue sandwiches, Lobster Thermidor, roast lamb kidneys, hamburger steak, jellied consommé, Thursday night chicken pot pies, and a three-ounce martini with a decanter riding shotgun. In 1919, Musso's already had competition, mostly from the Café Trocadero, which took to billing itself "the only high-class restaurant in Hollywood," one where you could view exclusive collections of "Spanish master paintings" while dining on "the best one-dollar dinner in California." If you chose to eat that dinner at home, the café would bring it to you "at all hours" not in a delivery bag, but on a tray direct from the kitchen.

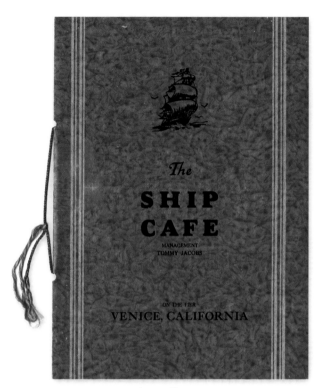

Ship Café • Venice Pier, Venice • 1930s
Anonymous Donor

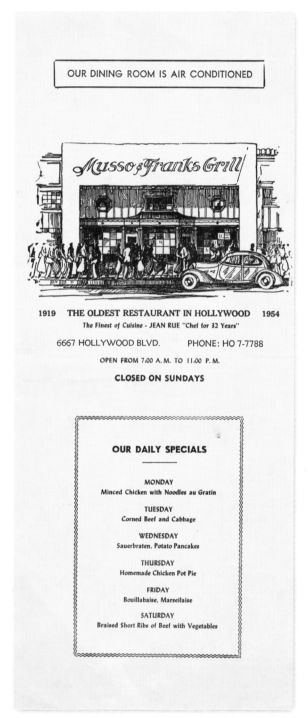

OUR DINING ROOM IS AIR CONDITIONED

1919   THE OLDEST RESTAURANT IN HOLLYWOOD   1954
The Finest of Cuisine - JEAN RUE "Chef for 32 Years"

6667 HOLLYWOOD BLVD.   PHONE: HO 7-7788

OPEN FROM 7:00 A. M. TO 11:00 P. M.

CLOSED ON SUNDAYS

OUR DAILY SPECIALS

MONDAY
Minced Chicken with Noodles au Gratin

TUESDAY
Corned Beef and Cabbage

WEDNESDAY
Sauerbraten, Potato Pancakes

THURSDAY
Homemade Chicken Pot Pie

FRIDAY
Bouillabaise, Marseilaise

SATURDAY
Braised Short Ribs of Beef with Vegetables

Musso & Frank's Grill • 6667 Hollywood Blvd.,
Hollywood • 1954

By 1922, seventy-five percent of the city reportedly ate out on a regular basis, and there was one restaurant for every 688 people. If we believe Duncan Hines, there were "twice as many good eating places in Los Angeles as San Francisco," including the Tam o' Shanter Inn, which opened that same year, serving prime rib and Yorkshire pudding inside a storybook cottage built by film studio carpenters. By 1923, the *Pacific Coast Record* warned housewives that their days cooking in the kitchen could be numbered: the "passing of the kitchen" was upon us. Thanks to advances in electric cooking equipment and industrial sanitation, the once exclusively domestic art and work of food preparation "will soon be contained almost entirely to restaurants." And at the 1923 conference held by *American Restaurant* magazine, it was Los Angeles—with its thirty thousand lunchrooms, eleven thousand fine-dining establishments, and five thousand tearooms and department store restaurants—that was declared the country's most diverse restaurant city. "When it comes to a variety of eating places," magazine publisher C.O. Patterson told

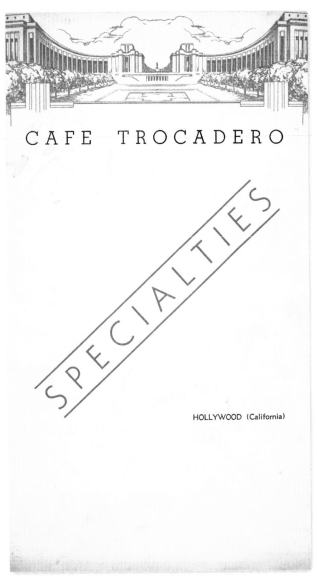

CAFE TROCADERO

SPECIALTIES

HOLLYWOOD (California)

Café Trocadero • 8610 Sunset Blvd., West Hollywood • 1930s

an audience that included Los Angeles restaurateurs Al Levy, M.L. Godfrey, John Tait, and Al Herbert, "I have never seen a city in the United States that can produce more types of restaurants than Los Angeles." By 1931, the cafés, cafeterias, restaurants, and lunchrooms of Los Angeles were responsible for the highest per capita restaurant sales in the country.

In these early days of the L.A. restaurant, menus as we now know them had not fully come into their own. Until the early 1900s, restaurants tended to write their fixed-price menus on boards or print them on small sheets which were then often reproduced in full in advertisements in local papers (the menu as print ad). In 1900, for example, the Royal Restaurant, on Spring between First and Second, printed its entire twenty-five-cent lunch ("dinner") menu in the *Los Angeles Record*—a meaty sampler that included English beef broth, Fricadellen on string beans, roast haunch of veal with dressing, with muskmelon for dessert.

More elaborately designed, handheld menus were typically reserved for luxury hotel dining rooms, banquets, and event dinners for Thanksgiving, Christmas, and New Year's. Hotel Raymond in Pasadena and Hotel Arcadia in Santa Monica both used printed menu cards before the turn of the century (an 1887 meal at the latter offered French peas, Spanish lamb, English Brawn, and Italian spaghetti). For its private banquets of 1905 and 1906, the members-only Jonathan Club printed menus offering Strained Gumbo, Roast Snow Bird, and Toke Point Oysters (a dish that was omnipresent on L.A. menus of the early 1900s) with original art and color illustration on its covers. The 1906 Hollenbeck Hotel Christmas menu had a wreath on the cover of a menu that alongside its Pomona farm-fed turkeys was stuffed with haughty epicurean flourishes like Calf's Sweetbreads à la Rothchild [sic], Saddle of Canadian Mutton with Currant Jelly, Monk's Beard Salad, and New England Suet Pudding with Sauce au Rhum.

Jonathan Club,

January Sixth, 1906

Jonathan Club • 610 S. Main St., Los Angeles • 1906

The earliest menu in the Los Angeles Public Library's collection, dated 1875, is also of this genre: a Bill of Fare for the first annual "Vintage Feast and Ball" held at Don Mateo Keller's personal ten-acre vineyard on Alameda and Seventh. Keller, an Irish immigrant who had taken on a Californio identity, was a successful vintner with tremendous real estate luck (he bought up the original land grant for a stretch of terrain called Malibu). His 1875 private invitation feast—which lasted all day and included both "dinner" and "supper" servings—was a carnivore's delight. There were cattle, sheep, and pig cooked various ways (including curried pig's feet) and served both hot and as "cold collations." A veal-and-ham pie was on hand for those who preferred multiple animals in a single bite.

· Christmas ·

HOLLENBECK HOTEL

Los Angeles, Cal.

A. C. BILICKE, PRESIDENT
JNO. S MITCHELL, VICE PRESIDENT

Hollenbeck Hotel Christmas Menu • Spring and Second Streets, Los Angeles • 1906

TO LIVE AND DINE IN L.A.

**A great deal has been written about the amenities of dining but few writers
have seen fit to comment on the very important problem of eating in a public place.**
—M.F.K. FISHER, *An Alphabet for Gourmets, 1949*

What *is* a menu? What work does it do? In a city like Los Angeles, famous for images and saturated by appearances, a city where the confusion of reality and fantasy is a way of life, a city where our top-grossing exports are representations, what does the restaurant menu represent?

The brute function of the menu is obvious. It tells you what you can order, and how much it will cost. It gives you choices. It advertises food that you can't see (or if it's after the 1950s, it might provide photos of the food you can't actually see). Menus are purposeful and never accidental, "instrumental texts" as sociologist Priscilla Parkhurst Ferguson has called them, in that "every menu seeks to guide the reader to a 'good' reading, which is, in effect, a 'good' meal." What makes a good reading and what makes a good meal, of course, is open to endless interpretation. The menu became the diner's guiding philosophical text: a gastronomic Talmud waiting for hungry rabbis to argue over its meaning.

Instant individualization has been the menu's purpose ever since it was first invented in Paris in the 1770s, when early restaurants began departing from the tavern and eating-house tradition of a fixed, single-priced *table d' hote* meal and led customers through individually priced options, all deliberately framed and arranged. "The restaurant," historian Rebecca Spang has written, "made it possible, for the first time, to partake of a meal in the company of others without actually sharing their provisions." The advent of the menu you could hold in your hand, printed just for you—"Tell me a little bit more about the halibut"—and your personal appetite—"I'll leave the menu on the table in case you want to order anything else"—formalized a shift in custom that became a social norm and an industry standard. As *Caterer and Household Magazine* put it in 1885, the menu may have been "originally intended merely for a medium through which the guest might learn of what his contemplated dinner was to consist," but before long the menu became a medium of much more, a medium with limitless possibility for design, storytelling, politics, and theater.

Chef Jeremiah Tower, who grew up acting out menus as if they were dramatic monologues, has described menus as entire, self-contained worlds. "They spoke to me as clearly as any childhood fantasy novel," he wrote in his 2003 memoir *California Dish*, "Reading an old menu slowly forms in my mind's eye its era, the sensibility of the restaurateur or the chef, even the physical details of the dining room. I can picture the guests even when I don't know who they were. Sometimes I can conjure up an entire evening, a three-act play orchestrated around the food."

The artistic possibility of the menu hasn't been lost on L.A. artists. Haruko Tanaka, for example, writes imaginary menus for the "invisible kitchens" of imaginary Japanese immigrant restaurants. At her make-believe Mammano, the menu consists of pop-tarts, energy bars, iceberg wedges with bleu cheese and other "uncomfortable classics: foods that scared us when we got here and some that still do." Tanaka says that menus are conceptual art, installations of ideas that can raise questions and provoke emotions. Allen Ruppersberg first played with this very idea back in 1969, when he created his Al's Café art installation in downtown Los Angeles. Using foraged materials that included chairs and tables from the Seahorse Inn Restaurant in Santa Monica, Ruppersberg created a performance art coffee shop where he cooked inedible, absurdist, and affordable meals for guests. The Al's Café menu was all concept and no utility, with dishes that included "toast and leaves," "grass patch with five rock varieties served with seed packets on the side," "desert plate and purple glass," "three rocks with crumpled wad," and "simulated burned pine needles à la Johnny Cash, served with a live fern."

Ruppersberg was riffing on the menu as a kind of writing: chefs don't assemble menus, they write menus. Menus are literature. Because menus are stories—stories about the chef, for sure, how they see the world, how they've been shaped, where they're from, where they're at—but also the stories the chef wants to invent and spin for us, the eager readers with napkins on our laps hungry for a trip outside ourselves. As little fictions, menus of course have their own rules of grammar and style—what linguist Robin Lakoff once dubbed "gastrolinguistics"—that change according to time and place. As you'll see, the *à la mode* and *du jour* virus known as "continentalizing" or "menu French" (so named by two other menu-studying linguists) infected the city's earliest restaurants with a vengeance.

The menus on these pages also provide plenty of evidence that historically menus have relied heavily on past participles—roasted, sautéed, boiled—with an on-again, off-again crush on more direct adjectives, one that gets more serious in the description-drenched wonder years of the 1970s and 1980s. Restaurant critic Arthur Schwartz has claimed that while menu language was generally spare and direct for most of the early 1900s, that all changed in the 1950s when the fine-dining group Restaurant Associates made it perfectly acceptable (and now expected) to offer a dish described as "Wild Fowl Cooked in Sherried Tomatoes under a Mantle of Musty Corn." The language of menus can be as important to our experience of the meal as the meal itself.

Menus were early forms of social media, not in the Instagram-a-picture-of-your-meal sense (though plenty of restaurant menus were designed to be take-home souvenirs or folded up into "I ate this" picture postcards ready to be sent to a friend), but in the sense that they mediate private and public lives. When we read a menu at the table, we make private decisions in public without worrying too much about what's going on at the next table. As historian Spang puts it, "Nobody has ever expected restaurant customers to reach a consensus, or even strive for one. Nobody has ever imagined that beef-eaters and chicken-eaters could agree for the common good to compromise on veal." And yet we do the occasional look-over, the menu our tip-toe into sociality, comparing the descriptions in front of us to the dishes we see all around us. The menu helps us interrupt, ask, and make friends (or enemies): "Excuse me, what is that? Is that the salmon? Where is that on the menu?" And then back into our shells we go.

In the narrowest sense, menus are things, but as anthropologists and materialist historians have shown for decades, there is nothing narrow about a thing. Things, they tell us, have social lives and biographies and get their identity through their circulation and use. Menus, then, are things par excellence. They exist only to be relational, to connect a customer to a chef, a chef to her cooks, her cooks to her kitchen staff, her customers to her food suppliers. They are there to help us—to convince us—to order something. Menus, in that sense, are unique in that they don't have any market value in themselves; they are not the commodities the restaurant is selling (their price tag comes later, when they land in the hands of collectors, antiquarians, and eBay auctioneers). Yet they play a key role in the business life of any restaurant. As restaurateur Mildred Pierce explains in the classic James M. Cain L.A.-restaurant novel that bears her name, "'What costs in a restaurant is waste, and the extras, like printing for menus.'" The extras matter. After the brief opening acts of lighting, interior decorating, acoustics and the social skills of a host, it falls to the menu to give the true first impression of the meal to come. A menu is the chef's handshake, the welcome mat, a mix of autobiography and manifesto.

In the broadest sense, menus are media; they play a key role in food as "a system of communication," an idea that Roland Barthes toyed with back in 1961. The primary information menus convey is, of course, culinary. For example, L.A. menus in the Library's collection tell us that Caesar Salads were everywhere in the 1930s, that jellied soups and cold meats in aspic were out of vogue by the 1960s, and being able to say your beef was corn-fed and shipped in all the way from Kansas City was once something to brag about. Yet the information menus communicate is not limited to the formats and data of available food options. Menus are central to what Georg Simmel called the "sociology of the meal" back in 1910. Eating at a restaurant is never just about eating at a restaurant, but about socialization, customs, ethics, and community. Or as pioneering food anthropologist Sidney Mintz has often claimed, besides the primary role of food as satisfying human need (we eat to stay alive) and human pleasure (we eat because it feels good), food is always about communication, and always about power.

Some of that power gets expressed in the menu's price columns. As economic texts, they are particularly rich. They tell us about changes in costs—from fifteen-cent meals to fifteen-cent steaks to fifteen-dollar beef tartare appetizers—and how recessions and wars dip prices, and economic booms push them back up. Ollie Hammond's used the back of one its menus to offer a Depression-era economic history of one of its specialties. "The World's Finest Small Steak was created," the menu explained, "to fill a need for a small piece of meat at a small price (forty cents) to fit the many small pocketbooks of the year 1934." By the 1940s, that price had jumped back up, but with a new set of World War II rationing limitations: there would be no Famous 13 Steak Sauce, 1000 Island Dressing, French Dressing, or Sesame Seeds on rolls.

World War II had significant impact on L.A. menus and their pricing, which followed the national lead by putting details of rationing and government-set pricing in fine print. The poppies on the cover of the California Kitchens menu tried to keep the California dream alive in

Ollie Hammond's • 3683 Wilshire Blvd., Los Angeles • 1950

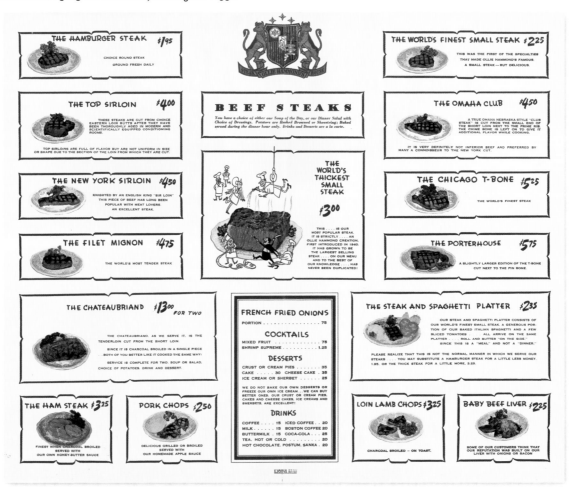

Ollie Hammond's • 3683 Wilshire Blvd., Los Angeles • 1960s

California Kitchens • (various locations) • 1943

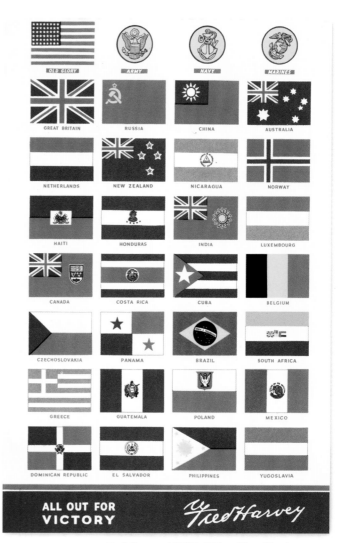

Fred Harvey / Aid To Ribbon Identification • 1943

the face of stark wartime realities: "We are very grateful for your patronage and patience during these war times." The Los Angeles Limited train menu urged customers to buy war bonds once they finished paying for their morning breakfast, and even Eaton's steakhouse observed Tuesdays and Fridays as "meatless days." The Brown Derby in Los Feliz announced that it was following the national Famine Emergency Program and was including no wheat, fats, or oil products on its menu. The Union Station location of Fred Harvey's western restaurant chain put service ribbons and soldier decorations on the cover of a 1945 menu that only listed American wines. Others used the war to shamelessly help boost their business. "Not all of us have a job as exciting as that of the Dawn Patrol—demanding super stamina and energy," read the cover of Thrifty's Fount 'n Grill "Dawn Patrol" breakfast menu, "but whatever your job is, it's just as important in our all-out war effort. Start the day with a good breakfast to help you do your job better and easier!" Inside, soldiers blew sound-off bugles next to the Wilshire Breakfast: toast, coffee, and your choice of fresh grapefruit, orange juice, or stewed prunes.

Or consider the 1942 menu of Van's Louisiana Barbecue at 142 East Florence Avenue. Above listings for fifty-cent pork spareribs and fifty-cent beef loin (ten cents more added salad, potatoes, and coffee, tea, milk, or buttermilk to the table), the restaurant included a reprint of

Los Angeles
LIMITED

Los Angeles Limited

DINNER
A LA CARTE

Fruit Cocktail 40

Today's Soup, Cup 25; Tureen 35

Available Fresh Fish   Domestic Sardines 60

Broiled Lamb Chops on Toast (2) 1.00; (1) 55
Corned Beef Hash with Poached Egg 85

Bacon and Eggs 90   Ham and Eggs 90
Bacon 80; Half Portion 45   Ham, Fried or Broiled 80; Half Portion 45
Boiled, Scrambled, Fried or Shirred Eggs (2) 35
Poached Eggs on Toast (2) 55
Plain Omelette 50   Spanish Omelette 75
Ham, Cheese or Jelly Omelette 70

Hashed Browned or Saute Potatoes 20
String Beans 20   Garden Spinach with Egg 25
Green Peas 20   Asparagus on Toast 45

THE SALAD BOWL 40
Head Lettuce 35   Potato Salad 30   Sliced Tomatoes 40
Chicken Sandwich 60   Chicken Salad 95
Cheese Sandwich 30   Tongue Sandwich 30

Bread and Butter 15   Milk Toast 35   Toast, Dry or Buttered 15

Ice Cream 25; with Wafers 35   Canned Fruits 30
Camembert Cheese 30   Roquefort Type Cheese 30

Milk (Individual Bottle) 15   Buttermilk 15   Postum (Pot) 25
Coffee (Pot) 25   Tea (Pot) 25
Decaffeinated Coffee (Pot) 25

All prices listed are our ceiling prices or below. By office of Price Administration
regulation, our ceilings are our highest prices from April 4, 1943 to April 10,
1943. Records of these prices are available for your inspection at the office of the
Manager, Dining Car & Hotel Department.

Los Angeles Limited

Select Dinners
Please order by number with items desired

SHRIMP COCKTAIL OR CHILLED APPLE JUICE
OR
SOUP: VEGETABLE JULIENNE

1.	GRILLED FRESH SALMON, MAITRE D'HOTEL	1.20
2.	BAKED INDIVIDUAL CHICKEN PIE	1.40
3.	OMELETTE WITH ASPARAGUS TIPS	1.15
4.	ROAST PRIME RIB OF BEEF, AU JUS	1.45

POTATOES RISSOLE   SEASONABLE VEGETABLE

OLD FASHIONED COMBINATION SALAD
FRENCH DRESSING

HOT CORN BREAD

RICE CUSTARD PUDDING WITH RAISINS, CREAM
BAKED APPLE   KADOTA FIGS, SYRUP
ROQUEFORT TYPE CHEESE, TOASTED CRACKERS

COFFEE   TEA   MILK   COCOA
DECAFFENATED COFFEE

THE CHALLENGER DINNER 75c

AVAILABLE FRESH FISH
OR
RAGOUT OF LAMB, VEGETABLES

POTATOES   VEGETABLES

BREAD AND BUTTER

ICE CREAM

COFFEE   TEA   MILK

Half bottle of red or white wine—special bottling—served with meals
where permissible, 50c extra; individual bottle, 30c extra.
Prices shown subject to Sales Tax in States where applicable.
Liquors, Wines or Beer Not Sold in Dining Car while Patrons are
Waiting to be Served, or After 10 P. M.   2W 2-28-46

Union Pacific Railroad / *Los Angeles Limited* • (Los Angeles to Chicago) • 1946

THRIFTY'S FOUNT 'N GRILL

Dawn Patrol

BREAKFAST MENU

Not all of us have a job as exacting as that of the Dawn Patrol — demanding super stamina and energy. But whatever your job is, it's just as important in our all-out war effort. Start the day right with a good breakfast to help you do your job better and easier!

BUY MORE U. S. WAR STAMPS AND BONDS

GOOD MORNING

BUY U. S. WAR SAVINGS STAMPS and BONDS

De Luxe Ham or Bacon and Eggs 55c
Tender Puritan Ham or Bacon, (2) Eggs, Potatoes, White or Whole Wheat Toast

Club Breakfasts

PLEASE ORDER BY NUMBER
WE DO NOT SUBSTITUTE
Cream Served with Prunes 5c Extra

BUY U. S. WAR SAVINGS STAMPS and BONDS

Wilshire Breakfast 21c
Fresh Grapefruit or Orange Juice or Stewed Prunes, Buttered White or Whole Wheat Toast, One Cup of Coffee

No. 1 - - - - - - - - - - 32c
Choice of: Fresh Grapefruit or Orange Juice, (1) Fried Egg or
(3) Slices of Bacon, Buttered Toast and One Cup of Coffee

No. 2 - - - - - - - - - - 27c
Choice of: Fresh Grapefruit or Orange Juice or Stewed Prunes, Two Hot Cakes, Maple Syrup and Butter, One Cup of Coffee

No. 3 - - - - - - - - - - 42c
Choice of: Fresh Grapefruit or Orange Juice, Two Hot Cakes, Stripped with Bacon, Sausage or One Fried Egg, Butter, Maple Syrup, One Cup of Coffee

No. 4 - - - - - - - - - - 32c
Choice of: Fresh Grapefruit or Orange Juice, Choice of: Any Dry or Cooked Cereal, Whole Wheat or White Buttered Toast, One Cup of Coffee

No. 5 - - - - - - - - - - 39c
Choice of: Fresh Grapefruit or Orange Juice or Stewed Prunes or Apple Sauce, French Toast, One Cup of Coffee

No. 6 - - - - - - - - - - 49c
Choice of Fresh Grapefruit or Orange Juice, Grilled Puritan Ham Steak, Potatoes, Buttered Toast and One Cup of Coffee

No. 7 - - - - - - - - - - 44c
Fresh Grapefruit or Orange Juice, Choice of: Ham, Bacon or Sausage, One Egg, Potatoes, Whole Wheat or White Buttered Toast and One Cup of Coffee

No. 8 - - - - - - - - - - 48c
Fresh Grapefruit or Orange Juice or Stewed Prunes, "3 Little Pigs" (Swift's Pork Sausage, Wrapped in Hot Cakes), Butter, Maple Syrup, One Cup of Coffee

No. 9 - - - - - - - - - - 44c
Fresh Grapefruit or Orange Juice or Stewed Prunes, Two Eggs, Any Style, Potatoes, Whole Wheat or White Buttered Toast and One Cup of Coffee

No. 10 - - - - - - - - - - 63c
Fresh Grapefruit or Orange Juice, Ham, Bacon or Sausage, (2) Eggs, Potatoes, Whole Wheat or White Buttered Toast, One Cup of Coffee

Toast, coffee cakes, etc.

Golden Brown Toast, 3 Slices 10
Cinnamon Toast 10
French Toast 30   Milk Toast 20   Cream Toast 30
Half and Half with Toast 25   Marmalade Filled 8
Danish Pastry 8   French Coffee Cake 8
One Large Doughnut 6   Two Small Doughnuts 6

Specials
(Potatoes and Toast Served with Orders)
Puritan Ham 40   5 Slices Puritan Bacon 35
Ham and Eggs 55   Link Sausage 35
Bacon and Eggs 55
Small Breakfast Steak, Potatoes and Toast 65
Steaming Hot Oatmeal or Cream of Wheat, Toast, One Cup of Coffee 27

We Make All of Our Own Doughnuts Coffee Cakes Layer Cakes Pies Rolls Danish Pastry
Made in our own sanitary bakery, from the same quality of ingredients as though made in your own kitchen at home. Delivered to our stores fresh daily with the morning sunrise!

Omelettes and **Eggs**
(Potatoes and Toast Served with Orders)
Eggs (2), Boiled 35   Eggs (2), Fried 35
Eggs (2), Poached 35   Eggs (2), Scrambled 35
Plain Omelette 35   Ham Omelette 50
Bacon Omelette 50   Jelly Omelette 40
Green Pepper Omelette 45   Tomato Omelette 40
Cheese Omelette 45   Spanish Omelette 40
All Side Orders of Ham, Bacon or Sausage 20c
One Cup Coffee 7c extra served with above orders

Special Blend Coffee 7   Postum 5   **Beverages**
Lipton's Tea, Per Pot 10   Tomato Juice 10
Hot Chocolate 12   Hot Ovaltine 10
Hot Malted Milk 10   Bottle Sweet Milk 8

TO PROTECT YOUR HEALTH — ALL GLASSES, DISHES AND SILVERWARE ARE WASHED AND STERILIZED IN AN ELECTRIC DISHWASHER

SD-5-43

All prices listed are at or below our ceiling prices. By O. P. A. regulation, our ceiling prices are our highest prices from April 4th, to April 10th, 1943. Records of these prices are available for your inspection.

Thrifty's Fount 'n Grill / Dawn Patrol Breakfast Menu • Los Angeles • 1943

Van's Louisiana Barbecue • 142 E. Florence Ave., Los Angeles • 1946

a *Daily News* article. The Southern California Restaurant Association had called for an end to "special dinner combinations" to reduce food waste during wartime rationing days. But the real story was the menu's other headline: "War is War! Every Defense Stamp That You Buy Pays The Postage To Send a Jap To Hell!" That the restaurant probably catered to the neighborhood's growing African-American community and that the menu was printed on a stock advertising menu card for Mexican brewery Carta Blanca with a watercolor of a Mexican bullfight on its cover didn't stop Van's from offering an anti-Japanese deathwish as a side order to pork loin and coleslaw. It's just one example of what L.A. menus can tell us about food's connection to larger social and cultural forces, the way social entrees like class, race, and gender shape the way the city eats and the way it thinks.

Menus are great indicators of gender norms as well. In the 1950s, Ships went after men with their Businessman's Lunch (soup, hamburger, sherbet, coffee, offered up through the 1970s) and Rothey's went after women by including the promotion "All Moms: Free Baby Food (National Brands)" in the middle of their menu. The 1915 menu for Jahnke's Tavern & Ladies Grill—the tavern for the men, the grill for the ladies—is a reminder that for much of early L.A. restaurant history, dining out was a male privilege. Before Prohibition's ban on alcohol in 1920, most restaurants

Ships Coffee Shop • Washington Boulevard at Overland Avenue, Culver City • 1960s

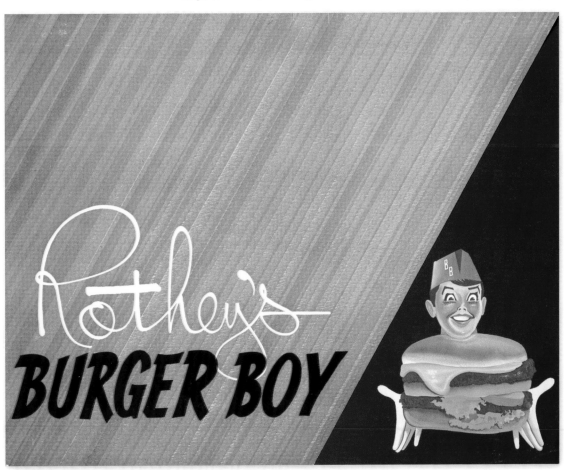

Rothey's Burger Boy • 1950s

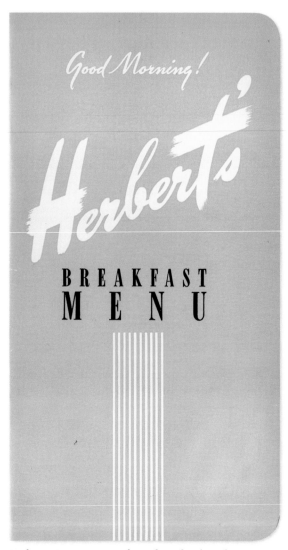

Herbert's Drive-In • Beverly Boulevard and Fairfax Avenue,
Los Angeles • 1940s

refused to serve women unaccompanied by men or only served them behind pulled curtains or in segregated ancillary "ladies" spaces. There was Herbert's Bachelor Grill, and there was Herbert's Café for Ladies and Gentlemen. For *Los Angeles Times* food writer Marian Manners (the pseudonym of Ethel Vance Morse) restaurant menus were most valuable to women as inspirations for their own kitchens, dramatic productions that L.A. housewives should study and imitate to keep their home tables lively. "There's something about eating out that makes the whole family anticipatory," she wrote in 1940, "The restaurateur knows how to dramatize his menus and, of course, he is able to offer an inspiring variety. Without in the least lessening the joy of dining out, the wise housewife takes a lesson from the chef with her everyday meals and both dramatizes their presentation and offers as much variety as she possibly can."

This all began to change during World War II when an industrializing labor force led more women to work—and by extension, to take their meals—outside the home. As we see with the waitresses-turned-restaurant owners portrayed in novels of the time like Shoson Nagahara's 1925 *Tale of Osato* and James M. Cain's 1941 *Mildred Pierce*, it also led to a rise in women as owners of restaurants and cafeterias, from Little Tokyo to Glendale. In *Tale of Osato*, originally serialized in the Japanese-language newspaper *Rafu Shimpo*, Osato goes from being a struggling waitress to the successful owner of two restaurants. "The owner of a small restaurant near the produce market was returning to Japan," she writes in a letter back home to her brother, "So I agreed to buy him out. I renamed the restaurant Shinfujitei and became the owner and manager of my own place." A similar plot unfolds in Cain's *Mildred Pierce*, when the fictional Drop Inn cafeteria in Glendale starts buying up Mildred's homemade pies, allowing the single mom to quit waiting tables at a Hollywood diner and open her own restaurant. When she does, she makes sure the menu is as easy to follow as possible. Instead of the diner's "jumble" of a menu—"There were fifty-five-and sixty-five-cent lunches on it, as well as appetizers, steaks, chops, desserts, and fountain drinks, most of these bearing fancy names that were unintelligible to her"—her restaurant's eighty-five-cent meal menus would be streamlined populist documents: fried chicken,

Tick Tock
TEA ROOM

1716 North Cahuenga Boulevard
Hollywood, Calif. • HEmpstead 7576
(Two Doors North of Hollywood Boulevard)

Tick Tock Tea Room • 1716 N. Cahuenga Blvd., Hollywood • 1938

waffles, vegetables, and pies.

Women also played key leadership roles in tearooms that offered "home-cooked" comfort food in restaurants designed to look like middle-class living rooms—cozy sites of culinary domesticity meant to appeal to women as both customers and entrepreneurs. There were Osatos and Mildreds everywhere: Helen Mosher opened the city's first cafeteria, local Californio Piedad Yorba owned the city's first elite Mexican restaurant, and Mexican immigrant Consuelo de Bonzo was on her second restaurant by 1930. The Copper Kettle was already in business as L.A.'s first all-women tearoom in 1908. As Agnes Gleason put it in the *Journal of Home Economics*, "The most successful tearoom is one that preserves the atmosphere of a pleasant, well-ordered home."

That was certainly the aim of the Tick Tock Tea Room, opened in 1930 by Helen Johnson and her husband Art, who served individual pot pies and pot roast with homemade noodles in a room she designed as a replica of the Minnesota living room they left behind—cuckoo clocks, fireplaces, fresh flowers and all. The Tick Tock was the focus of a 1936 *Restaurant Management* feature that, while titled "The Woman Executive," also included an ode to the female waitress: "delightful to look at, delicious as nougat and neat as a peppermint wafer"—a reminder that restaurant feminism was still a work in progress. The ode continued:

> This chic little maiden
> Her arms fully laden
> With dishes deliciously scenty
> Is doll-like and dainty
> But not a bit fainty,
> Of fortitude she has a plenty.

Ruder's Inn • Laurel Canyon, Los Angeles • 1911 • Anonymous Donor

Menus are also demographic media. They help us understand the making of neighborhoods and changing population demographics. In the first decades of the last century, nobody may have been living in bucolic, vacant Laurel Canyon but there were two restaurants there, both in hotels: The Lookout Mountain Inn and Ruder's Inn (which featured a rendering of the still rustic canyon on the front of its 1911 menu). The 1930s menu for Mme. Portier's French Restaurant proudly claims its East Los Angeles location on its cover (lesser known perhaps than Marcel and Jeanne's French Café in Montebello, French East L.A.'s longest hold-out). If the Breaded Pig's Feet and Beef Tongue Sauce Piquante of Mme. Portier's were to appear on a menu in contemporary East Los Angeles, where there are just a few more Mexican immigrants than French ones, they would be rewritten as *Manitas de Cerdo and Lengua en Salsa de Chile Morita*.

The vast majority of Chinese restaurant menus carry addresses near New and Old Chinatown until the 1980s, when they start to move east into Monterey Park with a new influx of Chinese immigrants and developers and a new Chinese restaurant trend: Chinese food for Chinese diners. In 1977, when Frederic Hsieh first pitched the world on the city of Monterey Park as a future Chinese immigrant suburb, he did it over lunch at one of the city's earliest Chinese restaurants. A year later, the neighborhood's first major Asian grocery store opened and a flood of restaurants quickly followed. As Hua Hsu describes it, restaurants were "the shock troops" of Monterey Park's middle- and upper-class Chinese immigrant makeover (into what some dubbed the "Chinese Beverly Hills") and, by 1990, it was the first city in the continental U.S. with a majority Asian population.

Within neighborhoods, menus tell us about the fragility and flexibility of community, about how we connect and disconnect. Menus can be exclusive information sources, designed to be legible to only specific audiences, and they can be open doors of translation, invitations to connect and cross over. A menu can be bridge and boundary both, a passport and a Keep Out sign. One of Old Chinatown's longest holdouts, Jerry's Joynt—best remembered for its Jade Lounge bar built of a 3600-year-old Chinese carving—liked to describe itself as "that strange place of elbowing."

All restaurants can be strange places of elbowing, junctions where communities bump up against each other, stare each other down, and size each other up over bowls of pho and plates of tacos. It's the menus that often contain the clues, treasure maps to lost, layered worlds. If you were to stop in for breakfast or lunch, say, at Tak's Coffee Shop on Crenshaw, in the heart of contemporary Inglewood, next to Denver Omelettes, French Toast, and Patty Melts, you would find all of this elbowing on its menu: Spam and Eggs, Grits, Tommy's Moco Loco, Chino's Special, Steak Ranchero, Cha-Shu Pork Sandwich, Hot Links, Oyako Donburi, Chicken Wings, and Saimin Noodles. The dishes are all traces of the restaurant's complicated cultural history shaped by war, immigration, demographic change, and urban development.

Tak's opened in 1996 as the child of the Holiday Bowl, the bowling alley and coffee shop launched by five Japanese-Americans whose World War II internment camp memories were still fresh in their minds. The Bowl became a beloved post-war hub for the growing Japanese community in what was then a still predominantly white Inglewood. Its iconic "Googie" architecture from Armét + Davis is now the site of a Starbucks and a Walgreens. Chino Bravo, who left Mexico in the 1970s and ended up washing dishes at the Holiday Bowl, later became the owner of Tak's. He learned to cook Japanese and Chinese dishes from the Bowl's Japanese chef (many of have remained on Tak's menu) and he added a few of his own Mexican breakfast recipes. Tak's head waitress, originally from Thailand, also worked at the Bowl as an immigrant teenager, learning to speak English on the job. Tak's clientele is now mostly African-American and Latino but get there before seven in the morning and a few of the old Bowl regulars will still show up and order the *cha-shu* sausage with eggs and a cup of coffee (the houses across the street on Bronson still have bonsai trees in their front yard).

Tak's Coffee Shop • 3870 Crenshaw Blvd. #101, Los Angeles • 1990s

A similar story of strange elbowing was set in motion when another set of former internees, Ito and Minoru Matoba, opened the Atomic Café in 1946. For the next forty years, they served teriyaki dinners, chow mein, and chop suey alongside in-house creations like the mysterious Hamburger Gacha to an ever-changing downtown crowd. When the Matobas' daughter Nancy took over the jukebox and the front of the house in the late 1970s, the Atomic became the L.A. punk

TO LIVE AND DINE IN L.A.

Atomic Cafe
LITTLE TOKYO

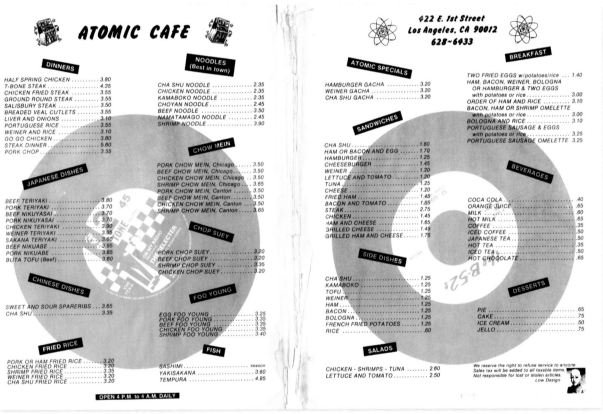

ATOMIC CAFE

422 E. 1st Street
Los Angeles, CA 90012
628~6433

DINNERS

HALF SPRING CHICKEN	3.80
T-BONE STEAK	4.35
CHICKEN FRIED STEAK	3.55
GROUND ROUND STEAK	3.55
SALISBURY STEAK	3.50
BREADED VEAL CUTLETS	3.55
LIVER AND ONIONS	3.10
PORTUGUESE RICE	3.55
WEINER AND RICE	3.10
GO GO CHICKEN	3.80
STEAK DINNER	5.60
PORK CHOP	3.55

JAPANESE DISHES

BEEF TERIYAKI	3.80
PORK TERIYAKI	3.70
BEEF NIKUYASAI	3.70
PORK NIKUYASAI	3.70
CHICKEN TERIYAKI	3.90
WEINER TERIYAKI	3.60
SAKANA TERIYAKI	3.60
BEEF NIKUABE	3.95
PORK NIKUABE	3.85
BUTA TOFU (Beef)	3.60

CHINESE DISHES

SWEET AND SOUR SPARERIBS	3.65
CHA SHU	3.35

FRIED RICE

PORK OR HAM FRIED RICE	3.20
CHICKEN FRIED RICE	3.20
SHRIMP FRIED RICE	3.35
WEINER FRIED RICE	3.20
CHA SHU FRIED RICE	3.20

NOODLES
(Best in town)

CHA SHU NOODLE	2.35
CHICKEN NOODLE	2.35
KAMABOKO NOODLE	2.35
CHOYAN NOODLE	2.45
BEEF NOODLE	3.50
NAMATAMAGO NOODLE	2.45
SHRIMP NOODLE	3.90

CHOW MEIN

PORK CHOW MEIN, Chicago	3.50
BEEF CHOW MEIN, Chicago	3.50
CHICKEN CHOW MEIN, Chicago	3.50
SHRIMP CHOW MEIN, Chicago	3.65
PORK CHOW MEIN, Canton	3.50
BEEF CHOW MEIN, Canton	3.50
CHICKEN CHOW MEIN, Canton	3.50
SHRIMP CHOW MEIN, Canton	3.65

CHOP SUEY

PORK CHOP SUEY	3.20
BEEF CHOP SUEY	3.20
SHRIMP CHOP SUEY	3.35
CHICKEN CHOP SUEY	3.20

FOO YOUNG

EGG FOO YOUNG	3.25
PORK FOO YOUNG	3.35
BEEF FOO YOUNG	3.35
CHICKEN FOO YOUNG	3.35
SHRIMP FOO YOUNG	3.40

FISH

SASHIMI	season
YAKISAKANA	3.60
TEMPURA	4.85

OPEN 4 P.M. to 4 A.M. DAILY

ATOMIC SPECIALS

HAMBURGER GACHA	3.20
WEINER GACHA	3.20
CHA SHU GACHA	3.20

SANDWICHES

CHA SHU	1.60
HAM OR BACON AND EGG	1.70
HAMBURGER	1.25
CHEESEBURGER	1.45
WEINER	1.20
LETTUCE AND TOMATO	1.20
TUNA	1.25
CHEESE	1.20
FRIED HAM	1.45
BACON AND TOMATO	1.55
STEAK	2.75
CHICKEN	1.45
HAM AND CHEESE	1.65
GRILLED CHEESE	1.45
GRILLED HAM AND CHEESE	1.75

SIDE DISHES

CHA SHU	1.25
KAMABOKO	1.25
TOFU	1.25
WEINER	1.25
HAM	1.25
BACON	1.25
BOLOGNA	1.25
FRENCH FRIED POTATOES	1.25
RICE	.60

SALADS

CHICKEN - SHRIMPS - TUNA	2.60
LETTUCE AND TOMATO	2.50

BREAKFAST

TWO FRIED EGGS w/potatoes/rice	1.40
HAM, BACON, WEINER, BOLOGNA OR HAMBURGER & TWO EGGS	
with potatoes or rice	3.00
ORDER OF HAM AND RICE	3.10
BACON, HAM OR SHRIMP OMELETTE	
with potatoes or rice	3.00
BOLOGNA AND RICE	3.10
PORTUGUESE SAUSAGE & EGGS	
with potatoes or rice	3.25
PORTUGUESE SAUSAGE OMELETTE	3.25

BEVERAGES

COCA COLA	.40
ORANGE JUICE	.65
MILK	.60
HOT MILK	.65
COFFEE	.35
ICED COFFEE	.50
JAPANESE TEA	.50
HOT TEA	.35
ICED TEA	.50
HOT CHOCOLATE	.65

DESSERTS

PIE	.65
CAKE	.75
ICE CREAM	.50
JELLO	.75

We reserve the right to refuse service to anyone.
Sales tax will be added to all taxable items.
Not responsible for lost or stolen articles.
Low Design

Atomic Café • 422 E. 1st St., Los Angeles • 1980s

scene's after-hours headquarters. Little Tokyo old-timers rubbed elbows with members of X and the Germs as the restaurant filled with songs by Roy Rogers, Yuzo Kayama, Henry Mancini, and the Weirdos. The jukebox became as famous as the food, and by the 1980s, listings for pork chop suey and a side of *kamaboko* were printed atop faded 45s by the B-52s and the Selecter.

**The menu is to the mood of a restaurant what the tie is to the dress ensemble . . .
a small detail but the most noticeable of all!"**
—"Menu Profit Maker," *Restaurant Management*, 1936

The Atomic jukebox motifs and the Japanese *maneki-neko* good-luck-charm cat on the cover of Tak's Coffee Shop menu point to one of the more obvious menu functions: to be a design object, the studied result of aesthetic choices and the blank slates for visual storytelling. Hand-written or printed? Victorian or Streamline Moderne? Embossed or matte? Helvetica or Futura? Photographs of a staged chicken dinner or a drawing of an unsuspecting chicken before it gets "unjointed" and "disjointed" into a basket? A single page on thick card stock says something different about the meal we're about to have than four marbled pages bound in leather with a gold tassel or four photocopied pages laminated in plastic still sticky with leftover syrup.

As design historian Jim Heimann has shown, menu design only becomes a priority in the 1830s. Advances in printing began to move menus from the hand-scrawled chalkboards of small restaurants (where every seat had a good view of it) to printed, hand-held menu cards that were typically designed by commercial artists and better suited to more spacious dining halls (the first printed menu in the United States is believed to date back to 1834). By 1885, *The Caterer and Household Magazine* declared that the age of the menu as "merely a medium through which the guest might learn of what his contemplated dinner was to consist" was already over. The menu was a business tool, but especially where upscale restaurants were concerned, it was also art. By the end of the 1800s, an elite cadre of menu designers began to emerge (The Philadelphia artist known as Dreka, for instance, was a popular choice because of the "dainty beauty" of his designs). In the 1920s, menus start to take cues from the popularity of poster art and become "small posters" using increasingly elaborate and sophisticated letterforms and illustrations to advertise meals as if they were films and plays.

When the rise of both urbanization and automobiles helps ignite the nationwide restaurant boom of the 1930s, the design of menus takes on an even greater monetary significance. They become seen as a key business asset that if approached strategically could be used to maximize profits. In 1936, *Restaurant Management* magazine even began running the monthly column, "Menu Profit Maker." Design and the visual aesthetics of "printed salesmanship" were common topics. "The menu from a physical appearance standpoint, is grossly under-estimated," the magazine wrote in its November issue. "Too often it is looked at as merely a somewhat readable list of food items . . . when actually it should be an asset and an earmark of the place it serves. The menu is to the mood of a restaurant what the tie is to the dress ensemble . . . a small detail but the most noticeable of all!" For the editors, a successfully designed menu should, first and foremost, be legible to all with unadorned typefaces and fonts (they recommend Futura Light, Bodoni Light, and Garamond) and ample spacing to make dishes easy to read.

Most twentieth century L.A. menus—which tended to favor the "cram in as many dishes as possible" approach—ignored the editors cardinal rule: "Feature three things on a page and you've featured none!" One column focused specifically on arrangement and food layout, and offered a full-page chart highlighting different design templates of "classical," "modern," and "ultra" fonts printed according to four different layout motifs (the urn, the triangle, the block, and the "dynamic balance"). The most expensive dishes or the dishes you most want to sell, the magazine preached, should be listed in the upper left of the menu and never in the lower left. But ultimately, no design can save a menu from its food: "Your menu can make or break you. It can be the most beautiful and offer rare bargains. But if it does not list interesting food, you don't make a sale."

In Los Angeles, where everything can be stage and spectacle, all this advice went out the window. Here the menu was a versatile character actor who could play any role. One of the earliest L.A. restaurants to invest in the menu form was the Angelus, part of the hotel of the same name that opened at the corner of Spring and Fourth in 1901. Two menus from January of 1903 feature radically different, yet equally elaborate and sophisticated, designs that both conveyed the promise of a carefully prepared and elegant meal. A New Year's Day menu floated

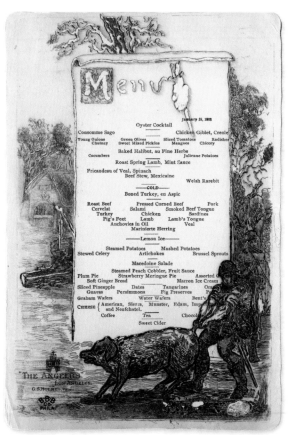

The Angelus • Fourth and Spring Streets, Los Angeles • 1903 • Anonymous Donor

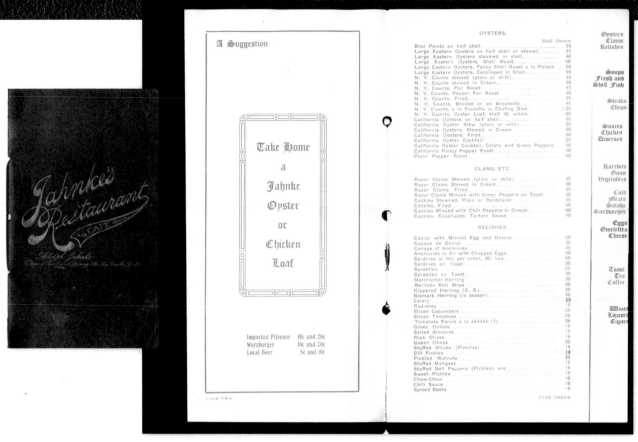

Jahnke's Restaurant & Café • First and Spring Streets, Los Angeles • 1915 • Anonymous Donor

trait of a blushing woman in a fur coat and bonnet on its cover and just seventeen days later switched to a single-card menu framed by an embossed, hand-drawn hunting landscape.

The 1920s menu for Jahnke's Restaurant & Café broke all of the minimalist *Restaurant Management* rules. It was pure extravagance and bounty, or as the cover page put it beneath a poem praising sharp knives, pickles, and good ale, "unsurpassed in appointments and cuisine." It was so long—twenty-eight pages—that it needed its own chapter tabs to separate the Rarebits/Game/Vegetables section from Sauces/Chickens/Diverses. The numbered pages were stuffed with dishes in five-point—yes, that's tiny—font. They listed thirty different relishes for twenty-two different oyster options. The thirty-four diverses, or sundries (Adolph Jahnke was German), included six variations on sweetbreads, six variations on calf's head, five variations on calf's liver, but just a single variation on Arabian Stew. Only half the menu belonged to the restaurant's dishes. The rest was devoted to advertisements for local food, drink, apparel, and cigar suppliers: A.K. Brauer & Co. tailors, Barber & Thomson butter, Palace Market Meat, the Franco-American Baking Company, Red Ribbon Beer, and more.

If you dined at the Paulais restaurant on March 13, 1925, there were two pages of fountain drinks to get through before even arriving at the food, which was broken up into four different *table d'hôte* meals (no. 4 featured Poached Barracuda and a laundry list of "choice of" options), two columns jammed with nearly two hundred à la carte dishes, and a specials menu with seven different "electric toasted sandwiches." Its vertical margins bragged about the coffee, its upper margins bragged about the courtesy and duty of "the young lady serving you," and its lower margins bragged about both moderate prices and the twice-daily screenings of the film *The Iron Horse* (1924) "with Sid Grauman's startling prologue including tribes of

TO LIVE AND DINE IN L.A.

THE YOUNG LADY SERVING YOU WAS SELECTED BECAUSE OF HER COURTESY AND ATTENTION TO DUTY

TABLE D'HOTE SERVICE

Served 11 to 9 p. m.

NO. 1—$1.25

Clam Chowder, Manhattan
Choice of
PLANKED N. Y. SIRLOIN
or
TENDERLOIN STEAK, Maitre d'Hotel
Vegetables   Potatoes
HEARTS OF LETTUCE, 1000 Island Dressing
French Rolls and Butter

Rice Custard Pudding   Fresh Apple or Cocoanut Custard Pie
Mocha, Devil's Food or Chocolate Cake   French Pastry
Raspberry, Orange or Pineapple Sherbet
Vanilla, Chocolate or Strawberry Ice Cream
Choice of Coffee, Pot of Tea, Iced Tea, Hot Chocolate
Bottle of Milk or Buttermilk

NO. 2—$1.00

Clam Chowder, Manhattan
Choice of
BROILED HAM STEAK, Country Gravy
or
LOBSTER a la Newburg   Mashed Potatoes
Carrots a la Vichy
HEARTS OF LETTUCE, 1000 Island Dressing
French Rolls and Butter
Choice of
Rice Custard Pudding   Fresh Apple or Cocoanut Custard Pie
Mocha, Devil's Food or Chocolate Cake   French Pastry
Raspberry, Orange or Pineapple Sherbet
Vanilla, Chocolate or Strawberry Ice Cream
Choice of Coffee, Pot of Tea, Iced Tea, Hot Chocolate
Bottle of Milk or Buttermilk

NO. 3—75c

ROAST LEG OF PORK
Carrots a la Vichy   Mashed Potatoes
LETTUCE, 1000 Island Dressing
French Rolls and Butter
Choice of
Rice Custard Pudding   Fresh Apple or Cocoanut Custard Pie
Mocha, Devil's Food or Chocolate Cake   French Pastry
Raspberry, Orange or Pineapple Sherbet
Vanilla, Chocolate or Strawberry Ice Cream
Choice of Coffee, Pot of Tea, Iced Tea, Hot Chocolate,
Bottle of Milk or Buttermilk

NO. 4—50c

POACHED BARRACUDA, Portugaise
Noodles in Butter   Boiled Potato
French Rolls and Butter
Choice of
Rice Custard Pudding   Fresh Apple or Cocoanut Custard Pie
Mocha, Devil's Food or Chocolate Cake   French Pastry, 5c extra
Raspberry, Orange or Pineapple Sherbet
Vanilla, Chocolate or Strawberry Ice Cream
Choice of Coffee, Pot of Tea, Iced Tea, Hot Chocolate
Bottle of Milk or Buttermilk

Extra Charge for Deviations

NOT RESPONSIBLE FOR LOST ARTICLES

A LA CARTE SERVICE

Friday, March 13, 1925

RELISHES

Jordan Almonds	.20	Oyster Cocktail	.30
Jumbo Ripe Olives	.25	Crab Cocktail	.35
Dill Pickles	.10	Lobster Cocktail	.35
Radishes	.10	Imported Sardines	.40
Hearts of Celery	.25	Canape of Caviar	.50
Alligator Pear Cocktail	.50	Canape of Anchovies	.40
Shrimp Cocktail	.35	Chutney	.20
California Fruit Cocktail	.25	Sweet Gherkins	.15

SOUPS

Clam Chowder, Manhattan 10
Consomme 10   Clam Broth 15   Chicken Broth 15
Cream of Tomato to order 15 Cream of Chicken to order 25

FISH AND SEA FOOD (Cooked to order)

Fried Filet of Sole, Tartar Sauce, F. F. Potatoes	.40
Broiled Salmon Steak, Maitre d'Hotel	.50
Grilled Barracuda, Maitre d'Hotel	.45
Baked Whitefish au Gratin	.50
Broiled Fresh Mackerel, Parsley Butter	.45
Sea Bass Saute Meuniere or Baked	.45
Steamed Finnan Haddie, Drawn Butter, Boiled Potato	.50
Halibut Steak au Gratin or Creole	.55
Steamed Alaska Cod, Drawn Butter, Boiled Potatoes	.50
Oyster Stewed or Fried	.40
Half Broiled Lobster, Drawn Butter	.75
Lobster, Shrimps or Crab Pattie	.65
½ Lobster Thermidor	.75
½ Cold Lobster, Mayonnaise	.75
½ Cracked Crab	.50

READY ENTREES AND ROASTS

Poached Barracuda, Portugaise	.40
Spaghetti, Italienne	.35
Spanish Enchiladas	.35
Calf's Liver and Bacon, French Fried Potatoes	.45
Paulais' Special Oyster	.60
Old Fashioned Steak, Country Gravy	.50
Chicken Patty	.50
Lobster a la Newburg	.75
Vegetable Dinner with Poached Egg	.50
Roast Leg of Pork, Apple Sauce	.50

STEAKS AND CHOPS

(10 minutes' notice)

N. Y. Cut Sirloin, F. F. Ptoes.	.90	Old Fashioned Steak, Country	
Planked N. Y. Cut Sirloin	1.15	Gravy, F. F. Potatoes	.50
T-Bone, F. F. Potatoes	.75	Ham Steak, F. F. Potatoes	.50
Steak, Minute, F. F. Potatoes	60	Hamburger Steak, F. F.	
Tenderloin, F. F. Potatoes	1.00	Potatoes	.40

Steaks Smothered with Onions 15c extra

Pork Chops (2)	.50	Veal Cutlet, Tomato Sauce	.60
Broiled Ham or Bacon	.40	Calf's Liver and Bacon	.45
English Mutton Chop	.75	Lamb Chops (2) with Peas	.65

French Fried Potatoes, Bread and Butter Served with above Orders
SAUCES TO ORDER—Spanish, Tomato or Creole | .15
Hollandaise, Bernaise or Bordelaise | .25

POULTRY

Chicken Pattie	.50	Chicken a la Maryland (½)	1.00
Chicken a la King	.75	Half Broiled Chicken	.85
Creamed Chicken on Toast	.50	Half Fried Spring Chicken	.85

Single Portions Served for 2 Persons, 10c extra

A LA CARTE SERVICE

POTATOES

Mashed	.10	Cottage Fried	.20
Boiled	.10	Au Gratin	.20
American Fried	.10	O'Brien	.20
French Fried	.10	Hashed in Cream	.20
Lyonnaise	.15	Fried Sweet Potatoes	.15
Shoestring (Julienne)	.15	Paulais Big Baked Potato	.15
Hashed Browned	.15	Candied Sweet Potatoes	.25

Long Branch | .15

VEGETABLES

Corn Saute 20; with Peppers	25	Sweet Corn	.15
June Peas	.15	Corn Fritters	.20
Stewed Tomatoes	.15	Brussels Sprouts	.15
Creamed Spinach	.20	Lima Beans	.15
Mammoth Asparagus,		Fresh Artichoke,	
Drawn Butter	.35	Drawn Butter	.30
Beets	.15	Asparagus Tips, Drawn Butter	30
String Beans	.15	Fried Egg Plant with Bacon	25
Boiled Rice	.15	French Fried Onions	.25

Spinach | .15

SALADS

Paulais De Luxe	.30	Pineapple and Cottage Cheese	25
Chicken	.50	Lettuce and Egg	.25
Crab Meat	.50	Banana and Nut	.25
Shrimp	.50	Lettuce and Tomato	.25
Fruit	.30	Potato and Egg	.25
Alligator Pear Salad	.50	Potato	.20
½ Alligator Pear	.60	Fruit Supreme	.30
Sliced Tomatoes	.20	Lettuce	.50
Sliced Cucumbers	.25	Mexican Cold Slaw	.20
Asparagus Tips, Mayonnaise	.35	Lobster, Shrimp, Crab, Louie	75
Mammoth Asparagus	.35	Fresh Artichoke	.50
Combination	.30	Tomato Stuffed with Chicken	45
Waldorf	.35	1000 Island or Roquefort	
Tomato Surprise	.35	Dressing, extra	.15
Tuna	.35	Lettuce	.20

HOT SANDWICHES

Paulais Club	.50	Fried Ham or Bacon and Egg	30
Paulais Ham Rarebit	.50	Fried Cheese	.35
Creamed Chicken	.40	Fried Egg	.20
Toasted Cheese	.25	Grilled Ham Steak	.40
Hot Cheese	.25	Hot Beef Steak	.35
Hot Roast Beef, Mashed		Hamburger	.30
Potatoes	.35	Denver	.30
Hot Pork, Mashed Potatoes	.35	Monte Cristo	.50

COLD SANDWICHES

Mother Hubbard	.60	Chicken (white meat)	.35
Deviled Egg	.20	Imported Swiss Cheese	.20
Deviled Ham	.15	Pimiento Cheese	.15
Minced Olives	.15	Tuna Salad	.20
Ham	.15	Peanut Butter	.15
Tongue	.15	Pimiento	.20
Paulais Assorted with Potato		Pork	.25
Salad	.50	Roast Beef	.20
Tuna	.20	Manhattan	.50
American Cheese	.15	Lettuce	.15
Chicken Salad	.25	Sardine	.25

DESSERTS

		Chocolate Eclair	.15
COCOANUT CUSTARD PIE	15	Paulais French Pastry	.15
Fresh Apple Pie	.15	Chocolate Layer Cake	.15
Raisin Pie	.15	Mocha Cake	.15
Boston Cream Pie	.15	Devil Food Cake	.15
Pie a la Mode	.25	Angel Food Cake	.15
Pie with Whipped Cream	.25	Assorted Petit Fours	.15
Pie with Cheese	.20	Raspberry, Pineapple or	
RICE CUSTARD PUDDING	15	Orange Sherbet	.15
English Tea Cake	.15	Banana Nut Ice Cream	.20
Coffee Cake	.15	French Vanilla, Chocolate or	
Baked Cup Custard	.20	Strawberry Ice Cream	.15

A la Carte Service Continued on Next Page

2:15—TWICE DAILY—8:15 "THE IRON HORSE" with Sid Grauman's Startling Prologue including tribes of Arapaho and Shoshone Indians

COMPARE OUR MODERATE PRICES WITH THE SUPERIOR QUALITY OF OUR FOOD

YOU WILL LIKE PAULAIS SPECIAL BLEND COFFEE, ORDER A SECOND CUP WITH OUR COMPLIMENTS

YOU WILL LIKE PAULAIS SPECIAL BLEND COFFEE, ORDER A SECOND CUP WITH OUR COMPLIMENTS

Paulais • 6702 Hollywood Blvd., Hollywood • 1925

Arapaho and Shoshone Indians." Or if you went out to eat at one of the four Mike Lyman's Grills on January 29, 1955, the choices before you were also daunting. There were fourteen sections (Dinner de Luxe, Eastern Steaks, and Radio Specials sponsored by KFI, among them), fourteen daily specials, twelve fish options, ten steak options, and twenty-four desserts. You might have needed every minute of the two-hour parking they validated (for fifteen cents) to make up your mind.

The menu for the Scotch Plaid Sweet Shop in Glendale may have listed its dishes with clarity and strategy—featured dinner suggestions in the upper left, the Scotch Plaid fountain special set off in a red box on the lower right—but it went rogue on its back cover. Instead of focusing on daily specials, it explained the seventeenth-century Anglo-Saxon paintings and drawings on the restaurant's walls with a twenty-six point "wall

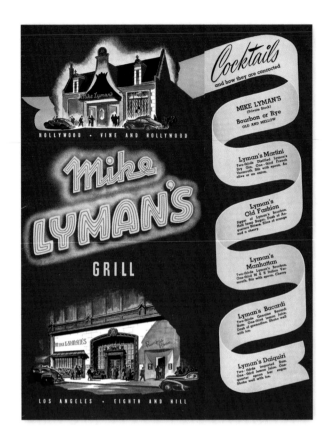

Mike Lyman's Grill • Hill and 8th Street, Los Angeles • 1955

The Scotch Plaid Sweet Shop • 412 N. Glendale Ave., Glendale • 1950s

AL LEVY'S
FAMOUS
$1.00 DINNER $1.00
SERVED NIGHTLY

CLOSED SUNDAYS

Exhilarating
CHAMPAGNE
COCKTAIL - 50¢
The Sparkling Queen
of All Cocktails!

Intimate Affairs

BANQUET
FACILITIES

Dinners
Bridges
Teas

Our Banquet Manager
Will Gladly Discuss
Further Details

HEINEKEN'S
IMPORTED
HOLLAND
BEER
50¢

617 So. Spring St. Los Angeles

Al LEVY'S GRILL

LOS ANGELES' FOREMOST RESTAURATEUR • FROM STAGECOACH DAYS TO STREAMLINE ERA • NOW CATERING TO MY FOURTH GENERATION

Al Levy's Grill • 617 S. Spring St., Los Angeles • 1930s

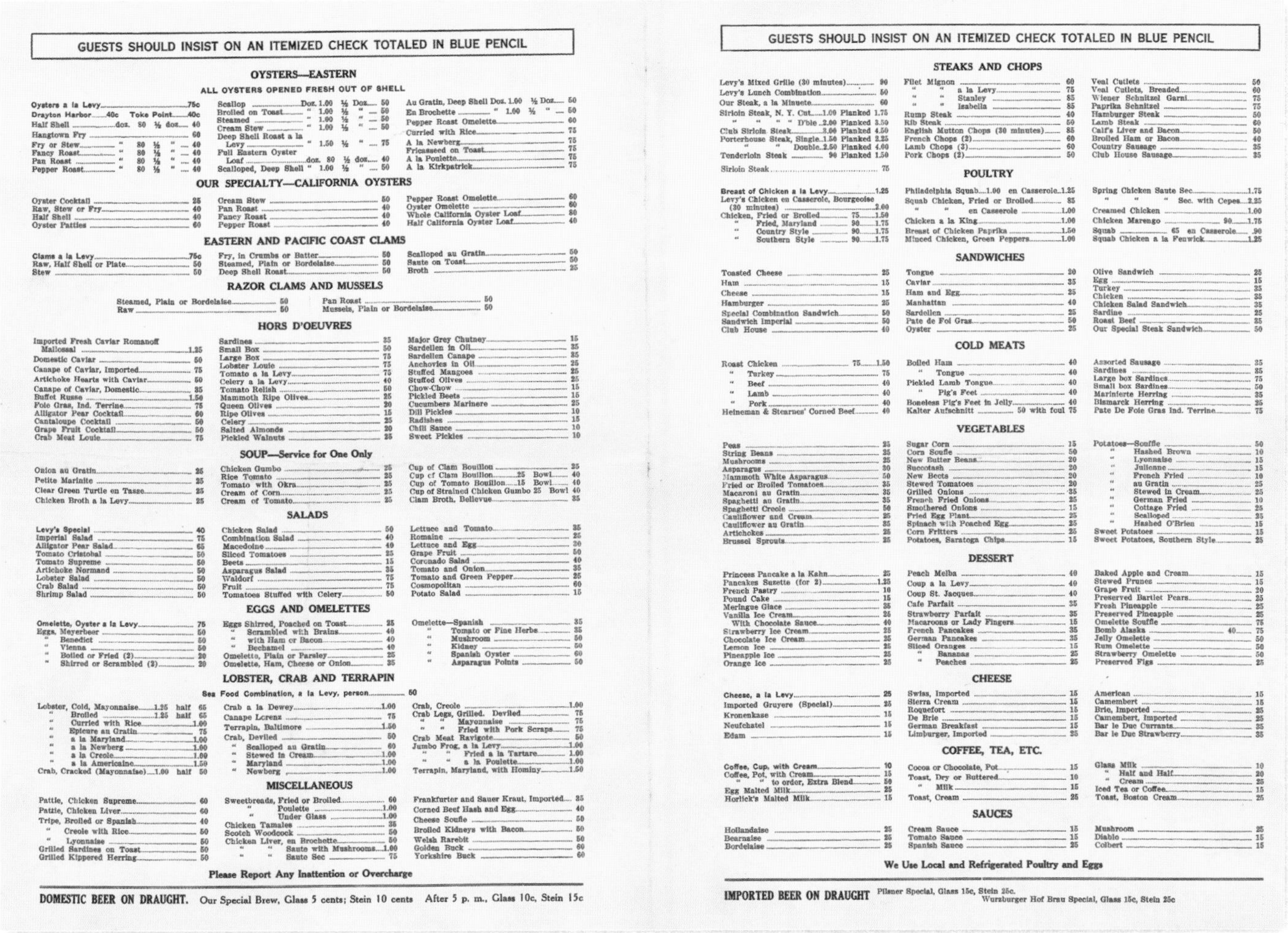

GUESTS SHOULD INSIST ON AN ITEMIZED CHECK TOTALED IN BLUE PENCIL

OYSTERS—EASTERN

ALL OYSTERS OPENED FRESH OUT OF SHELL

Oysters a la Levy ... 75c
Drayton Harbor ... 40c Toke Point ... 40c
Half Shell ... doz. 80 ½ doz. ... 40
Hangtown Fry ... 60
Fry or Stew ... " 80 ½ " ... 40
Fancy Roast ... " 80 ½ " ... 40
Pan Roast ... " 80 ½ " ... 40
Pepper Roast ... " 80 ½ " ... 40
Scallop ... Doz. 1.00 ½ Doz. ... 50
Broiled on Toast ... " 1.00 ½ " ... 50
Steamed ... " 1.00 ½ " ... 50
Cream Stew ... " 1.00 ½ " ... 50
Deep Shell Roast a la Levy ... " 1.50 ½ " ... 75
Full Eastern Oyster Loaf ... doz. 80 ½ doz. ... 40
Scalloped, Deep Shell " 1.00 ½ " ... 50
Au Gratin, Deep Shell Doz. 1.00 ½ Doz. ... 50
En Brochette ... " 1.00 ½ " ... 50
Pepper Roast Omelette ... 60
Curried with Rice ... 75
A la Newberg ... 75
Fricasseed on Toast ... 75
A la Poulette ... 75
A la Kirkpatrick ... 75

OUR SPECIALTY—CALIFORNIA OYSTERS

Oyster Cocktail ... 25
Raw, Stew or Fry ... 40
Half Shell ... 40
Oyster Patties ... 60
Cream Stew ... 50
Pan Roast ... 40
Fancy Roast ... 40
Pepper Roast ... 40
Pepper Roast Omelette ... 60
Oyster Omelette ... 60
Whole California Oyster Loaf ... 80
Half California Oyster Loaf ... 40

EASTERN AND PACIFIC COAST CLAMS

Clams a la Levy ... 75c
Raw, Half Shell or Plate ... 50
Stew ... 50
Fry, in Crumbs or Batter ... 50
Steamed, Plain or Bordelaise ... 50
Deep Shell Roast ... 50
Scalloped au Gratin ... 50
Saute on Toast ... 50
Broth ... 25

RAZOR CLAMS AND MUSSELS

Steamed, Plain or Bordelaise ... 50
Raw ... 50
Pan Roast ... 50
Mussels, Plain or Bordelaise ... 50

HORS D'OEUVRES

Imported Fresh Caviar Romanoff Mallossal ... 1.25
Domestic Caviar ... 50
Canape of Caviar, Imported ... 75
Artichoke Hearts with Caviar ... 50
Canape of Caviar, Domestic ... 35
Buffet Russe ... 1.50
Foie Gras, Ind. Terrine ... 75
Alligator Pear Cocktail ... 60
Cantaloupe Cocktail ... 50
Grape Fruit Cocktail ... 50
Crab Meat Louie ... 75
Sardines ... 35
Small Box ... 50
Large Box ... 75
Lobster Louie ... 75
Tomato a la Levy ... 75
Celery a la Levy ... 40
Tomato Relish ... 50
Mammoth Ripe Olives ... 25
Queen Olives ... 20
Ripe Olives ... 15
Celery ... 25
Salted Almonds ... 20
Pickled Walnuts ... 25
Major Grey Chutney ... 15
Sardellen in Oil ... 35
Sardellen Canape ... 35
Anchovies in Oil ... 25
Stuffed Mangoes ... 25
Stuffed Olives ... 25
Chow-Chow ... 15
Pickled Beets ... 15
Cucumbers Marinere ... 25
Dill Pickles ... 10
Radishes ... 15
Chili Sauce ... 10
Sweet Pickles ... 10

SOUP—Service for One Only

Onion au Gratin ... 25
Petite Marinite ... 25
Clear Green Turtle en Tasse ... 25
Chicken Broth a la Levy ... 25
Chicken Gumbo ... 25
Rice Tomato ... 25
Tomato with Okra ... 25
Cream of Corn ... 25
Cream of Tomato ... 25
Cup of Clam Bouillon ... 25
Cup of Clam Bouillon ... 25 Bowl ... 40
Cup of Tomato Bouillon ... 15 Bowl ... 40
Cup of Strained Chicken Gumbo 25 Bowl 40
Clam Broth, Bellevue ... 35

SALADS

Levy's Special ... 40
Imperial Salad ... 75
Alligator Pear Salad ... 65
Tomato Cristobal ... 50
Tomato Supreme ... 50
Artichoke Normand ... 50
Lobster Salad ... 50
Crab Salad ... 50
Shrimp Salad ... 50
Chicken Salad ... 50
Combination Salad ... 40
Macedoine ... 40
Sliced Tomatoes ... 25
Beets ... 15
Asparagus Salad ... 35
Waldorf ... 75
Fruit ... 75
Tomatoes Stuffed with Celery ... 50
Lettuce and Tomato ... 35
Romaine ... 25
Lettuce and Egg ... 30
Grape Fruit ... 50
Coronado Salad ... 40
Tomato and Onion ... 35
Tomato and Green Pepper ... 25
Cosmopolitan ... 60
Potato Salad ... 15

EGGS AND OMELETTES

Omelette, Oyster a la Levy ... 75
Eggs, Meyerbeer ... 50
" Benedict ... 50
" Vienna ... 50
" Boiled or Fried (2) ... 20
" Shirred or Scrambled (2) ... 20
Eggs Shirred, Poached on Toast ... 25
" Scrambled with Brains ... 40
" with Ham or Bacon ... 40
" Bechamel ... 40
Omelette, Plain or Parsley ... 25
Omelette, Ham, Cheese or Onion ... 35
Omelette—Spanish ... 35
" Tomato or Fine Herbs ... 35
" Mushroom ... 50
" Kidney ... 50
" Spanish Oyster ... 60
" Asparagus Points ... 50

LOBSTER, CRAB AND TERRAPIN

Sea Food Combination, a la Levy, person ... 60

Lobster, Cold, Mayonnaise ... 1.25 half 65
" Broiled ... 1.25 half 65
" Curried with Rice ... 1.00
" Epicure au Gratin ... 75
" a la Maryland ... 1.00
" a la Newberg ... 1.00
" a la Creole ... 1.00
" a la Americaine ... 1.50
Crab, Cracked (Mayonnaise) ... 1.00 half 50
Crab a la Dewey ... 1.00
Canape Lorenz ... 75
Terrapin, Baltimore ... 1.50
Crab, Deviled ... 50
" Scalloped au Gratin ... 60
" Stewed in Cream ... 1.00
" Maryland ... 1.00
" Newberg ... 1.00
Crab, Creole ... 1.00
Crab Legs, Grilled. Deviled ... 75
" " Mayonnaise ... 75
" " Fried with Pork Scraps ... 75
Crab Meat Ravigote ... 50
Jumbo Frog, a la Levy ... 1.00
" " Fried a la Tartare ... 1.00
" " a la Poulette ... 1.00
Terrapin, Maryland, with Hominy ... 1.50

MISCELLANEOUS

Pattie, Chicken Supreme ... 60
Pattie, Chicken Liver ... 60
Tripe, Broiled or Spanish ... 40
" Creole with Rice ... 50
" Lyonnaise ... 50
Grilled Sardines on Toast ... 50
Grilled Kippered Herring ... 50
Sweetbreads, Fried or Broiled ... 60
" Poulette ... 1.00
" Under Glass ... 1.00
Chicken Tamales ... 35
Scotch Woodcock ... 50
Chicken Liver, en Brochette ... 50
" " Saute with Mushrooms ... 1.00
" " Saute Sec ... 75
Frankfurter and Sauer Kraut, Imported ... 35
Corned Beef Hash and Egg ... 40
Cheese Soufle ... 50
Broiled Kidneys with Bacon ... 50
Welsh Rarebit ... 50
Golden Buck ... 60
Yorkshire Buck ... 60

Please Report Any Inattention or Overcharge

DOMESTIC BEER ON DRAUGHT. Our Special Brew, Glass 5 cents; Stein 10 cents After 5 p. m., Glass 10c, Stein 15c

GUESTS SHOULD INSIST ON AN ITEMIZED CHECK TOTALED IN BLUE PENCIL

STEAKS AND CHOPS

Levy's Mixed Grille (30 minutes) ... 90
Levy's Lunch Combination ... 50
Our Steak, a la Minuete ... 60
Sirloin Steak, N. Y. Cut ... 1.00 Planked 1.75
" " " " D'ble ... 2.00 Planked 3.50
Club Sirloin Steak ... 3.00 Planked 4.50
Porterhouse Steak, Single ... 1.50 Planked 2.25
" " Double ... 2.50 Planked 4.00
Tenderloin Steak ... 90 Planked 1.50
Sirloin Steak ... 75
Filet Mignon ... 60
" " a la Levy ... 75
" " Stanley ... 85
" " Isabella ... 85
Rump Steak ... 40
Rib Steak ... 50
English Mutton Chops (30 minutes) ... 85
French Chops (2) ... 60
Lamb Chops (3) ... 60
Pork Chops (2) ... 50
Veal Cutlets ... 50
Veal Cutlets, Breaded ... 60
Wiener Schnitzel Garni ... 75
Paprika Schnitzel ... 75
Hamburger Steak ... 50
Lamb Steak ... 60
Calf's Liver and Bacon ... 50
Broiled Ham or Bacon ... 40
Country Sausage ... 35
Club House Sausage ... 35

POULTRY

Breast of Chicken a la Levy ... 1.25
Levy's Chicken en Casserole, Bourgeoise (30 minutes) ... 2.00
Chicken, Fried or Broiled ... 75 ... 1.50
" Fried, Maryland ... 90 ... 1.75
" Country Style ... 90 ... 1.75
" Southern Style ... 90 ... 1.75
Philadelphia Squab ... 1.00 en Casserole ... 1.25
Squab Chicken, Fried or Broiled ... 85
" " en Casserole ... 1.00
Chicken a la King ... 1.00
Breast of Chicken Paprika ... 1.50
Minced Chicken, Green Peppers ... 1.00
Spring Chicken Saute Sec ... 1.75
" " " Sec. with Cepes ... 2.25
Creamed Chicken ... 1.00
Chicken Marengo ... 90 ... 1.75
Squab ... 65 en Casserole ... .90
Squab Chicken a la Fenwick ... 1.25

SANDWICHES

Toasted Cheese ... 25
Ham ... 15
Cheese ... 15
Hamburger ... 25
Special Combination Sandwich ... 50
Sandwich Imperial ... 50
Club House ... 40
Tongue ... 20
Caviar ... 35
Ham and Egg ... 25
Manhattan ... 40
Sardellen ... 25
Pate de Foi Gras ... 50
Oyster ... 25
Olive Sandwich ... 25
Egg ... 15
Turkey ... 35
Chicken ... 35
Chicken Salad Sandwich ... 35
Sardine ... 25
Roast Beef ... 35
Our Special Steak Sandwich ... 50

COLD MEATS

Roast Chicken ... 75 ... 1.50
" Turkey ... 75
" Beef ... 40
" Lamb ... 40
" Pork ... 40
Heineman & Stearnes' Corned Beef ... 40
Boiled Ham ... 40
" Tongue ... 40
Pickled Lamb Tongue ... 40
" Pig's Feet ... 40
Boneless Pig's Feet in Jelly ... 40
Kalter Aufschnitt ... 50 with foul 75
Assorted Sausage ... 35
Sardines ... 35
Large box Sardines ... 75
Small box Sardines ... 50
Marinierte Herring ... 35
Bismarck Herring ... 25
Pate De Foie Gras Ind. Terrine ... 75

VEGETABLES

Peas ... 25
String Beans ... 25
Mushrooms ... 25
Asparagus ... 30
Mammoth White Asparagus ... 50
Fried or Broiled Tomatoes ... 35
Macaroni au Gratin ... 35
Spaghetti au Gratin ... 35
Spaghetti Creole ... 50
Cauliflower and Cream ... 25
Cauliflower au Gratin ... 35
Artichokes ... 25
Brussel Sprouts ... 25
Sugar Corn ... 15
Corn Soufle ... 50
New Butter Beans ... 20
Succotash ... 20
New Beets ... 20
Stewed Tomatoes ... 20
Grilled Onions ... 35
French Fried Onions ... 25
Smothered Onions ... 15
Fried Egg Plant ... 25
Spinach with Poached Egg ... 25
Corn Fritters ... 25
Potatoes, Saratoga Chips ... 15
Potatoes—Souffle ... 50
" Hashed Brown ... 10
" Lyonnaise ... 15
" Julienne ... 15
" French Fried ... 10
" au Gratin ... 25
" Stewed in Cream ... 25
" German Fried ... 10
" Cottage Fried ... 25
" Scalloped ... 25
" Hashed O'Brien ... 15
Sweet Potatoes ... 15
Sweet Potatoes, Southern Style ... 25

DESSERT

Princess Pancake a la Kahn ... 25
Pancakes Suzette (for 2) ... 1.25
French Pastry ... 10
Pound Cake ... 15
Meringue Glace ... 35
Vanilla Ice Cream ... 25
With Chocolate Sauce ... 40
Strawberry Ice Cream ... 25
Chocolate Ice Cream ... 25
Lemon Ice ... 25
Pineapple Ice ... 25
Orange Ice ... 25
Peach Melba ... 40
Coup a la Levy ... 40
Coup St. Jacques ... 40
Cafe Parfait ... 35
Strawberry Parfait ... 35
Macaroons or Lady Fingers ... 15
French Pancakes ... 35
German Pancakes ... 35
Sliced Oranges ... 15
" Bananas ... 25
" Peaches ... 25
Baked Apple and Cream ... 15
Stewed Prunes ... 15
Grape Fruit ... 20
Preserved Bartlet Pears ... 25
Fresh Pineapple ... 25
Preserved Pineapple ... 25
Omelette Souffle ... 75
Bomb Alaska ... 40 ... 75
Jelly Omelette ... 50
Rum Omelette ... 50
Strawberry Omelette ... 50
Preserved Figs ... 25

CHEESE

Cheese, a la Levy ... 25
Imported Gruyere (Special) ... 25
Kronenkase ... 15
Neufchatel ... 15
Edam ... 15
Swiss, Imported ... 15
Sierra Cream ... 15
Roquefort ... 15
De Brie ... 15
German Breakfast ... 15
Limburger, Imported ... 25
American ... 15
Camembert ... 15
Brie, Imported ... 25
Camembert, Imported ... 25
Bar le Duc Currants ... 35
Bar le Duc Strawberry ... 35

COFFEE, TEA, ETC.

Coffee, Cup, with Cream ... 10
Coffee, Pot, with Cream ... 15
" " to order, Extra Blend ... 50
Egg Malted Milk ... 25
Horlick's Malted Milk ... 15
Cocoa or Chocolate, Pot ... 15
Toast, Dry or Buttered ... 10
" Milk ... 15
Toast, Cream ... 25
Glass Milk ... 10
" Half and Half ... 20
" Cream ... 25
Iced Tea or Coffee ... 15
Toast, Boston Cream ... 25

SAUCES

Hollandaise ... 25
Bearnaise ... 25
Bordelaise ... 25
Cream Sauce ... 15
Tomato Sauce ... 15
Spanish Sauce ... 25
Mushroom ... 25
Diablo ... 15
Colbert ... 15

We Use Local and Refrigerated Poultry and Eggs

IMPORTED BEER ON DRAUGHT Pilsner Special, Glass 15c, Stein 25c. Wurzburger Hof Brau Special, Glass 15c, Stein 25c

Al Levy's Grill • 617 S. Spring St., Los Angeles • 1930s

picture sequence." The curatorial essay by owner Ralph C. Weihe was more suited to a museum exhibition catalog than a place that sells Hot Fudge Banana Royales and Hot Butterscotches and had a Scottish Terrier as its design mascot.

The gatefold 1930s menu for Al Levy's Grill opened up into a crowded three-page world of choices (including "Lent Specials") overlaid with separate small-card attachments pushing a half-broiled, spring chicken dinner as the "biggest bargain in town," a special steak plate, and a twenty-five-cent Manhattan on a cut-out shaped like a cocktail glass. Another cocktail cut-out advertising an "exhilarating" champagne cocktail was glued to the menu's cover, which was already packed with illustrations of a prop airplane and a stagecoach forging the Overland Trail. Al Levy, the city's first street vendor to flip a pushcart into a restaurant empire, opened his first oyster cart on the streets of downtown L.A. in 1897. With his restaurants, he wanted his customers to know that they were not just eating a meal, they were eating the history of the American west.

There were plenty more L.A. improvisations on the menu template. Nate's, a downtown deli and coffee shop, designed one of its 1953 menus as an "Eater's Digest" magazine that kicked off with a lengthy and cheeky "Editor's Note" from its owner Nathan Steinberg. "If by any chance there should arise any cause for complaint as to food, service, or price (or something

Hotel
ST. CATHERINE
E. H. BERNEGGER, MANAGER

BREAKFAST

STEWED SEEDLESS GRAPES
RASPBERRIES WITH CREAM   CHILLED CANTALOUP   SLICED BANANAS
SLICED VALENCIA ORANGES   GRAPEFRUIT
ORANGE JUICE   STEWED CALIFORNIA PRUNES   BLACKBERRY JAM
COMB OR STRAINED HONEY   HOME MADE JELLY
ORANGE MARMALADE   CATALINA FIGS IN SYRUP

CLAM BOUILLON IN CUP

WHEAT MUFFETS   SHREDDED WHEAT BISCUITS
CORN FLAKES   ARMOUR'S ROLLED OATS   PUFFED WHEAT
KELLOG'S BRAN   GRAPENUTS   PUFFED RICE

EGGS

BOILED   SHIRRED   FRIED   POACHED   SCRAMBLED   SUISSE
SUR LE PLAT   VIENNA
PLAIN OMELET   CHEESE OMELET   HAM OMELET
EGGS FROM ST. CATHERINE CHICKEN RANCH

FISH

FRIED CATALINA SAND DABS, PARSLEY BUTTER
BOILED FINNAN HADDIE, STEAMED POTATOES

BROILED

BREAKFAST STEAK, PLAIN OR RASHER OF BACON
SUGAR CURED HAM   BREAKFAST BACON
LAMB CHOPS ON TOAST   CERTIFIED PORK SAUSAGE
CALF'S LIVER AND BACON

SPECIALS

CREAMED ALASKA SABLE FISH ON TOAST
ROAST BEEF HASH, SOUTHERN STYLE
MINCED HAM WITH SCRAMBLED EGGS
FRIED CORN MEAL MUSH WITH SYRUP

AMERICAN FRIED POTATOES   BAKED POTATOES

BREAKFAST ROLLS   DRY TOAST   BUTTERED TOAST   CORN MUFFINS
FARINA CAKES, MAPLE SYRUP OR STRAINED HONEY

COFFEE   TEA   MILK   COCOA   HORLICK'S MALTED MILK

SERVICE TO ROOMS 50 CENTS EXTRA FOR EACH PERSON
Thursday, July 5, 1928

CATALINA ISLAND

Hotel St. Catherine • Catalina Island • 1928

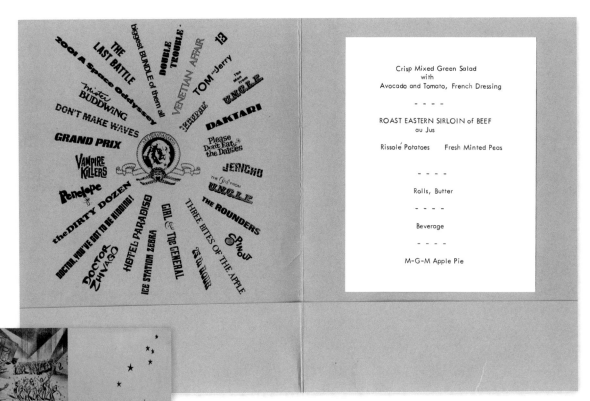

The radiating design includes titles: THE LAST BATTLE, 2001 A Space Odyssey, Mister BUDDWING, DON'T MAKE WAVES, GRAND PRIX, VAMPIRE KILLERS, Penelope, the DIRTY DOZEN, DOCTOR, YOU'VE GOT TO BE KIDDING!, DOCTOR Zhivago, HOTEL PARADISO, ICE STATION ZEBRA, GIRL & The GENERAL, THREE BITES OF THE APPLE, SPINOUT, LA HORA, THE ROUNDERS, JERICHO, THE Girl FROM U.N.C.L.E., Please Don't Eat the Daisies, DAKTARI, The Man FROM U.N.C.L.E., TOM and Jerry, VENETIAN AFFAIR, 13, DOUBLE TROUBLE, biggest BUNDLE of them all

Crisp Mixed Green Salad
with
Avocado and Tomato, French Dressing

- - - -

ROAST EASTERN SIRLOIN of BEEF
au Jus

Rissolé Potatoes   Fresh Minted Peas

- - - -

Rolls, Butter

- - - -

Beverage

- - - -

M-G-M Apple Pie

M-G-M STUDIOS

M-G-M Studios • 10202 W. Washington Blvd., Culver City • 1964

else as trivial), contact me at once, I will be found around the corner at Berliner's or the Downtowner having a sandwich." The 1928 menu of the Hotel St. Catherine on Catalina Island was both a "fold here to mail" postcard souvenir, and a tourist advertisement for the island's glass-bottom boat trips, mountain hikes, and fishing launches. A 1964 luncheon menu at M-G-M was really a press release for the studio's new TV season. Far less imagination went into presenting the drab luncheon selection (green salad, roast beef, buttered rolls, beverage, and apple pie) than into the promo stills and production stories announcing *Flipper* and *The Man From U.N.C.L.E.*

The former Brooklyn pants presser born in Lithuania, Hershel Gerguzin, used his restaurant menus to help perpetuate his own myth and sustain the L.A. restaurant world's greatest wink of a con, that he was actually Prince Mike Romanoff of Russia. A 1948 lunch menu for Romanoff's, his exclusive Beverly Hills restaurant where he reserved tables for unannounced celebrity walk-ins, devotes more space to inflating Romanoff's ego on its oversized pages than to his Brochette of Lamb Tenderloin à la Turk and Patty of Sweetbread à la King. On the cover he's wearing ripped and tattered clothes on a princely throne, scepter in hand and crown on head. Inside was a limited-edition poster of Romanoff on the ski slopes with a bottle of pricey French champagne tied around his waist, and a full-page gossip column—"Romanoff's Round-Up: Imperial Greetings"—about his inside scoop on why John Houston left Warner Bros. Following "royal" tradition, Romanoff always referred to himself in the third person.

ROMANOFFS

Romanoff's • 326 N. Rodeo Dr., Beverly Hills • 1948

UNITED STATES SHIP IDAHO

The Committee wishes to call attention to the fact that all Printing for the Ball,—Invitations, Admission Tickets and Programs, with exception of the embossed covers, is a product of the Printing Office on board the U. S. S. IDAHO

✢

CHOW CARD

SALAD A LA SEA GULL

LETTUCE HAVE PEACE

IRISH PLUMS   KELP A LA SHARK

RING BUOYS   JA-MOCH

RED SHELLAC

PARALYZED MILK

PIPE DOWN FOUR TO EIGHT BELLS

Committees

Executive Committee

H. A. OLIVER, C. Q. M., President
H. J. PINDELL, W. T., Vice-President
J. M. ELIAS, Yeo. 1c, Secretary
T. G. SWETZ, Sgt., U.S.M.C., Treasurer

Arrangement Committee

J. T. OLIVER, C. Q. M., Chairman
V. A. BARRON, C. Y., Asst. Chairman
G. S. FORTE, C. Std.   H. R. ROBERTS, Q. M. 1c
M. E. REINHOLD, Sea.   C. W. UPCHURCH, Q. M. 2c
R. A. MACHT, Shpftr. 1c

Floor Committee

G. T. MAIER, C. T. C., Chairman
C. W. SKEHAN, B. M. 2c   J. M. PLANAGAN, Sea.
J. J. MULLEN, Q. M. 2c   H. A. RIDER, Cox.
A. H. BERG, Sea.

Publicity Committee

R. E. DUMON, C. Prtr., Chairman
E. T. CROOKER, Sea., Assistant

Division Representatives

F. A. MALINOSKI, G. M. 1c   .   .   .   First Division
J. O. LLOYD, B. M. 1c   .   .   .   Second Division
W. E. MYATT, B. M. 2c   .   .   .   Third Division
P. G. GORTH, G. M. 2c   .   .   .   Fourth Division
J. M. PLANAGAN, Sea.   .   .   .   Fifth Division
C. W. SKEHAN, B. M. 2c   .   .   .   Sixth Division
G. SEGNIT, Eng. 1c   .   .   .   Engineer's Division
H. A. GANGAWARE, Yeo. 1c   .   .   .   Supply Division
R. A. MACHT, Shpftr. 1c   .   .   .   Repair Division
B. B. GRIFFIN, Q. M. 3c   .   .   .   Navigator's Division
A. H. BERG, Sea.   .   .   .   Fire Control Division

First Annual Ball

and

Reception

Given by the crew of the

United States Ship Idaho

On Wednesday, the twenty-sixth of November Nineteen hundred and nineteen

In honor of

Captain Theodore Vogelgesang
and
Commander R. S. Holmes

At Shrine Auditorium
Los Angeles

U.S.S. *Idaho* • (United States Navy) • 1919

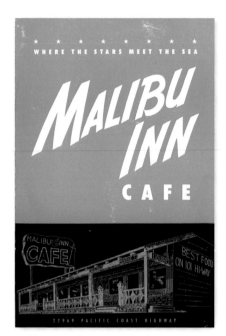

Malibu Inn Café • 22969 Pacific Coast Hwy.,
Malibu • 1950s

Fox and Hounds • 2900 Wilshire Blvd., Santa Monica • 1950s

Of more humble scale is the pocket-sized and tasseled menu, or "Chow Card," for the 1919 ball hosted by the crew of the U.S.S. *Idaho* at the Shrine Auditorium. The evening's dishes were all delivered in cryptic seaman speak: "salad à la sea gull" followed by "lettuce have peace," "kelp à la shark" followed by "ring buoys," all topped off with "paralyzed milk." The miniature menu included an even more miniature souvenir: a

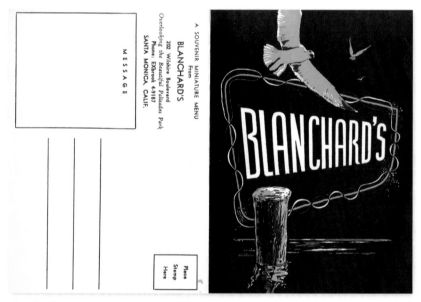

Blanchard's • 202 Wilshire Blvd., Santa Monica • 1950s

photograph of the *Idaho* that was no bigger than a commander's thumb. Souvenir miniature menus were a national trend that L.A. restaurants glommed onto with glee. From the Malibu Inn on the coast to Blanchard's and Fox and Hounds in Santa Monica to Grandview Gardens in New Chinatown, the goal was to squeeze the regular full-size menu—often as many as 150 different dishes—down to fit a small index card. These were menus for squinting, not reading. The prize for smallest menu in the Library's collection goes to Phillip's Whiz Inn in Inglewood. Its Chicken in the Basket and Dude Ranchburger were all in magnifying-glass-required fine print, laid out with tweezers on the backsides of two folded, cut out chickens.

Phillip's Whiz Inn • 2901 W. Manchester Blvd., Inglewood • 1943

Grandview Gardens • 951 Mei Ling Way, Los Angeles • 1980s

For most of the twentieth century, menus were manufactured by professional printing companies and in many cases delivered to restaurants on a daily basis to accommodate rotating specials and seasonal offerings. The largest menu printing company in the country, the Lord Printing Company, opened in 1909 in downtown Los Angeles, where its factory/warehouse full of letterpresses and linotype machines served as a "daily menu press" that supplied restaurants throughout the city with over five hundred menus a day (as well as to restaurants in San Diego, Phoenix, Lake Tahoe, and Las Vegas). It was Lord that first put full color photographs into the visual menu lexicon, an art they mastered with their menus for the Bob's Big Boy chain, which next to their hat designs for the Brown Derby menus and regal portraiture for Romanoff's, were probably their most famous. In some cases, restaurants brought their own designs already completed, but for most, it was Lord employees like Albert Abram, a seasoned lithographer who hand-carved each menu's linoleum printing blocks, in-house designer José Martinez, and Lord's resident photographers who were responsible for imagining and executing a restaurant's menu design identity. They also printed their own promotional materials and advertisements, including mock Luncheon and Dinner postcard menu mailers. In 1944, they distributed a full-size "menu" that sold the company's services atop a collage of their most visually arresting work. "A well designed menu pays two ways," went the company's sales motto, "It works for you both inside and outside your restaurant."

It not only serves as a menu but it also serves as an advertisement for your restaurant.

With food still an item of public concern, restaurant owners have greater need than ever for a well-designed menu that will merchandise the items they have to sell.

The hungry diner wants to know what he can eat, and what it will cost, clearly and quickly.

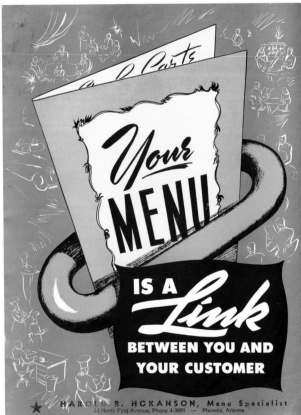

Lord Printing Company advertising material and sample menu

Original Lord menu templates for Bob's Big Boy and its franchise, Shoney's Big Boy • 1950s

**Wanted: a dish that will make Los Angeles and
California distinctive in the science of cookery.**

—Los Angeles Times, 1910

Etymologically speaking, the menu and the map have a lot in common. In French, *carte* refers to both. L.A. menus map the historical urban geography of eating out: they double as cartographies of where people ate, where restaurants have thrived, and in the case of menus for the Brown Derby, Ollie Hammond's, and Bullock's Tea Room that all put illustrated city maps on their covers, how restaurants subjectively envisioned the borders and limits of the city that surrounded them (what's on their maps was just as important as what was left off). As

part of the research for this book, we began pinning menus from the Library's collection to a city map by street address and quickly were able to see where these menus—as just one small sample of the city's restaurant population—were distributed across L.A. sprawl since the late nineteenth century.

Turns out, not so sprawling. The menus tend to cluster in dense pockets in key restaurant zones (food oases, let's say, not deserts): downtown, Chinatown, East Los Angeles, Hollywood, West Hollywood, Beverly Hills, Culver City, Venice, Santa Monica. Menu geography roughly follows the growth of "the fragmented metropolis" itself, beginning around the Plaza in downtown along Commercial and Los Angeles streets in the nineteenth century (with the exception of those cross-town hotel restaurants on the coast), and then moving out in

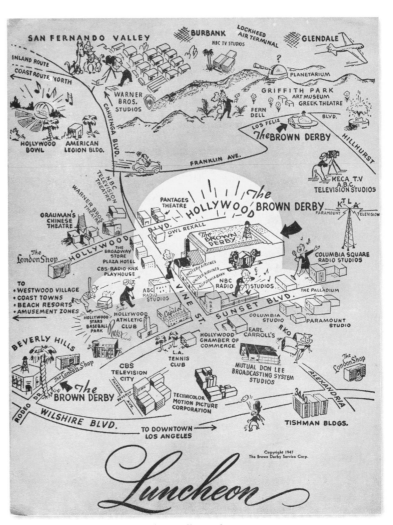

The Brown Derby • 1628 N. Vine St., Hollywood • 1953

wider downtown circles before stretching various points east and west by the 1920s. With the rise of the automobile in the 1930s, the geography of eating was no longer limited to local convenience. By 1939, there were Adams-Sheetz drive-in restaurants in the middle of downtown, in Inglewood and Huntington Park, and on the corner of Florence and Vermont, and they all featured cars and car-hops on their covers. Wilshire became the city's first mobile restaurant row and soon the glamorous glow of the Hollywood restaurant boom was well under way. There are only two menus in the Library's collection that identify themselves as being in Watts, though there are plenty from surrounding South Los Angeles communities, especially in the years before 1965. Scully's, Eleda, and The Clock, are just a few of the menus that in the 1940s and 1950s proudly proclaimed South L.A. addresses. The Clock had locations on both Atlantic Boulevard and Long Beach Boulevard and wrapped its menu map of Slauson, Florence, Bell, Huntington Park, Walnut Park, and Maywood in a big red "Southeast District" heart. During the post-World War II years leading up to the Watts uprising, however, the inequalities of South Los Angeles boiled over into a series of sweeping economic and demographic changes that would change the area's food culture for decades to come. In the 1960s and 1970s, restaurant menus from working-class and low-income African-American neighborhoods throughout South L.A. begin to dwindle, and we start to see hints of what some activists and policy organizations have dubbed the "food deserts" and "food swamps" of contemporary South Los Angeles.

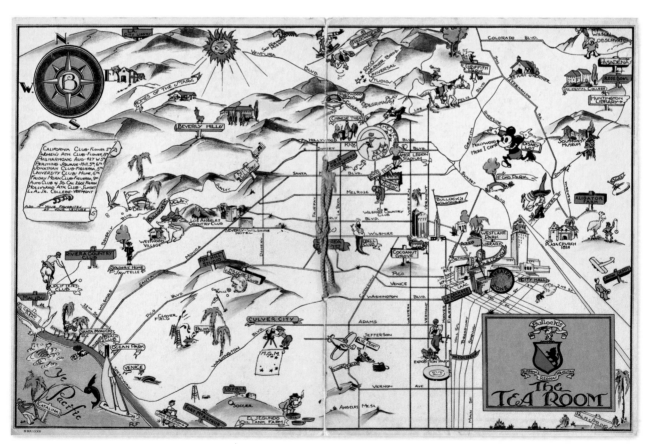

Bullock's Tea Room • Seventh at Broadway and Hill Streets, Los Angeles • 1937

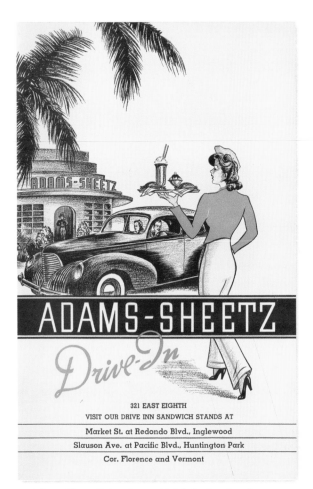

Adams-Sheetz Drive-In • 321 E. 8th St., Los Angeles • ca. 1945   McDonnell's • 4700 Huntington Dr., Los Angeles • 1940s

Yet these are not the only city maps these menus chart. Menus also offer maps of immigrant, refugee, and exile communities in the city. The city's nineteenth century French immigrant population was instrumental in the birth of the city's food and wine industry, Chinese and Japanese immigrants made L.A. a dining hub before 1900, and a tight-knit circle of Croatian immigrants ran over twenty restaurants in the 1870s (including Marcovich & Toppan's Italian Restaurant right on the original Plaza). During the World War II years, the arrival of European exiles—many of whom went straight to work in film studios and orchestras—gave the Hollywood dining scene a boost. The passage of less restrictive immigration laws in 1965 pumped Los Angeles full of new diaspora dishes—Indonesian, Mandarin Chinese, Thai—and generic "Spanish" and "Mexican" menus developed a new-found regional identity as "Oaxacan" and "Sonoran." Armenians ordered from countless menus in Glendale and from restaurants like the immigrant outpost Kavkaz, the Sunset Boulevard Armenian restaurant where Sharon Tate ate her last meal before the Manson murders (and also the restaurant eventually sold to become the first Spago). And of course, there'd be no doughnut shops left without the generation of Cambodian refugees who arrived in 1975 and cornered the market on strip-mall crullers and apple fritters.

Once the Library's collection turns to the 1980s, we see menus representing that the city

Eleda • 4296 Crenshaw Blvd., Los Angeles • 1946

Christopher Jencks once dubbed a "heteropolis," a city that is really a federation of countries: the largest Mexican city outside of Mexico, the largest Korean city outside Korea, the largest Vietnamese city outside Vietnam, and the largest Filipino city outside the Philippines. Or as the city's always-perceptive restaurant bard, Jonathan Gold, has put it, "The greatest Los Angeles cooking, real Los Angeles cooking, has first a sense of wonder about it, and only then the sense of place, because the place it has a sense of is likely to be somewhere else entirely."

While the immigrant, working-class restaurants of Los Angeles blossomed in the 1980s (alongside the wood-fired ovens and locavorism of that other, more famous California food revolution), culinary multinationalism has always been a part of the city's food profile. In the 1850s, tamale wagons and taco carts on the streets of the original Plaza—helmed by early food entrepreneurs

The Clock • 5930 Atlantic Blvd., Maywood • 1941

like Nicholas Martinez who also sold ice cream—fed Mexican migrant railroad and streetcar workers, laying the foundations for early twentieth century community restaurants like El Progreso, La Esperanza, and El Veracruzano. Tamale wagons, or "peripatetic restaurants" as the *Los Angeles Times* dubbed them in 1901, were not always simple creations. The paper reported one wagon that was two stories high, "and it looked as though the proprietor had arranged sleeping apartments on the upper floor, either for rental or living purposes." In 1881, Hilario Preciado opened a restaurant that was just advertised as "Mexican Restaurant" and was—nearly a century before El Torito opened in Encino—perhaps the first attempt to formally introduce Mexican dishes to non-Mexican diners. He served tamales, enchiladas, *carne con chile*, and *albondigas*, alongside "Spanish, French, and American cooking." The first Italian restaurant opened on Calle de los Negros in the 1850s; the first Chinese eateries opened in the 1860s; and some of the very first formal, sit-down restaurants downtown were places like Restaurant du Commerce, LaRue's, and Restaurant Français (which served pastries all day and had a corral with enough grass and water to keep its customers' horses happy).

By 1922, the *Los Angeles Times* could run a headline proclaiming "All Nations' Food Served Here" and declare the city "a melting pot of epicures." Turkish, Dutch, Chinese, Japanese, and Mexican restaurants abounded, "almost every nation of the universe without passing beyond

El Torito • (various locations) • 1979

the city limits." Six years later, the paper celebrated L.A. as a Mecca of "foreign-eating" where "the foreign-born population is more varied ... than in any other city in the world, and the spirit of its native life is concentrated in its typical restaurants." There were Greek cafés on Fourth, Mexican cafeterias on North Main, Hungarian kosher restaurants on Spring (full of "dark, thin, aesthetic Jews; plump, twinkling Germans; hatless, intense women"), and Japanese restaurants on First that served raw fish and bean-curd soup.

Throughout the 1930s, the *Times*'s regular "Southland Cafés" restaurant review column made repeated references to the city as a hub of "faraway lands." Without leaving downtown, you could eat equally well in "the Old World" and "the orient," and if you were willing to go to Hollywood, Sweden awaited. A 1934 feature in the *Times* similarly promoted the city's global menus: sukiyaki with imported shoyu at Kawafaku, *kabba* and *baba ganoush* at the Cairo Café, mustard greens soup and rice imported from South China at Yee Hung Guey, chicken enchiladas and Mexican chocolate at Los Monitos, and sauerbraten at the Hofbrau Garden. In 1937, The Weekly Publishing Service of Los Angeles provided a free menu guide focused on all the "Foreign Cooking" that could be had without leaving Los Angeles (unless you wanted to get aboard the French Line cruise ship advertised on its back page and eat the Chief Steward's *crêpes suzette*). It provided a menu for each of its restaurant recommendations: Lucca for Italian, Paris Inn for French-Italian, Rene and Jean for French, Little Hungary for Hungarian, Soochow Café for Chinese, Café Caliente for Spanish, and La Merienda (a "Genuine Café of Old Mexico" stationed, appropriately, in the Crossroads of the World building) for Mexican.

Rene and Jean • 639 S. Olive St., Los Angeles • 1938

It was during this period that a question began to be asked that dogs the city's food culture to this day: if everything here is from everywhere else, if menus are maps of ethnic regionalism and odes to faraway homes, then is there even such a thing as an L.A. menu? Do menus reveal a distinctly local L.A. culinary character?

What is now typically used to define and celebrate Los Angeles cuisine—a globalized culinary network of immigrants and refugees—was in the early twentieth century seen as an outside, "foreign" influence that often threatened the very possibility of an indigenous and unified L.A. food identity. The *Los Angeles Times* wondered as much in a 1910 article that began: "Wanted: a dish that will make Los Angeles and California distinctive in the science of cookery." New York has its meat pie and Boston has its baked beans, the paper surmised, "but Los

Slapsy Maxie's • 5665 Wilshire Blvd., Los Angeles • 1940s

Paris Inn • 210 E. Market St., Los Angeles • 1930s

Angeles with French chefs and limitless markets of meats, fruits, vegetables, and what not at all seasons, has so far failed to produce even a salad to lend it conspicuity in the culinary art." In that early-twentieth century "cosmopolitan" city that was a "strange mosaic" of people and cultures, there were places to eat, but no eating that was defined by place. Were there simply too many restaurants, the *Times* wondered, because there were too many unmarried people eating out? Was French food too popular because chefs could get fresh produce and fresh flowers all year long? Were there too many "foreigners" eating too much "foreign" food? Why, in 1910, were there three Chinese restaurants—the Oriental, the New China, and the Canton—within a block of each other on Main Street?

By 1913, the anti-gastronomic smear of L.A. had only become more popular. Writing in *Smart Set*, Willard Huntington Wright added provincialism and populist simplicity to the list. "Cooking in Los Angeles," he declared, "has none of the essentials of an art. There is no delicacy, no desire to please the eye, no imaginative combination, no rare and savory dishes copied from the astrological lore of European kitchens. No item on the bill of fare will cause an Iowan to hesitate and ponder as to its meaning. . .The atrocity of cooked food in one restaurant is only surpassed by the offering of the one down the street." Two more decades' worth of significant restaurant openings—Musso and Frank (1919), Tam o' Shanter (1922), Brown Derby (1926), Taix French Restaurant (1927), La Golondrina (1930), Canter's Delicatessen (1931), Don

Tam o' Shanter Inn • 2980 Los Feliz Blvd., Los Angeles • 1959

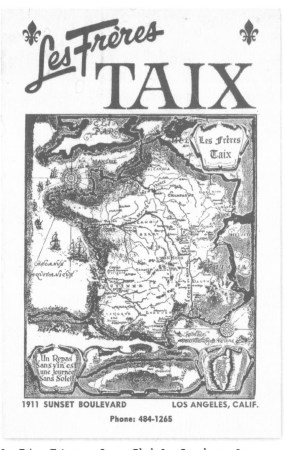

Les Frères Taix • 1911 Sunset Blvd., Los Angeles • 1960s

the Beachcomber (1934), Dragon's Den (1935), Chasen's (1936)—did little to convince many distinguished commentators that L.A. had any culinary character. James M. Cain took his shots in his 1933 essay "Paradise":

> You can go from Santa Barbara to the border, and you will not strike one place where you can get a really distinguished meal. There are, to be sure, the various Biltmores, and in Los Angeles the Ambassador, a restaurant called the Victor Hugo, a hotel called the Town House, and Bernstein's sea-food place. All of them have their points, and the Town House, I must say, really knows how to put a meal together. But they suffer from two circumstances. The first is that they can't sell liquor. If you want food and drink at the same meal, you have to go to a speak, and a California speak is so bad that there is nothing to say about

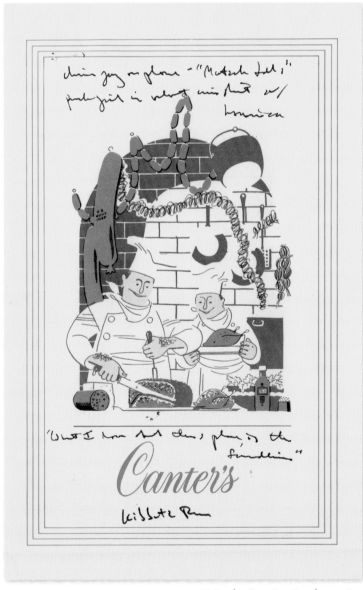

Canter's • 419 N. Fairfax Ave., Los Angeles • 1980s

Bernstein's Fish Grotto • 424 W. 6th St., Los Angeles 1937

it. The other is that they really have nothing to make a distinguished meal with. Meats are obtainable here, and vegetables, the best you can get anywhere; but when it comes to fish, and particularly shellfish, those indispensable embellishments that transform eating into dining, they are simply not to be had. Brother, God hath laid a curse on this Pacific Ocean, and decreed that nothing that comes out of it shall be fit to eat; and anybody who tells you different has simply never fished in another ocean.

The humorist S.J. Perelman picked up where Cain left off when he lampooned the L.A. lunch in 1937. "One day not long ago in Los Angeles I found myself, *banderillas* in hand, facing the horns of a dilemma," he wrote in the *New Yorker*, "Issuing into the hot sunlight of the street, I was dismayed to find that it was time for lunch, and since I had forgotten to bring along a bag of pemmican, I would have to eat in Los Angeles—a fairly exact definition of the term 'kiss of death.'" Even Lois Dwan, the restaurant critic for the *Los Angeles Times* throughout the 1970s and 1980s, confessed her own bias in an introduction she wrote to *Super Los Angeles Restaurant Guide*, a 1968 compendium of nearly two hundred L.A. restaurant menus: "But what will you write about—asked a friend (from New York) when she heard I was about to start a regular restaurant column—in Los Angeles? I wasn't too sure myself."

Restaurants and chefs have grappled with these issues for nearly as long as the city has existed. In the 1880s, local restaurants suffered from a case of what we might call "Delmonico's anxiety," the nagging desire to prove that they were just as good, just as elegant, as New York's pioneering and premiere dining palace. Both the Hollenbeck and the Commercial restaurants each advertised themselves as "the Delmonico's of Los Angeles," and Harris Newmark called the Commercial's Victor Dol "the Delmonico of his day." For the Commercial, that meant playing up its farm-to-table menu of sole, turbot, and sea trout, caught daily on the coast, and chickens "just in from the ranches." The owner, French immigrant Victor Dol, also featured a *fromage de brie* that he tried to turn into an L.A. specialty, a cheese "which can only be had at his restaurant."

In one of its earliest L.A. incarnations, the formal menu was just one more weapon in the booster arsenal. Restaurant food was the stuff of civic pride. On the menu for the 1895 L.A. Chamber of Commerce banquet dinner, each dish was named for a local landmark, regional theme, or historical event. There were "Olives à La Fiesta de Los Angeles," "Crackers and Cheese á Los Angeles Press," "Lime Frappé à la Mount Lowe Railway," and least sensibly of all "Roast Lamb with Mint Sauce à la Harbor at San Pedro." A glass of Claret-Schramsburger was served "To the Glorious Climate of California," and a plate of figs, nuts, and raisins was "à la Good Roads." In the 1920s, the 250-plus-seat Stillwell Cafeteria on Main, the one that charged a cent for napkin service and boasted washing its dishes "in fresh scalding water in our $3,000 machine," used its menu to connect their twenty-cent spareribs—with sauerkraut and five-cent sugar corn—to promotional city pride and regional climate hype. They included a "California Catechism" interrogation on its back page that included jabs at East Coast heat waves and blizzards. "What things

CALIFORNIA CATECHISM

Question—Where is the state of California located?
Answer—On the front side of the American continent, between the rest of the United States and the Pacific Ocean, and near the Panama canal.

Q.—Why is Southern California famous?
A.—It produces annually $154,000,000 worth of oil and contains Los Angeles.

Q.—What is Los Angeles?
A.—The climatic capital of the United States.

Q.—To what has it been likened?
A.—To paradise, heaven Eden and the Riviera.

Q.—Which does it most resemble?
A.—It is a happy combination of all of them.

Q.—What is the population of Los Angeles?
A.—1,100,000 boosters (Will be more tomorrow).

Q.—What is a booster?
A.—One who knows a good thing and wants others to come and share it.

Q.—Of whom does the population consist?
A.—Mostly of people from Iowa, together with many former residents of other states and a sprinkling of native sons.

Q.—Into what two classes may the people of the United States be divided?
A.—Those who have already seen Southern California and those who intend to see it soon.

Q.—What are Eastern visitors called while visiting Los Angeles? A.—Tourists.

Q.—What is a tourist?
A.—A permanent resident in the bud.

Q.—What things may a tourist see in and around Los Angeles that he does not see back East?
A.—Oranges, ostriches, lemons, alligators, olives, missions, sardines, aqueducts, harbors, tunas, bungalows, abalones, loquats, casaba melons, horned toads, snow-covered peaks, submarine gardens, yuccas, eucalyptus, palms, pepper trees, cafeterias, Thanksgiving celery and Christmas strawberries.

Q.—Does L. A. hide its light under a bushel?
A.—It does not. In addition to showing the light it sets fire to the bushel and makes a conflagration that attracts the attention of the whole world.

Q.—Has L. A. any agents working for it in the East?
A.—Yes. Mr. Cyclone, Mr. Blizzard, Mr. Thunderstorm and the two Wave brothers, Messrs. Cold and Hot.

Q.—Are they successful?
A.—Highly so. They are sending thousands of people to Los Angeles every year.

Q.—When is the best time to come to Los Angeles?
A.—At once. "Everybody's doing it."

Q.—What is the only way to leave Los Angeles?
A.—With a return ticket.

Q.—When will Los Angeles cease to exceed the speed limit in growing? A.—When Gabriel blows his horn.

Q.—Where is the best place to eat in Los Angeles?
A.—STILLWELL'S "NONE SUCH" CAFETERIA. 633 So. Main St. Phone, TRinity 1971. Los Angeles
G. W. & J. E. STILLWELL, Inc.

17th Year
Stillwell Cafeteria

633 South Main Street
Los Angeles

Nearly Opposite Pacific Electric Depot
New, Enlarged Up-to-date Equipment
Seating over 250

All our glasses, silverware and dishes are thoroughly washed, sterilized and *rinsed in fresh scalding water* in our $3,000 machine.

3 Serving Counters
Quick Service
6 a. m. to 7:30 p. m.

Sundays 11 to 7:45

We serve the Best at a Low Price

GEO. W. & J. E. STILLWELL, Props.
SAM PETRUCELLI, Chef.
JOHN S. COBB, Manager.

STILLWELL CAFETERIA

BREAKFAST

6 A. M. to 10:30 A. M. Except Sunday

Fried Egg	5c to 7c	Milk Toast	10c
Fried Ham	10c	All Breakfast Cereals	5c
Pork Sausage	5c	Fried Potatoes	5c
Fried Mush, 3c, 2 for 5c		3 Hot Cakes, 1 Syrup, 1 Butter, 1 Cup Coffee with Cream	10c
Boiled Egg	5c to 7c		
Fried Bacon	5c	Apple Sauce	5c
Coffee with Cream	5c	Stewed Prunes	5c
Oat Meal	5c	Rhubarb Sauce	5c
Cream of Wheat	5c	Stewed Figs	5c
Roman Meal	5c	Grape Fruit	5c to 10c
Toast, 2c, 3 for	5c	Sliced Oranges	5c to 10c
Hot Milk	5c	Napkin Service	1c

SALADS

Potato	5c
Cold Slaw	5c
Macaroni	5c
Fruit	10c
Shrimp	10c
Cream Cheese	3c
Celery	5c
Pickles	5c
Green Onions	3c
Head Lettuce	5c
Asparagus	10c
Beets	3c
Combination	5c & 10c
Egg Salad	10c
Chicken Salad	20c
Stuffed Tomato	10c
Cold Ham and Potato Salad	20c
Sliced Tomatoes	5c
Stuffed Pepper	10c
Mayonaise Dressing	2c
Olive Oil	2c
1000 Island Dressing	5c
Tomato Ketchup	2c
Cottage Cheese	5c
Napkin Service	1c

BREAD

Corn Bread	2c
Bran Muffins	2c
Rye	1c
White	1c
Raisin	2c
Bran Bread	2c
Biscuit	2c
Whole Wheat	2c
Butter (1)	2c
French Rolls	3c
Graham	1c

DESERTS

Pies	5c & 10c
Bread Pudding	5c
Rice Custard	7c
Indian Pudding	5c
Cocoanut Pudding	10c
Fruit Pudding	10c
Apple Cobbler	7c
Peach Cobbler	7c
Berry Cobbler	10c
Jello	5c
Apple Dumpling	10c
Ice Cream	5c
Preserved Figs	10c
Layer Cake	5c
Stewed Prunes	5c
Apple Sauce	5c
Rhubarb Sauce	5c
Melba Peaches	10c
Whipped Cream	5c
Sliced Pineapple	5c
Cranberry Sauce	5c
Comb Honey	10c
Strained Honey	5c
Jam and Jelly	5c
Orange Marmalade	5c
Cantaloupe	5c to 10c
Watermelon	5c to 10c

MEATS

Soups	5c
Meat Loaf	10c
Beef Hash	5c
Pork Chops	10c
Hamburger	10c
Roast Beef	15c
Sausage	5c

Pork and Dressing	15c
Roast Lamb and Dressing	20c
Macaroni & Cheese	5c
T-Bone Steak	30c
Top Sirloin	25c
Pounded Steak	20c
Country Gravy	
Fried Fish	15c
Tarter Sauce	3c

VEGETABLES

Sugar Corn	5c
Stewed Tomatoes	3c
Carrots	3c
Lima Beans	3c
Peas	5c
String Beans	5c
Spinach	5c
Boiled Rice	3c
Spaghetti	5c
Sweet Potatoes	10c
Chili Sauce	5c
Squash	5c
Chili Beans	3c
With Chili	5c
Boiled Potatoes	5c
Fried Potatoes	5c
Baked Potatoes	7c

HOT AND COLD DRINKS

Coffee with Cream	5c
Grade A Milk, ½ pt.	7c
Fresh Butter Milk	5c
Iced Tea	5c
Black & Green Tea	5c
Chocolate	5c
Postum	5c
Orange Juice	5c

EVERY DAY SPECIALS

Monday

Spare Ribs, Sauer Kraut	20c
Beef Stew	15c

Tuesday

Wieners & Kraut	15c
Beef Stew Spanish	15c

Wednesday

Pig Hocks and Cabbage	20c
Goulash & Noodles	20c

Thursday

Corned Beef and Cabbage	15c
Lamb Stew	15c

Friday

Creamed Cod Fish	10c
Fried Fish	15c
Tartar Sauce	3c

Saturday

Short Ribs Beef, Brown Potato	20c
Veal Stew	15c

Sunday

Chicken Fricassee with Dumplings	40c
Roast Veal with Dressing	20c
Baked Ham and Honey Sauce	25c

Stillwell Cafeteria • 633 S. Main St., Los Angeles • ca. 1925

may a tourist see in and around Los Angeles that he does not see back East?" the menu asked. Among the answers were "Thanksgiving celery" and "Christmas strawberries." (In light of their hosting a "Red Supper" dinner in 1919, they might have also asked: "Where can Marxists serve themselves an affordable, not-so-capitalist meal?")

Beyond culinary boosterism, menus lead us to the pantheon of L.A. food "originals." At the turn of the twentieth century, when L.A. was the premiere sanitorium destination for the infirm and the invalid—a TB tourist hot-spot—the restaurant dishes L.A. was notorious for were vegetarian. At early health-conscious haunts like the Vegetarian Restaurant (which opened at the bottom of Bunker Hill in 1903) and the Nut Kettle (home of the nut burger) in the 1930s, plant and vegetable dishes fed the city's thriving vegetarian and raw food movements. At Hain's Health Foods on W. Third Street, you could order off the "you're not in Iowa anymore" menu and put away a lunch of alfalfa candy, seaweed, and veggie bologna with a chaser of either fresh-pressed loganberry juice or "Potassium Broth" (a celery and spinach remedy). In the middle of the Depression, local citrus companies even had the gall to push a weight-loss regime, the "Hollywood Eighteen-Day Diet," that cobbled together six hundred calories a day out of grapefruit, raw veggies, melba toast and coffee. (This wasn't true everywhere. Some menus flaunted their un-healthiness. At the Lick Pier Coffee Shop, you could get any breakfast dish "fried in butter" for an extra five cents.)

Eating healthy, pure, and raw turned L.A. dining into a national punch line. "Los Angeles!" the WPA exclaimed in its 1930s report on how L.A. eats, "Where religion turns into thousands of obscure cults; where by street dress men and women merge into a common sex; and where the fine art of eating becomes a pseudo scientific search for a lost vitality hidden in the juice of a raw carrot." In his *New Yorker* takedown, Perelman mocked L.A. menus boasting of ice cream made with "no fillers," "cane sugar," and "real fruits." "One thing I'll have in my ice cream or it's no dice," he quipped in the piece he titled "Avocado, or the Future of Eating," "and that's fillers." By the 1940s, a version of the California Salad—avocados and cottage cheese a must—was as ubiquitous on L.A. menus as were the pre-Atkins "Dieter's Delight" or "Weight Watcher" options, which usually went something like this: burger patty, cottage cheese, sliced tomatoes, a ring of pineapple, and Melba toast or a RyKrisp on the side. A similar version was available at

Lick Pier Coffee Shop

- We serve the finest foods at reasonable prices . . .
- We make our own waffle and pancake batter .
- We serve Breakfast at all hours . . . . . .
- We make our own chili . . . .

30 OCEAN FRONT
Phone Santa Monica 6-2131
VENICE
•
SAMUEL PORTNOY, Prop.

Lick Pier Coffee Shop • 30 Ocean Front, Venice • 1921

The Source • 8301 Sunset Blvd., West Hollywood • 1960s

La Golondrina, only there it was offered as the "Mexican Weight Watcher."

An early guru of the L.A. vegetarian menu and organic food movement was Jim Baker, an ex-Marine and failed Tarzan actor. In 1957, during the heyday of processed and frozen foods, he and his wife Elaine opened the Aware Inn on Sunset Boulevard, which featured organic fruit and vegetables and free-range chickens. When *Gourmet* critic Caroline Bates ate there in 1974, she called its use of raw sugar, whole-wheat flour, and locally sourced milk and cream "alarmingly nutritious." In the 1960s, Baker remade himself as Father Yod, the leader of the Hollywood Hills spiritualist cult the Source Family, and opened the Source restaurant so his devotees could share raw combinations of carrots, beets, and sprouts like the Higher Key Salad and the Aware Salad with the city at large. It too became a punch line. "I'm gonna have the alfalfa sprouts," Woody Allen joked when he ate there in *Annie Hall* (1977), "and, uh, a plate of mashed yeast."

In her 1935 tour of Los Angeles restaurants in *Curious California Customs*, Elisabeth Webb-Herrick called L.A. the home of "the vitamin-minded," where lunch meant salad and sprouts. She also noticed that the vitamin-minded were a fickle bunch. "Your native Californian has a very great regard for his vitamins for luncheon," she wrote. "But we betide the dietician who tries to part him from his beefsteak at night!" Yes, the beefsteaks come out at night.

L.A. has always been beefsteak country. We are an adventurous burgeropolis, a sandwich sanctuary. The hamburger wasn't born here, but the cheeseburger was (originally called the "Aristocratic Hamburger Sandwich" at Sternberger's the Rite Spot in Pasadena), as was the chili burger or "chili size" (at Ptomaine Tommy's in Highland Park), the spaghetti burger or "royal size" (at O'Dell's on Figueroa), the hickory burger (at the Apple Pan on Pico), and the burger-hot dog combo or "Hamburger-Bologna sandwich" at Perry's Brass Rail in Hollywood (not to be confused with Tommy's Willy Burger which included cheese and a grilled hot dog). At the Clock Broiler, the hamburger was anthropomorphic, a smiling burger boy with a wide smile and skinny legs named Chubby the Champ. Fatty Arbuckle allegedly invented the steak sandwich at the Vernon Country Club, Tip's invented the pancake sandwich in 1925, and two

L.A. restaurants, Cole's and Philippe's, claim to have invented the French Dip beef sandwich. "Los Angeles," Don Dolan reported from his visit to L.A. for the Works Progress Administration, "retains the art of the sandwich; in so doing, it is guilty on at least three counts of providing the *piéce de resistance* of an eat-and-run meal." Just look at the sandwich showroom on the 1937 menu for the Globe Coffee Shop: ten "three deck" sandwich options, twenty single-deck sandwiches, and a fifteen-cent "hamburger sandwich."

Of course, the "only in L.A" claims don't stop at burger behemoths and skyscraper sandwiches. Our restaurants hold the birthright citizenship papers to Veal Oscar (Scandia), hard-shell tacos (Mitla Café in San Bernardino), the Cobb Salad (Brown Derby), BBQ Chicken Pizza and Jewish Pizza (Spago), the California Roll (Tokyo Kaikan), the ice cream sundae (C.C. Brown's), and most recently, the Korean Short-Rib Taco and Kimchi Quesadilla (Kogi). There were early sushi bars in Little Tokyo as early as 1906, but it's Kawafuku that is still credited as being the first

O'Dell's • 4922 S. Figueroa, Los Angeles • 1928

restaurant in the U.S. to open a contemporary style sushi bar in 1966. The 1980s might get credit for "Asian-fusion" but the style had its roots in early twentieth century Chinatown and Little Tokyo menus that spliced veteran homeland dishes with tamales and spaghetti.

The cafeteria menu was perfected here, the carhop drive-in menu was invented here, the "thick steaks and thin pancakes" trend started here (at Tip's in the 1930s), and the theme restaurant menu was turned into graphic-design high art here (menus shaped like monkeys, baseballs, and the faces of clowns). We are the capital of burgers, tacos, and pastrami sandwiches advertised together on menu boards next to car washes. We are the home of the apostrophe restaurant (Carl's, Ricky's, Daisy's, Bob's, Simon's, Herbert's, Rothey's, Foxy's). We are the U.S. laboratory of the taqueria, the pop-up bacon-wrapped hot dog *puesto*, the taco truck, and since it began trending in the 1940s, the taco stand: Taco House, Alice's Taco Terrace, Tito's Tacos, King Taco, Bert's Taco, Taco Junction, Frank's Taco Inn, to name but a few (and to not even mention Taco Bell).

La Scala
BEVERLY HILLS

FULL PARKING
Two hours with validation
George Payne Parking
Catered by Le Grill and L'Orangerie Pkwy

La Scala
Luncheon Menu

Appetizers
Mozzarella Marinara 2.25   Half Cantaloupe 1.25   Little Neck Clams 3.45
Fresh Cracked Crab 3.95   Prosciutto and Melon 3.95
Pate de Foie Gras de Strasburg 8.50   Nova Scotia Salmon 3.45
Fresh Asparagus 2.65   Caviar "Beluga Malossol" (1 oz.) 13.50

Soup
Zuppa all'Ortolana 1.45   Minestrone 1.25

Salads
Leon Salad 1.75   California Salad 2.45   Mixed Green 1.50
Mushrooms and Watercress 1.95   Hearts of Romaine, Roquefort 2.45

Entrees
Fettuccine Leon 4.95
Coquille de Crab Portofino 4.95   Cotoletta Milanese 5.95
Scaloppini di Vitello Piccata 5.95   Eggs Benedict 4.25   Poached Salmon 5.25
Omelette Port Salut 3.95   Calf's Liver al Vino Bianco 5.45
Spaghetti al Gusto 4.25   Vitello Tonnato 5.95   Lasagne Verdi al Forno 4.45
Chicken La Scala 4.95   Omelette aux Champignon 3.95   Steamed Clams 4.65
Linguine alle Vongole 4.95   Filet of Sole al Cabernet 5.65
Cannelloni La Scala or Gigi 4.45

Broiler
Chopped Sirloin of Beef 5.45   Prime New York Steak 9.50
Veal Steak 9.50   Lamb Chops, Ver Pre 9.50   Scampi Grille 5.95

Cold Plates
Roast Sirloin of Beef 6.45   Fisherman Salad 4.95   Half Broiled Chicken 4.45
Leon's Chopped Salad 4.25   Fresh Fruit Salad with Cottage Cheese 4.25

Desserts
Mousse au Chocolat 1.25   Cheese and Fruit 1.75   Cheese Cake 1.25
Zuppa Inglese 1.25   Fresh Fruit Tart 1.25   Sherbet 1.25
Ice Cream 1.25   Macedonia of Fruit al Champagne 1.75

Beverage
Caffe Expresso .60   Cappuccino 1.75
Coffee .35   Tea .35
House Wine "Pitcher" 3.25

Special of the Day
5.25

For Private Parties
Inquire About The Piazza Room And The President Room

La Scala • 9455 Santa Monica Blvd., Beverly Hills • 1960s

Something Tastes Divine!

C. C. BROWN'S: A SOUTHLAND TRADITION

Hot fudge, the dieter's dream! Just the thought of it inspires a feeling of bliss. There's nothing that tastes as luscious or leaves you as smugly satisfied, and the one place that is synonymous with this glorious concoction is C. C. Brown's famed establishment at 7007 Hollywood Boulevard.

When you enter Brown's, you are immediately enveloped in the rich, nostalgic smell of the candy kitchen—bringing back childhood memories of watching chocolate frosting bubbling on the stove and clamouring for the privilege of "licking the bowl." After an initial heavenly whiff, the whole atmosphere of Brown's settles gently down, putting you on the side of the angels as you prepare to consume each exquisite mouthful. This wonderful confectionery retains the distinctive personality of an old-fashioned ice cream parlor with high-backed black walnut and mahogany booths, looking as chocolate as the fudge, pink leather seats, and warm lighting—no flashy chrome, fluorescent lights, or lack of privacy. The charming and affable proprietor allows that his customers wouldn't let him change a thing (and we quite agree with them). Every day a dozen or more tell him how nice it is that everything is the same at Brown's—happily remembering it from their days at Hollywood High School twenty years ago.

For Brown's grew up with Hollywood. In 1929 when they moved to the present location, two major landmarks—Grauman's Chinese Theatre and the Hollywood Roosevelt Hotel—had not long been built. For years the most celebrated names in the entertainment business have frequented the sweet shop. During the halcyon days of the big premiere, fans used to line up outside Brown's for hours while great screen stars like Joan Crawford signed autographs. Mr. Brown's reminiscence of the 70-year-old institution's colorful history would make an interesting story in itself.

It all started in 1906 when the first C. C. Brown opened a candy store at 7th and Hill in downtown Los Angeles. His son, the present C. C. Brown, joined him in 1922, and his was the idea of creating the now famous fudge sauce. He started making a gallon a day in the back of the store, stirring and tasting, blending sugars as well as flavorings. (Blending the sugar is the secret of the sauce's incomparably smooth taste.) Brown changed the formula every day for twenty years until he had just the right consistency and flavor. Having achieved perfection, he hasn't changed the recipe for the last 20 years. Today, 35 gallons a day are made in the kitchen; some of it is put up in small containers and sold over the counter. In the near future, Mr. Brown hopes to open a larger canning facility and distribute his unique fudge sauce through fancy groceries.

Brown's also has their own delicious candy, once known in the vernacular of an earlier era as "Ragtime Chocolates." Now called "C. C. Brown's Originals," the candies are made of dark and light chocolate mixed with the same freshly roasted and chopped almonds that top the sundaes and filled with fifteen different flavors. In addition to the fudge, there is a sensational hot caramel sundae, made with sauce just as thick, and a hot coffee sundae. Other fancy ice cream delights are legion—sandwiches, too, for those who can manage a preface to the "Last Act."

This "Last Act"—a hot fudge sundae at C. C. Brown's—has become a cherished Southland tradition, which we may all hope to enjoy for the next fifty years.

After the war another member of the Brown family, Mr. John A. Schumacher and his beautiful wife and their eight little children took over the operation.

Again every day dozens of customers tell them how nice it is that everything is the same at Brown's.

To celebrate our 70 years of service, Brown's opened in the Woodland Hills Promenade, serving all the specialties.

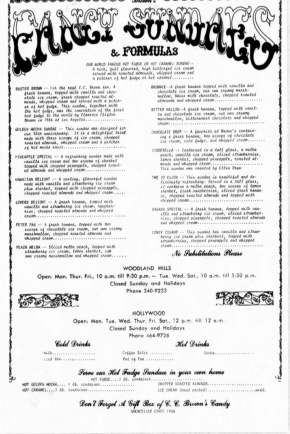

C.C. Brown's • 7007 Hollywood Blvd., Hollywood • ca. 1980s

Tip's • 921 Broxton Ave., Westwood • 1943

Cook's Steak House • 645 S. Olive St., Los Angeles • 1960

Knott's Berry Farm • Buena Park • 1940

The Owl Drug Company
(various locations) • 1940s

Zamboanga South Sea Café and Nite Club
3828 W. Slauson Ave., Los Angeles • 1940s

Ricky's
323 W. Valley
Blvd., Alhambra
1969

The menu cover
illustration for a
1958 meeting of
the Wine and Food
Society of San
Francisco is
repurposed on
menu covers of
Ricky's and Carl's
restaurants.

Carl's • S. Flower and S. Figueroa Streets at W. 38th Street, Los Angeles • 1961

Appetizers

Shrimp or Crab Meat Cocktail 1.25
Chilled Tomato or Orange Juice 45
Clam Juice 75

TUNA SALAD (All White Meat Albacore) Garnished with Hard Boiled Egg, Sliced Tomato, Pickle and Lettuce	1.75
AVOCADO Stuffed with Tuna Salad	1.95
TUNA SALAD SANDWICH	1.25
COLD ALBACORE (All White Meat), Potato Salad and Sliced Tomato	1.95

Luncheon

SERVED 11:00 A.M. TO 4:00 P.M.

SOUP: Vegetable — Cup .50; Bowl 65
French Onion au Gratin — Cup .50; Bowl 65
FRIED FILET OF SEATTLE HALIBUT,
   Tartar Sauce 1.75
GRILLED SWORDFISH STEAK, Lemon Butter . 1.85
ABALONE STEAK, Fried in Butter, Creamed
   Cole Slaw, Tartar Sauce 2.45
BRAISED SHORTRIBS OF STEER BEEF,
   Oven Browned Potato 1.85
ROAST PRIME RIB OF STEER BEEF, au Jus 3.35
COLD PRIME RIB OF STEER BEEF, Sliced
   Tomato, Potato Salad 2.75
CHICKEN SALAD, Sliced Tomato and
   Hard Boiled Egg 1.75
COLD ALASKAN RED SOCKEYE SALMON,
   Potato Salad and Sliced Tomato 1.85
COTTAGE CHEESE with Sliced Pineapple,
   Choice of Dressing 1.65
ASSORTED COLD CUTS with American
   Cheese and Potato Salad 2.10
AVOCADO FILLED WITH FRESH SEA FOOD,
   1000 Island Dressing 1.65
CHEF'S MIXED GREEN SALAD with Alaskan
   King Crab Meat, 1000 Island Dressing 1.85
FRESH ALASKAN KING CRAB MEAT
   a la Louie, 1000 Island Dressing 2.25
SHRIMP A LA LOUIE, 1000 Island Dressing . . . 2.65
COLD BARBECUED ONE-HALF CHICKEN 1.95

Absolutely No Substitutions

MINIMUM CHARGE PER PERSON — 75c

●●●●●●●●

SPECIAL DESSERTS

Homemade Cheese Cake 65
French Vanilla, Chocolate or Special Ice Cream 45
Wine Jell-O Whipped Cream 50
Hot Green Apple Pie 45   Sherbet 45
Chocolate Sundae 70   Half Fresh Grapefruit . . .45
French Whip Chocolate Chip Pie 45

For Many Years You Have Made Us Famous for the Following

HAMBURGER STEAK 1.85
HOT PRIME RIB SANDWICH 2.55
HAMBURGER SANDWICH 1.15
STEAK SANDWICH ON TOAST 1.35
AVOCADO STUFFED with FRESH SEA FOOD . 1.65
CENTER CUT HAM and (3) RANCH EGGS 2.45

Special Salads

Head Lettuce . . .60   Sliced Tomatoes . . .70
Chef's Salad Bowl, Ham and Turkey . . 1.95
Special Avocado Salad 1.45
Cottage Cheese, Chopped Green Onions 1.35
Avocado with Crab Legs 2.50
   with Shrimp 2.65

Cold Dishes

**Smoked Alaska Red Salmon,
Hard Boiled Egg** 1.95
**Cold Pickled Ox Tongue,
Swiss Cheese** 1.85
**Assorted Cold Meats with
American Cheese** 1.95
**Baked Honey-Cured Ham,
Swiss Cheese** 2.10
**Imported Kosher Salami
with Assorted Cheese** 1.85
Potato Salad Served with Above Orders

CLOSED SUNDAYS

**FILET MIGNON STEAK
SANDWICH**
on Toasted Bun with French Fried Potatoes
and Mixed Green Salad with Choice of Dressing
$2.55

HOT PRIME RIB SANDWICH
Potatoes du Jour, Mixed Green Salad with
Choice of Dressing
$2.55

**DINING CAR SPECIAL THREE-DECK
TOASTED SANDWICH**
Consisting of Ham, Prime Rib of Beef, Swiss Cheese
$1.85

SPECIAL CLUB SANDWICH
Sliced Chicken, Bacon, Tomato and Mayonnaise
$1.75

**CENTER CUT HAM, OR BACON
or PAN FRIED STEAK
and (3) RANCH EGGS**
$2.45

**NEW YORK CUT STEAK
SANDWICH**
on Toasted Bun with French Fried Potatoes
and Mixed Green Salad with Choice of Dressing
$2.75

Sandwiches

HOT SANDWICHES

(No Deviation)

Dining Car Steak Sandwich on Toast 1.35
Dining Car Special Hamburger 1.15
Fried Egg 85
Grilled Cheese 1.15

Sliced Turkey or Chicken 1.55
Boiled Ham   .95   Prime Rib of Beef 1.75
American Cheese .95   Liverwurst 1.15
Swiss Cheese 95   Ham and Cheese 1.35
Corned Beef . . . . 1.15   Sardine 1.35
Ox Tongue . . . . . 1.15   Avocado 1.15

We Reserve the Right to Refuse Service to Anyone
Not Responsible for Wearing Apparel or Lost Articles
California Sales Tax and City Sales Tax will be Added to Above Prices

OVER 38 YEARS
IN
SAME
LOCATION

Pacific Dining Car

1310 West Sixth Street   Phone: HU 3-6000

Pacific -1

We will not go
fishing this summer.
We're now open for lunch
and dinner year 'round.

Best Ptg. LA

Pacific Dining Car • 2700 Wilshire Blvd., Santa Monica • 1990s

We are the only city where in the 1970s, a Mexican chef could serve *higados Yucatan* and *pollo verde* stuffed chorizo in a Beverly Hills cottage built in a faux New England village (as La Cantina did) only blocks from where, decades earlier, the Hungarian immigrant Mama Weiss opened an old-fashioned *czadra* in her bungalow home on Rodeo Drive. It's safe to presume that only in Los Angeles would a restaurant, like the one at the Ambassador Hotel in the 1950s, offer a menu for dining not *by* the pool, but *in* the pool. And of course, what's more L.A. than an L.A. restaurant in a Hollywood film, a set-piece for the whole world to see, whether it's the Formosa Café (*L.A. Confidential* [1997]), the Pacific Dining Car (*Training Day* [2001]), Pat & Lorraine's (*Reservoir Dogs* [1992]), Henry's (*Mildred Pierce* [1945]), Far East Café (*Farewell, My Lovely* [1975]), and perhaps more than any other, Johnie's Coffee Shop (*Miracle Mile* [1988], *Volcano* [1997], *The Big Lebowski* [1998], *American History X* [1998]), whose owners kept its prime Fairfax and Wilshire location long after it closed as an eatery and preserved the space strictly as a film and event location (a restaurant turned starlet).

Yet as one prominent L.A. menu collector told me, there might actually be only one thing that differentiates the L.A. menu from all others. Out here we like our menus big.

> At Lang's. He again praises Atlantis to the ersatz skies.
> He sees a special lifestyle where I only see high capitalism:
> possible I can't see the "real" Atlantis for the high capitalism.
> —BERTOLT BRECHT, 1942

Los Angeles has always been a republic of eaters, but one where you're a welcome citizen only if you can afford what the menus are selling. The earliest menus in the Library's collection are not documents of where and what the city ate, but of where and what the city's upper-classes ate—more high capitalism than everyman Atlantis. Many early L.A. menus promised "the finest" to only the most discerning "first-class" palates, like the Commercial which billed itself "the rendezvous of all wealthy strangers." Don Mateo Keller's 1875 banquet menu was just the beginning of a tuxedoed tradition of formal L.A. banquet meals that used their gourmet menus—rarely without a few dishes in untranslated French—to exude prestige, class, and exclusivity. If you threw a lavish wedding party at the Commercial Restaurant in 1881, you made sure to have the *Los Angeles Times* print the menu of Halibut à la Hollandaise, Fillet de Boeuf à la Rothschild, and Pigeons à la Rebecca on its front page. In the early 1900s, the dining room of the Hotel Alexandria was elite L.A.'s banquet location of choice, hosting dinners—Toke Point Oysters, Sand Dabs Papillote, and Roast Squab—for the likes of the Southern California Medical Society, the Southern California Association of the Companions of the M.O.L.L.U.S., and J.A. Graves, the president of the Farmer and Merchants National Bank. The latter was served Caviar Canapés and Guinea Chicken à L'Anglaise while being celebrated by an intimidating lineup of L.A. heavies: Pasadena District Attorney George S. Patton, engineer William Mulholland, U.S. District Attorney George Denis, and California Bankers Association President Stoddard Jess. By the 1920s, the Ambassador Hotel took over banquet duties, and over the next three decades feted everyone from Albert Einstein (Essence of Chicken aux Quenelles, Salad Beaudry) and Haile Selassie (Melon Balls Orientale, Stuffed Boneless Squab Chicken) to General Douglas MacArthur (Mixed Colossal Olives, Broiled Filet Mignon) and Nikita Khrushchev (*Tournedos Bolshoi*, Romaine Salad *Caucasienne* with Lorenzo Dressing).

As was the case with other growing urban centers across the country, fine-dining restaurants in Los Angeles generally prospered up until the passage of Prohibition laws in 1920. Without wine, gourmet tables emptied, and cafés, lunch counters, and cafeterias took over. Restaurateur Al Levy was worried that any chance the city had at emerging as a gastronomic superpower was now buried. "People have forgotten how to dine: they merely eat," he told the *Los Angeles Times* in 1933; "Where is the Los Angeles café that could serve a full banquet to 3000 people?" The oyster magnate shouldn't have worried too much. Gourmet fever was still in

His Imperial Majesty
ƐMPEROR ℋAILE ＄ELASSIE I
OF
ETHIOPIA

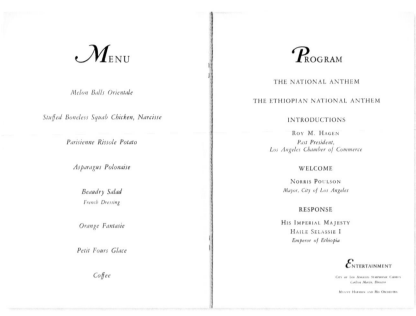

*ℳ*ENU

Melon Balls Orientale

Stuffed Boneless Squab Chicken, Narcisse

Parisienne Rissole Potato

Asparagus Polonaise

Beaudry Salad
French Dressing

Orange Fantasie

Petit Fours Glace

Coffee

*𝒫*ROGRAM

THE NATIONAL ANTHEM

THE ETHIOPIAN NATIONAL ANTHEM

INTRODUCTIONS
ROY M. HAGEN
Past President,
Los Angeles Chamber of Commerce

WELCOME
NORRIS POULSON
Mayor, City of Los Angeles

RESPONSE
HIS IMPERIAL MAJESTY
HAILE SELASSIE I
Emperor of Ethiopia

*ℰ*NTERTAINMENT
CITY OF LOS ANGELES SYMPHONIC CHORUS
Carlton Martin, Director

MOUNT HARMON AND HIS ORCHESTRA

Ambassador Hotel / Haile Selassie menu/program • 3400 Wilshire Blvd., Los Angeles • 1954

the air, finding a home amidst the private rooms and pink chandeliers of Victor Hugo's, where M.F.K. Fisher first followed her mother's palette to a plate of Chicken à la King. The vaunted Victor Hugo legacy would prove hard to kill: the Victor Hugo Inn brought gourmet French cooking to a seaside cliff in Laguna Beach in 1938, and the Beverly Hills branch of Victor Hugo would decades later be reborn as Joachim Splichal's Max au Triangle before it too closed, only to be replaced in 1989 by a new version of Victor Hugo.

Perino's had just opened on Wilshire in 1932 and, over the next three decades, would grow into the city's most revered fine-dining French restaurant and bone-china clubhouse for the

GENERAL OF THE ARMY DOUGLAS MACARTHUR

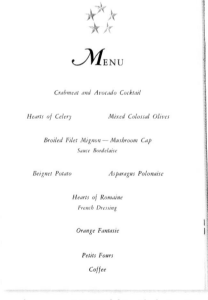

*ℳ*ENU

Crabmeat and Avocado Cocktail

Hearts of Celery   Mixed Colossal Olives

Broiled Filet Mignon — Mushroom Cap
Sauce Bordelaise

Beignet Potato   Asparagus Polonaise

Hearts of Romaine
French Dressing

Orange Fantasie

Petits Fours
Coffee

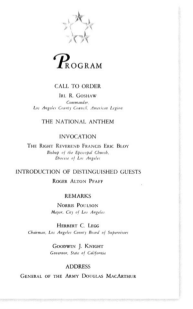

*𝒫*ROGRAM

CALL TO ORDER
IRL R. GOSHAW
Commander,
Los Angeles County Council, American Legion

THE NATIONAL ANTHEM

INVOCATION
THE RIGHT REVEREND FRANCIS ERIC BLOY
Bishop of the Episcopal Church,
Diocese of Los Angeles

INTRODUCTION OF DISTINGUISHED GUESTS
ROGER ALTON PFAFF

REMARKS
NORRIS POULSON
Mayor, City of Los Angeles
HERBERT C. LEGG
Chairman, Los Angeles County Board of Supervisors

GOODWIN J. KNIGHT
Governor, State of California

ADDRESS
GENERAL OF THE ARMY DOUGLAS MACARTHUR

Ambassador Hotel / Gen. Douglas MacArthur menu/program • 3400 Wilshire Blvd., Los Angeles • 1955

PERINO'S

LUNCHEON

Saturday, February 21, 1942

COCKTAILS

Crab Cocktail .70   Crab Legs .90
Shrimp Cocktail .70   with Avocado .85
Lobster .90   Blue Points .90
Crab Legs with Avocado .90
Oyster Rockefeller 1.30   Fresh Fruit Supreme .60

Cotuits 1.00
Crab Louie 1.25
Cherry Stone Clams .90
Tomato Juice .30

Olympia Oyster Cocktail .90
Clam Juice Cocktail .45
Half Cracked Crab, Mustard Sauce 1.00
Half Avocado .65   Sauerkraut Juice .30
Avocado Cocktail, 1000 Island Dressing .80

HORS D'OEUVRES

Nova Scotia Salmon 1.10
Mackerel in White Wine .80
Smoked Sturgeon .90
Marinated Herring .75
Filets of Tuna Fish .75
Imported Russian Fresh Caviar, p.p. 2.90

Assorted Hors d'Oeuvres 1.00
Prosciutto 1.00
Stuffed Celery au Roquefort .65
Celery Victor .65
Celery en Branche .40   Green Olives .40
Au Blinis 3.25   Canape 2.50

Tarrine Pate de Foie Gras 1.20
Boneless French Sardines 1.15
Antipasto .90   Salami .60
Crab Meat Ravigott 1.00
Colossal Ripe Olives .40; Stuffed w. Anchovie .70
Canape Lorenzo 1.20

SOUPS

Puree of Lentil Conty .35

Consomme .30   Chicken Broth .30
Tomato Bouillon .30
Clam Broth .40   Consomme Bellevue .45

Onion Soup Gratin .55
Petite Marmite .50
Green Turtle au Sherry .75
COLD: Vichysoisse .50   Cream Senegales .55   Madrilene .35   Consomme .35

Vermicelli a l'Uovo .55
Cream of Fresh Tomato .50
Cream of Fresh Peas .55

EGGS

Eggs Benedict .95   Perinos 1.10
Omelette with Chicken Livers 1.25

Eggs Florentine 1.15
Spanish Omelette 1.20

Eggs with Bacon or Ham .90
Eggs Mornay 1.15

FISH

Whitefish Saute Meuniere 1.50
Frog Legs Saute Fines Herbes 1.40
Fried Eastern Scallops 1.15
Filet of Sole Florentine 1.20
Lobster Thermidor 1.60

Filet of Sole Bonne Femme 1.20

Brook Trout Saute Meuniere 1.20
Filet of Sole Colbert 1.25
Lobster Americaine 1.85

Crab Legs a la Turque 1.60
Filet of Sole Marguery 1.30
Fried Filet of Sole, Tartar Sauce 1.15
Crab Leg with Marrow Bordelaise 1.50
Lobster a la Newburg $1.60

PLATS DU JOUR

Veal Saute Marengo .95
Calf's Brains and Artichoke Doree 1.15
Lamb Kidney Saute Chippolata Spinach 1.20
Grenadine of Beef Tenderloin Bernaise, String Beans 1.15
Chicken a la King en Casserolette Peas 1.50

Home Made Mexican Enchiladas .90
Fresh Mushrooms Saute Colbert 1.15
Deviled Sliced Turkey Virginia 1.50
Chicken Curry a l'Indienne 1.75
Genuine Calf's Liver Saute, Bacon Spinach 1.15

FROM THE GRILL

French Lamb Chop 1.25; with Bacon 1.40
Brochette Chicken Livers Colbert 1.30
Half Milk Fed Chicken 1.30
Jumbo Squab 1.40

½ Baby Squab Turkey, Colbert Sauce (for 2) 3.50
English Mixed Grill 1.40
Mushrooms on Toast 1.15
Breast of Capon, Sauce Diable Virginienne 1.60
Sauce Bernaise .35

Filet Mignon 1.90; w. Fresh Mushrooms 2.25
Eastern Corn Fed Beef Sirloin (for 1) 2.10
Special Corn Fed Steer Sirloin (for 1) 3.25
Steak Minute 1.60; with Bordelaise Sauce 1.90
Mushroom Sauce .50

TO ORDER

Breast of Chicken under Glass Queen Sheba 1.50
Breast of Guinea Hen under Glass Lucullus 1.75
Chicken en Casserole Paysanne (for 2) 3.75
Chicken Jerusalem 1.60   A la King 1.40
Chicken Saute Sec Perino's 1.60
Chicken Cacciatora 1.60
Squab en Casserole Paysanne 1.75

Gnoicchi Piedmontaise .85
Spaghetti Bolognaise .95
Spaghetti Tetrazzini 1.25
Ravioli Genovese .95
Tagliarini Bolognaise 1.10
Risotto Milanaise 1.00
Piedmontaise 1.25

Lamb Kidney Saute au Madere with Mushrooms 1.30
Veal Scallopine Marsala .95   Scallopine Perinos 1.30
Veal Escallop Bon Femme 1.15
Sweetbreads Saute Sec with Mushrooms 1.30
Sweetbreads Saute Financiere 1.40   Sweetbreads Eugenie 1.40
Rack or Saddle of Lamb en Casserole Paysanne (for 2) 3.50
Tournedos of Beef Medici 2.00   Tournedos Hawaiian 2.25

SALADS

Lettuce .30-.50   Romaine .35-.55   Sliced Tomatoes .40-.60
Mixed Greens .30-.50   Escarole .35-.55   Sliced Cucumber .60-.90
Heart Romaine with Grapefruit or Avocado .60   Endive .60-.90

Chiffonade .45-.70
Combination .45-.80
Roquefort Cheese Dressing .25 p.p.

Watercress .40-.65
Celery Root .35-.50
Lorenzo Dressing .20

SPECIALS

Chef Special .95
Lorenzo 1.15   Avocado Salad .75

Perinos 1.00
Pineapple and Cottage Cheese .85

Fresh Fruit .85
Fresh Vegetable .85
Stuffed Tomato Surprise with Chicken 1.15   With Crab 1.10

Heart of Palmes, 1000 Isl. Dressing 1.00
Colossal Asparagus, Mustard Sauce 1.00

Lobster Salad 1.35

Chicken Salad Parisienne 1.40

Crab Salad 1.30

Shrimp Salad 1.25

Breast of Chicken: Isabelle 1.30   Jeanette 1.65   Cold Roast Beef, Potato Salad 1.30
Sliced Chicken or Turkey 1.25   With Virginia Ham 1.40   Assorted Cold Cuts 1.00

Half Cold Roast Chicken 1.30
With Chicken 1.25

VEGETABLES

Garden Peas .35-.60   Paysanne .40-.65
String Beans .35-.60   Au Gratin .45-.70
English Spinach .30-.50   Creamed .40-.65
Spinach a la Provenciale .50
Broccoli Hollandaise .50

Colossal White Asparagus, Hollandaise .90
Cauliflower, Hollandaise or Au Gratin .40-.65
Heart of Palms .90   Artichoke .45
Corn Saute .35-.50   Au Gratin .45-.70

Lima Beans .45-65   Carrots Vichy .25-40
Zucchini Florentine .40-.65   Provencale .40-.65
Egg Plant Fried .40-.65   Portugaise .40-.60
French Fried Onions .50-.75
Artichokes Doree .50-.75

POTATOES

Baked Potato .30
Au Gratin .40-.60   Hashed in Cream .35-.50

Hashed Brown .35-.50
Cottage Fried .40-.70   Souffle .50-.75
Grilled Sweet .40-.65   Candied Sweet .45-.70

Lyonnaise .40-.60   Minute .30-.45
French Fried, Long Branch or Julienne .30-.50

DESSERTS

CHEESE TRAY .45 per person

FRESH FRUIT in Season .40

Coupe au Marrons .70
Coupe St. Jacques .50
Roman Punch .65
French Pastry .25
Parfaits: Cafe .50   Strawberry .50   Marron .60
Ice Creams: French Vanilla .30   Chocolate .35   Coffee .35
Sherbets: Lemon .30   Pineapple .30   Orange .30   Raspberry .30

Meringue Glace .50
Crepe Suzette 1.50
Cherry Jubilee 1.10
Pie .25

Strawberry Romanoff 1.35
Baked Alaska .80
Zabaglione .75
Spumoni .50

French Pancake .75
Compote of Fruit .50
Peach Melba .65
Wild Strawberries .75
Chocolate or Vanilla Souffle (for 2) 2.20
English Toffee .35

BEVERAGES

Pot of Coffee with Cream .25   Demi Tasse .15
Cafe Diablo 1.25   Orange Pekoe, Green, Oolong, Black Tea .25

Chocolate or Cocoa .30
Milk .15

Kaffee Hag .30
Buttermilk .15

Sanka or Postum .30
Peppermint Tea .30

Continental Lunch Served Daily Except Sunday $1.25, Including Beverage
In Addition to the Quoted Prices There Is a Charge of 3% Sales Tax
Minimum Charge, 50c

Perino's • 3927 Wilshire Blvd., Los Angeles • 1942

The Chestnut Room

RIEN SUPÉRIEUR

The Magnolia Room

Chasen's • 9039 Beverly Blvd., Beverly Hills • March 6, 1955

Epicurean Club
OF LOS ANGELES

Dinner and Dance
OF THE EPICURUS AND CONNOISSEURS OF GASTRONOMY

BEVERLY HILLS HOTEL
CRYSTAL
ROOM

SATURDAY EVENING
FEBRUARY SEVENTH
1948

"MAN SHALL NOT LIVE BY BREAD ALONE"
—New Testament
(Matthew IV)

Beverly Hills Hotel Crystal Room / Epicurean Club banquet • 1948

rich and famous. It's where Bette Davis had a permanent booth, where Sinatra played the piano, and where Cadillac chose to set its 1959 print ad for a car unmatched in "beauty and elegance . . . luxury and comfort." It was part of a larger 1930s culture of gourmet tastes that included *Hollywood Reporter* owner Billy Wilkerson's upscale "fine foods" emporium Vendome Café, and Young's Market Company, a high-end grocery that had been selling Danish bleu cheese and Columbia River smelt to distinguished palates and fat wallets since 1888. The 1930s also saw a six-table Southern Pit Barbecue joint transformed into the legendary Hollywood haunt, Chasen's; witnessed the birth of the Los Angeles chapter of the national epicurean organization the Food and Wine Society; and produced the first issue of the monthly *Bohemian Life* newsletter. Decades before food blogs, *Lucky Peach*, and Chowhound, *Bohemian Life*—which was published by local high-end liquor distributor the Bohemian Distributing Company—covered L.A. gourmet eats and drinks (its reviews and gossip were penned by Touring Topics editor Phil Hanna under the goofy Jean Anthelme Brillat-Savarin *nom de plume* "Savarin St. Sure"). It became the essential reading material of the city's rising epicurean class.

The fine dining scene had mostly moved west of downtown by the 1940s, centered on La Cienega's "Restaurant Row." Lawry's opened in 1938 as the row's flagship destination, a place where a standing rib roast and a spinning salad became blue-chip, upscale signatures. A menu

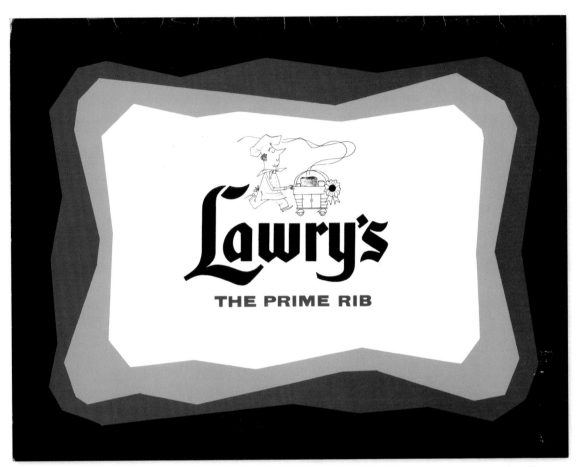

Lawry's the Prime Rib • 100 N. La Cienega Blvd., Beverly Hills • 1957

from Richlor's included its own self-promotion as part of the Row's exclusive gastronomic club: "An uncommon concentration of high-end eating establishments in a comparatively small area." In case the customer hadn't looked in the mirror, they included an illustration of the ideal L.A. gourmand—an older, white couple dressed to the nines in furs and fedoras, the same pair who might also frequent the Fontainebleau or be members of the Los Angeles Epicurean Society.

A bit farther east at the Ambassador Hotel, where fine dining had been a priority ever since the hotel opened in 1921, the gourmet commitment was so strong that even its room service menu kept it excessively formal. If you stayed there in 1954, after a night of drinking and dancing at its star-studded Cocoanut Grove

Ciro's • 8433 Sunset Blvd., West Hollywood • 1951

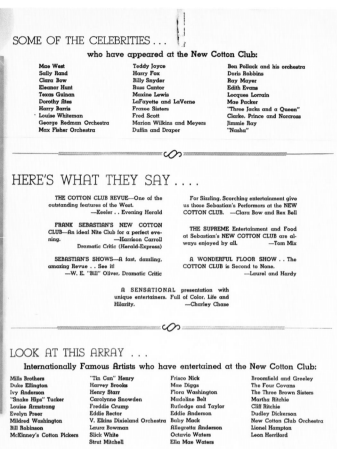

Frank Sebastian's Cotton Club • 6500 Washington Blvd., Culver City • 1930s • Anonymous Donor

nightclub, you could retire to your room to watch the *Jimmy Durante Show* in your satin pajamas and monogrammed velvet slippers while you ate Beluga caviar, Breast of Capon with Glazed Pineapple in a Madeira sauce, and Broiled Calf's Liver Sauteed with Crisp Bacon.

The Ambassador's gourmet sensibilities and its celebrity magnetism (it was the frequent home of the Academy Awards) was no accident. Hollywood helped keep L.A. fine dining afloat. As Jim Heimann has documented, Hollywood and fine dining were mutually supportive industries. Celebs gave restaurants the glamor, and restaurants gave celebs the appearance of taste, distinction, and class. One of Hollywood's earliest haunts, the Sunset Inn in Santa Monica, exploited the connection explicitly on its menus, listing the week's upcoming film premieres. Warren's advertised itself as "The Talk of Hollywood" in 1921. Culver City was star central in the 1930s, with hot spots like Frank Sebastian's Cotton Club billing its location as "In [the] Heart of Screenland," and putting name jazz acts like Louis Armstrong on its stage and veal scaloppini, Monte Cristo sandwiches, and alligator pear on its menus. Romanoff's was so indebted to its star clients that when film producer Walter Wanger ended up in jail, legend had it that Romanoff and his head waiter would come by nightly to lay down a tablecloth and serve him a gourmet meal.

In Budd Schulberg's 1942 short story "A Table at Ciro's," the famed Sunset Strip restaurant itself was a microcosm of Hollywood's star machine and all of its clipped dreams.

> At half-past five, Ciro's looks like a woman sitting before her dressing table, just beginning to make up for the evening. The waiters are setting up the tables for the dinner trade, the cigarette and hat-check girls are changing from slacks to the abbreviated can-can costumes which are their work clothes, and an undiscovered Rosemary Clooney making her debut tonight is rehearsing. Don't let the stars get in your eyes . . . A telephone rings and the operator, who is suffering from delusions of looking like Ava Gardner, answers, "Ci-ro's. A table for Mr. Nathan? For six. His usual table?" This was not what she had come to Hollywood for, to take reservations over the telephone, but even the small part she played in A.D. Nathan's plans for the evening brought her a little closer to the Hollywood that was like a mirage, always in sight but never within reach. For, like everyone else in Hollywood, the telephone operator at Ciro's had a dream.

The tradition of the restaurant as an after-hours Hollywood dream factory lived on for decades at Chasen's and was eventually reborn at Ma Maison and Spago in the 1970s and 1980s with a new generation of A-listers rehearsing the next day's scenes in corner booths.

When the celluloid dreams die, when high capitalism fails, we end up where L.A. culinary life has always thrived, at the real Atlantis of the lunch counter, the burger stand, the taqueria, and the noodle shop—those humble landmarks of Los Angeles as a city where anyone can get a tasty meal on a laborer's wage. After all, it was here that the Georges Braque-inspired gourmet collage that the Food and Wine Society of San Francisco put on one of its 1958 dinner menus (the same one that dons the cover of David Strauss's 2011 history of gourmet dining in America) was recycled on menu covers for Carl's and Ricky's, where chicken pot pie and pot roast were easier to find than a 1929 bottle of Dom Perignon.

In fact, the Library collection's first individually dish-priced bill of fare—from March 22, 1905—comes not from an up-scale restaurant but from Tait's Coffee Shop. A thirty-five cent deal got you cold salmon, veal, spaghetti, a cup of coffee, and either beer (a Busch pale lager) or wine (the Claret Bordeaux that was on just about every L.A. menu at the turn of the century). Its fifty-cent steaks and sixty-five cent chicken were average prices for the time, affordable for the growing middle-class lunch crowds of the new century and indicative of just how much L.A. was literally, not pejoratively, a cowtown. The lower the prices, the more beef you were bound to see. Which isn't to say that chicken or fish were rare sightings. On a 1915 menu from the more tony Nat Goodwin Café, which was perched above the waves on the Crystal Pier in Santa Monica, you could get chicken served eight different ways (including "County style" and "Stuffed With Oysters"), all of them nearly twice as expensive as the fifteen fish choices—lobster, barracuda, shad roe, and local Catalina sand dabs among them.

By the early 1900s menus with middle-class sensibilities began to take over. This was the L.A. version of a national trend: the revolt of middle-class diners against the aristocratic Francophilic pomp of the nascent restaurant trade. As Andrew Haley so thoroughly documented in his 2011 study *Turning the Tables*, the biggest change in restaurant culture from the 1800s to the 1900s was the shift in class-consciousness, what he calls "the middle-classing of the restaurant." A hungry urban middle-class office pool was done with French dishes they couldn't afford or pronounce (that might not have even been written in actual French at all but in "menu French") and ready for a democratic option: quicker service, ethnically diverse meals, and lower prices.

In an 1892 feature for the *Los Angeles Times* on "Los Angeles Restaurants," the mysteriously billed writer Alessandro acknowledged that while the city had a respectable cadre of "first-class" gourmet

Globe Coffee Shop · 1317 E. 7th St., Los Angeles · 1937

haunts, its true identity as a food town in the making just might lie in the twenty-five cent beef-steak, chop-house lunches gobbled up by its "wage-workers of both sexes" and steady streams of mechanics, managers, and clerks. "It is this class who are the mainstay of the smaller and most numerous of the eating-houses," he wrote,

> Where meals are served for fifteen or twenty cents. To the uninitiated such a scale of prices may be suggestive of poverty and squalor, but such an idea will be dispelled by a visit to any of the bright little parlors where any ordinary dishes can be called for and served by neat and intelligent attendants.

Three years later, the *Times* made affordable meals a matter of civic pride:

> If you told a man in Boston that he could get an excellent meal in Los Angeles composed of soup, meat, two sometimes three kinds of vegetables, bread and butter ad libitum, with a pot of tea or coffee and milk, or if preferred a small bottle of claret, all for fifteen cents, he would look at you as if he would like to tell you that the truth was not in you.

Three Deck Sandwiches

PLAIN OR TOASTED

No. 1 —Ham, Olive, Lettuce and Tomato	.25
No. 2 —Deviled Egg, Ham, Lettuce and Tomato	.25
No. 3 —Crisp Bacon, Sliced Tomato, Lettuce, Mayonnaise	.25
No. 4 —Peanut Butter and Jelly	.20
No. 5 —Sliced Ham and Egg Salad	.25
No. 6—Swiss Cheese, Sliced Ham and Lettuce	.15
No. 7 —Beef, Ham, Lettuce and Tomato	.30
No. 8 —Pimento Cheese and Pineapple, Lettuce, Dressing	.20
No. 9 —Ham, Pineapple, Lettuce and Dressing	.25
No. 10—Club House (Chicken, Bacon, Tomato, Lettuce, Dressing)	40

Sandwiches

ON WHITE, WHOLE WHEAT OR RYE BREAD

Chicken Salad on Toast	.25	Boiled Ham or Bacon with Tomato	.15
Boiled Ham with Lettuce	.15	Sliced Avocado and Tomato on Toast	.25
Combination Ham and Cheese on Toast	.20	Corned Beef or Tongue	.15
Sliced Chicken	.30	Minced Ham, Lettuce	.15
Tomato and Lettuce	.15	Liverwurst Sausage	.15
Minced Olive	.15	Kosher Salami	.15
Peanut Butter	.15	Sardines, Imported	.15
Deviled Egg	.15	Pimento Cheese	.15
Beef or Pork with Lettuce	.15	Imported Swiss Cheese	.20
Salmon Salad or Tuna Salad	.15	American or Domestic Swiss Cheese	.15

HAMBURGER SANDWICH on Toasted Bun, Tomato and Pickle **15c**

Cold Meats

Served with Potato Salad, Sliced Tomato, Bread and Butter

Roast Beef	.35	Corned Beef or Tongue	.35
Roast Pork	.35	Sliced Chicken	.50
Boiled Ham	.35	Liverwurst Sausage	.30
Kosher Salami	.30	Assorted Cold Cuts	.40
Red Salmon	.30	Sardines, Imported	.30

CALIFORNIA SALAD 35c
Mixed Fruit, Cottage Cheese and Whipped Cream

Salads

Served with Mayonnaise, French Dressing or 1000 Island Dressing
Roll and Butter Served with Salads 25c or over

Globe SPECIAL SALAD 35c
Sliced Tomato, Hearts of Artichoke, Green Asparagus Tips, Young Baby Beets, Chopped Lettuce

VEGETABLE SALAD (Ground Carrots, Peas, Celery, Lettuce, Mayonnaise) 25

Head Lettuce and Tomato	.25	Fruit, Whipped Cream	.25	Tuna Fish Salad	.25
Combination Salad	.30	Avocado with Fruit	.35	Salmon	.25
Sliced Tomatoes	.15	Pineapple and Cheese	.25	Crab Meat	.35
Sliced Cucumbers	.15	Pineapple and Banana	.25	Shrimp	.35
Head Lettuce	.15	Chicken Salad	.35	Potato	.10
Cole Slaw	.10	Egg and Potato Salad	.25	Stuffed Tomato with Chicken	35

ICE CREAMS 10c   ICE CREAM SUNDAES 15c   ICE CREAM SODAS 10c
DOUBLE MALTED MILK (ANY FLAVOR) 15c, WITH EGG 20c

Plain Lemonade	.10	Ovaltine (hot or cold)	.15	Hot Chocolate with Wafers	10
Coca Cola	.05	(with Egg 20)		Milk Shake	15
Root Beer	.05	Banana Split with Crushed Nuts	.20	Bromo Seltzer	10

—— WINE and BEER ——

Claret, Sauterne, Burgundy,		Eckert's Beer, bottle 10	Eastside, Acme or Rainier Beer, bottle	15
Sherry or Muscatel, glass	.10	Lucky Lager Beer 15	Rainier Ale, per bottle	15

No. 10

Globe Coffee Shop • 1317 E. 7th St., Los Angeles • 1937

The democratization of the L.A. restaurant was nowhere more visible than in the popularity of no-nonsense cafeterias. Helen Mosher opened the city's first in 1905 in the heart of downtown and used its posted and advertised menu to assure customers she had a "no tips" policy (save it for a slice of pie) and that all the food was prepared by women (code for the "American home cooking" white Midwesterners might be homesick for). The Boos Brothers super-sized the cafeteria a year later and turned it into the first cafeteria chain in L.A. In 1919, the Venice Cafeteria took the "woman cooks only" concept to the beach, promising non-stop service, seven-cent bacon and fish specialties. The trend became so inevitable that in 1922, even the once elite and exclusive Mission Indian Grill at the Hotel Alexandria gave in and traded its table service for trays. For Carey McWilliams, the abundance of accessible cafeterias was as much about populism as it

ABOUT
CLIFTON'S

NOVEMBER, 1937 — INFORMATION

ISSUED WHENEVER WE HAVE NEW SERVICES TO ADD

"We pray our humble service be measured, not by Gold, but by the Golden Rule," Clifton's; 618 So. Olive St. and 648 So. Broadway, L. A., TR-1673. Suggestions and criticisms appreciated—Drop in Bowl at Cash Desk. Happy to be at your service.—Clifford E. Clinton.

A STATEMENT OF ASSETS AND LIABILITIES

CLIFTON'S

"The Cafeteria of the Golden Rule"

"618" SOUTH OLIVE STREET — Open 6 A.M. to 8 P.M.
"648" SOUTH BROADWAY — Open 6 A.M. to Midnight
Phone TRinity 1673 8 A.M. to 8 P.M.
Los Angeles

INASMUCH as Clifton's is operated upon our humble conception of the Golden Rule—which teaches us that we should share with others even as we might wish others to share with us, if our positions were reversed, we present this Statement of Assets and Liabilities which we sincerely offer to share with you, who have chosen to be our guests even this once.

We consider each guest a partner in our business. As such you inevitably share in our losses and gains—our mistakes and successes.

At the tap of the tiny Bell on your table—or a word to one of us—there are nearly 600 Associates of Clifton's at your service—we will leave no effort undone to make your visit to us enjoyable.

Our guarantee shall always be—"Pay What You Wish" and

"DINE FREE UNLESS DELIGHTED"

EXPLANATION OF PARTNERSHIP

THE NAME—Clifton's—is a compound from the name of Clifford E. Clinton—Who in 1931, after many years in the Cafeteria business in San Francisco, came to Los Angeles and established Clifton's, for the purpose of applying the Golden Rule to the business in which he had devoted his life.

OWNERSHIP—Clifton's is owned 75% by Clifford E. Clinton and 25% by General Manager Ransom M. Callicott, who came with Mr. "Clifton" in 1932. Prior to this he was 13 years with the famous Boos Bros. Cafeteria Co.

PRICES—All our foods are priced at cost—That is cost of the food and all costs necessary to bring it to you. One cent is added to each check above this cost—which constitutes Clifton's entire profit (averaging ½c per meal) and costs of social security taxes. The statement printed on each check—"Regardless of amount of this check—our cashier will cheerfully accept whatever you wish to pay—or you may dine free" is sincerely meant. It is designed to allow guests the privilege of adjusting their check to suit their idea of a fair service—not ours. It is designed, too, to make it possible for guests who do not wish to pay us a profit on our service to remove that or any other portion of our charges.

"WHY THIS POLICY?"—is often asked; Because we are anxious to render a genuine service — At a price within reach of any who wish this service —And because we have proven that we are less apt to continue mistakes or poor service if our guests have the right to refuse to pay us for that service. In other words—when we have to pay in cash for our mistakes—we correct them more quickly. The last portion of the statement on the check, ". . . our cashier will cheerfully accept . . . or you may dine free" is to assure you that our cashiers will not act snippy— and will graciously and unquestionably receive what you feel you wish to pay.

IN REALITY—PARTNERS—Clifton's has no great outstanding stock, obligations, etc. Does not pay excessive rentals, or other fixed charges considered normal to similar organizations. Pays dividends, only to Clifton Guests, Associates (Employees) and Mr. "Clifton." This simplicity of ownership and operation—and the determination to operate at a very small fixed profit, coupled with the fact that Clifton's are serving more meals than any two similar places

---

The Clifton Tray...of
FOOD 4 THOT

"A TRA-FUL FOR A TRI-FUL"   Sept. 29, 1938.   Issue No. 342

"We pray our humble service be measured, not by Gold, but by the Golden Rule," Clifton's: 618 So. Olive St. and 648 So. Broadway, L. A., TR-1673. Suggestions and criticisms appreciated—Drop in Bowl at Cash Desk. Happy to be at your service.—Clifford E. Clinton.

THESE SERVICES at "618" South Olive St.—"Free Meals to Deserving," "Meal Credits," "How to Find a Friend," "Free Advisory Service," "Guests' Exchange," "Travel Service," "Clifton Chaplain, Your Friend," "CIVIC Information," "Phone, Mail and Notary Service," "Food 4 Thot Mailing," "Gold, Silver and Diamonds Bought," "Barber Shop," "Beauty Salon," "Free Tourists and Residents Official Information, Maps, etc." "Complete Hotel and Housing Accommodations," "Daily Free and Paid Sightseeing Trips," "Gerry's Get-Together Club"—For fuller information—See:

'About Cliftons'—An informative folder available at front desk answers questions.

HEAR CLIFFORD E. CLINTON

KEHE — Four Times Daily — Monday through Friday — 9:30 A. M., 12:30 Noon, 7 P. M., 11 P. M.

A CHALLENGE — LOS ANGELES
"HOLD HIGH THE TORCH"

Hold high the torch! Do not forget its glow;
It was given you from other hands, you know.
'Tis only yours to keep it burning bright,
Yours to pass on to those who need its light.
   I guess the world is movin' on;
     A lot of good old things are gone.
   But why be sad and why be glum?
     A lot of good new things have come!
       —Douglas Malloch.
     Copyright, McClure Syndicate.

MEN OF EARTH - *Edwin Markham*

We men of the earth have here the stuff
Of Paradise. We have enough.
We need no other stones to build
The stairs into the unfulfilled
No other marble for the floors
No other ivory for the doors
No other cedar for the beams
And dome of men's immortal dream.

Here on the path of everyday
Here on the common human way
Is ALL the stuff the gods would take
To build new heavens. To mould
And make New Edens
Out of the stuff sublime
To build Eternity in Time.

The gates of yesterday are closed behind us and the fields of the other years we shall till no more. We gather no harvests from the acres of Tomorrow. But Today is ours to use and to enjoy. Are there heights to be climbed, are there wrongs to be righted, are there deeds to be accomplished. Then let us attempt to do them now.

This is our hour for labor, for liberality, for service. Today is our day for worship, for friendship, and for love. Let us make the most of it while it is ours.—Rev. Willsie Martin.
      —Compliments of Elihu W. Sargent.

Clifton's Cafeteria reading material: "About" pamphlet, 1937, and "Food 4 Thot" newsletter, 1938.

was about L.A. melancholy. "I am convinced that the popularity of the cafeteria in Los Angeles," he wrote, "is primarily due to the loneliness of the people."

The lonely had a group home at Clifton's, the apex of the cafeteria as a culinary, class, and even spiritual sanctuary, which served food as much as social philosophy when it opened downtown on Olive in 1931 as an answer to the Depression. At Clifton's, nobody was turned away for lack of funds. "Pay what you wish—Dine free unless delighted" was its guiding principle. After you finished your pie and coffee, you could also meditate and seek spiritual enlightenment in "The Garden," a built-in replica of the Garden of Gethsemane, complete with life-size statues of Christ and

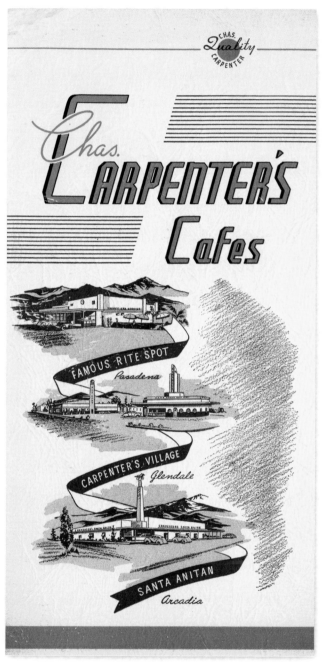

Chas. Carpenter's Cafés • (various locations) • 1930s

Wich Stand • 7111 S. Figueroa St., Los Angeles • 1950s
Anonymous Donor

Clifton's employees in costume as Jerusalem weavers. Its Penny Cafeteria downstairs (so it quickly became disparagingly nicknamed the "Caveteria") offered entire meals for a cent and the homeless ate free. The extravagant Clifton's Brookdale on Broadway—a themed woodland paradise with mock redwoods, streams, deer, and its own two-seat chapel—continued the Clifton's practice of both issuing the weekly "Food 4 Thot" inspirational newsletter geared toward the spiritual uplift of what the restaurant called "a still finer Los Angeles" and a posted statement of community services ("enter a trade—Clifton's Food Service School") and policies ("No guest shall go hungry for lack of funds"). In the face of the Depression and the upper-class leanings of the city's earlier restaurant culture, Clifton's was a radical culinary and social project: it approached feeding people, across the class divide, as a spiritual mission.

WILSHIRE BOULEVARD AT WESTERN AVENUE
Los Angeles

Melody Lane • 9454 Wilshire Blvd., Beverly Hills • 1950s

Working-class and middle-class eating in Los Angeles was equally transformed by the drive-in restaurant. As L.A. ascended into its car culture heights, driving your car to eat in a restaurant was soon replaced by driving your car to eat *in your car*. Proto drive-ins like Harry Carpenter's, the Pig Stand, and Montgomery's Country Inn set the stage for the 1930s boom, when architectural icons like the Wich Stand, Simon's, Robert's, Herbert's, and Melody Lane exploded along or near Wilshire Boulevard, the city's first automotive urban spine. In his 1949 novel *The Little Sister*, Raymond Chandler famously described drive-ins as being "gay as circuses with the chipper hard-eyed carhops, the brilliant counters, and the sweaty, greasy kitchens that would have poisoned a toad."

Throughout the 1940s and 1950s, the drive-ins were flanked by curbside armies of white carhops—"a new variety of the Southern California girl" as Kevin Starr put it—who also frequently graced the covers of drive-in menus. If it wasn't the women, it was cars. Scrivner's bragged of its modernity by putting a cartoon

Scrivner's • (various locations) • 1950s

Van de Kamp's Coffee Shops • (various locations) • 1963

The Keg • 11002 Ventura Blvd., Studio City • 1940s

Model T from the 1920s on its cover. "Come as you are . . . Eat in your car" the menu beckoned, while also reminding customers that while they ate Chicken à la King, pepperoni pizza, or a Virginia baked-ham plate in their front seat, they could also be interviewed by pioneering rock-radio DJ Art Laboe for his daily K-POP show.

The rise of the automotive eater in the 1930s was also responsible for one of L.A.'s most infamous contributions to urban architecture: the themed, roadside restaurant. Reyner Banham described it in 1971 as "symbolic packaging," in which "the building and the symbol are one" (not long after David Gebhard came up with the term that's since stuck, "programmatic architecture"). By now, the iconic examples are well-known to any casual student of L.A. fantasy: the Tamale restaurant shaped like a tamale, the Donut Hole that is half of a doughnut (you drive through the hole), the Brown Derby that is a massive brown derby, the Tail o' the Pup shaped like a hot dog. If the double-dutch reference in the name of the Van de Kamp's Holland Dutch bakeries, coffee shops, and drive-ins wasn't enough, they built large-scale windmills atop their front doors that were impossible to miss from the street (and put Dutch dresses on their waitresses who were hard to miss once you were inside). At the Jail Café on Sunset Boulevard—"Let's go to jail!," a 1928 advertisement beamed—a prison guard surveilled the street from a watchtower. Inmate waiters served chicken and steak dinners for a buck and a quarter (no knives or forks allowed, naturally) inside mock jail cells. Perhaps the first large-scale programmatic restaurant was Baron Long's Ship Café, built into the terminus of the Venice Pier in 1905, in the shape of the Spanish galleon that brought the first European to California.

The Redwood House • 234 W. 1st St., Los Angeles
1945

Hangman's Tree Café • 18671 Ventura Blvd., Tarzana • 1960s

Programmatic architecture led to what could be called "programmatic menus," where the symbol and the menu are one. The menu for the Keg was in the shape of a keg, the menu for the Redwood House was a circular tree stump, and the menu for Cap 'n' Quill was a quill tucked into the band of a large, red Robin Hood cap. The 1959 menu for Cook's Steakhouse was a tribute to the Los Angeles Dodgers, so why shouldn't the menu be an oversized baseball autographed by the team? Other menus were slightly less on the nose. The Blarney Castle went with a menu shaped like a coat of arms instead of a castle, Zamboanga tried to represent its vague "South Seas" theme and Philippines namesake by turning its menu into a tailless pipe-smoking monkey, and both Smith's Wood BBQ and Eaton's designed their menus to look like the wood that smoked their meat and chicken.

Hangman's Tree Café on Ventura Boulevard—named after an Old West hangman's tree in Calabasas—thankfully just went with a drawing of the tree and an empty loop of rope instead of reproducing the faux corpse dangling from a noose that adorned the restaurant's actual exterior. The menu, clearly written by a chef who would have rather been doing a set at Ciro's, described the restaurant as "the rendezvous for those who enjoy lousy food." The veal cutlets were "raised on our own ranch (*no tengo rancho*)" and if you chose the Caesar Salad, "the chef will hate you for ordering it." The wine list was "seasoning for the Town's most tasteless food!"

The programmatic menu tradition had clearly lost steam by the 1980s, when the menu for O'Shaugnessy's was neither shamrock nor leprechaun, but a "downtown tax-relief menu" entered onto a 1040 tax return form.

What complex bastardies!

—ALDOUS HUXLEY, *After Many A Summer Dies A Swan*, 1939

After the white British archivist Jeremy Pordage arrives at Union Station in Aldous Huxley's 1939 novel, *After Many a Summer Dies the Swan*, he gets into the backseat of a car driven by a black chauffeur and takes in Los Angeles from his rolled-down window. What he sees is a city of billboards and flashing signage, much of it having to do with food and restaurants: EATS. COCKTAILS. OPEN NITES. JUMBO MALTS . . . DRIVE IN FOR NUTBURGERS . . . CLASSY EATS. MILE HIGH CONES. JESUS SAVES. HAMBURGERS . . . FINE LIQUORS. TURKEY SANDWICHES.

In many ways, the passage is rightfully cited as a classic portrait of 1930s L.A. urban space and architecture, and a classic slice of L.A. restaurant lit we could roll into a syllabus alongside *Mildred Pierce, Lament in the Night, The Little Sister, Ask the Dust*, and every James Ellroy novel that ends up at the Pacific Dining Car. Yet all the signs for all the restaurants he sees, all the urban spaces that roll past his window, have what he calls a "Caucasian tinge." They belong not to L.A. but to white L.A. The segregation of the city is what he first notices as his driver takes him southwest out of downtown, "a slum of Africans and Filipinos, Japanese, and Mexicans. And what permutations and combinations of black, yellow, and brown! What complex bastardies!"

The newcomer has stumbled upon the ghost in the machine of L.A. as a modern city: race. When vintage L.A. obsessionists and mid-century kitsch collectors talk of the quintessential L.A. restaurants and wax nostalgic about classic L.A. menus, the L.A. they look back on is more often than not, a middle- and upper-class white L.A., a city with a Caucasian tinge. Up through the 1960s, for example, most of the city's top restaurants and popular "golden age" Hollywood haunts (the Brown Derby, Perino's) welcomed few black clientele. The same was true for most Hollywood studios: the commissary on the Fox lot offered a "special little restaurant" for Lena Horne and other members of the black cast of *Stormy Weather* (1943). Booker T. Washington stayed at the Hollenbeck Hotel when he visited L.A. in 1903 but was asked to take his meals in his room, not in the restaurant. In 1912, when white Angelenos formed the "Anti-Color League" they called for a boycott of every restaurant that employed Blacks. Duke Ellington riffed on the problem in his 1940 musical *Jump for Joy* (staged downtown at the Mayan) with a song that said it all in its title: "Uncle Tom's Cabin is a Drive-In Now." "There used to be a chicken shack in Caroline," it went, "but now they've moved it up to Hollywood and Vine . . . Jemima don't work no more for RKO, she's slinging hash for Uncle Tom and coinin' dough. Just turn on your headlights and she'll take a bow, 'cause Uncle Tom's Cabin is a drive-in now." (He might

Nickodell • 5511 Melrose Ave., Los Angeles • 1955

have been referring to Melody Lane, which opened at Hollywood and Vine in 1940, though it wasn't technically a drive-in.) The color line of L.A. dining was also on full display downtown at Bullock's Tea Room, where only whites could order a "United Nations Buffet Luncheon" until a series of protests that very same year forced the restaurant's integration.

Many remember the Wich Stand as an iconic coffee shop, especially because of its Googie-style architecture courtesy of Wayne McAllister, but few remember its Figueroa and Florence location as the site of one of the city's very first sit-ins in 1952. Notorious for not serving black customers and not allowing its carhops to roll their skates up to the windows of cars driven by blacks, it became a landmark of L.A. protest when Andrew Murray, a black teenager, was denied service and then organized a sit-in in response. Around the same time, famed Watts-born jazz musician Buddy Colette was working in the *You Bet Your Life* house band on the Paramount lot. On a break, he went where most studio regulars went, to the Nickodell restaurant on Melrose. Colette's lunch

Bullock's Tea Room • Seventh at Broadway and Hill Streets • 1943

partner was his white girlfriend, which offended the restaurant's host. He sent the couple to a spot in the room where they could be gawked at, and stir up whispers, from all angles. The restaurant's massive menus that packed in everything from filet of sole and liver steak to sweetbreads, sautéed ox joint, Lobster Thermidor, and corned beef hash, came in handy. "It was a good thing they had big menus," Collette remembered, "the noises lasted throughout dinner." He didn't need big menus down on Fifty-eighth and San Pedro, where, at the Crystal Tea Room, Collette held Sunday jam sessions open to musicians of any color.

Among white-owned restaurants, there were of course exceptions, and places to eat became places to imagine social change. It was part of the "Golden Rule" policy of Clifton's Cafeteria to serve African-Americans as they would serve any other customer; all tables were open seating, meant to encourage "strange elbowing" between customers of different backgrounds, classes, and races. When the Hamburger Hamlet opened its doors in 1950, its owners made a point of promoting racial openness by hiring African-American women who were paid respectable wages and benefits.

The "Caucasian tinge" of classic L.A. restaurants also meant they weren't shy in using food and menu design to promote racial hierarchies and represent their own versions of black, Chinese, Japanese, Filipino, and Mexican life. They were everywhere, in abundant and romantic caricature, and the menus tell the tale in full-color illustrations. In the case of Black America,

L.A. produced its fair share of blackface gastronomy and minstrel menus. Mrs. McEwen's Quality Cafeteria on Western advertised its Fricasee of Chicken and its free desserts with a minstrel caricature of a black chef. The Keg in North Hollywood listed its ½ Fried Disjointed Chicken With French Fries, Cole Slaw, Hot Biscuits & Honey with a drawing of an Al Jolson-esque blackface singer shouting "Mammy."

A 1947 menu for Carolina Pines, which put a Southern Colonial square in the middle of Melrose, bragged of bringing "the Deep South" to Los Angeles in 1923 "with its darky help and Southern Cookery." A black woman whose head was wrapped in a kerchief donned the menu's cover, which promised authentic Baked Virginia Ham, Carolina Mixed Green Salad, and Southern-style Prime Rib. But the inclusion of filet mignon and Northern halibut—not to mention an ad for private mah-jong rooms—were a good hint of just how far away Carolina really was. "There is nothing pseudo about the Southern air," the *Los Angeles Times* wrote in its "Famous Southland Cafés" review column, "South-

Carolina Pines • 7315 Melrose Ave., Hollywood • 1943

ern hospitality at Carolina Pines means, for instance, being served a helping by a mammy of crunchy, sweet, spiced pickles." The menu for the Old Dixie Southern Barbecue on Western Avenue went a step further and presented its "genuine hickory wood" smoked barbecue dinners, pork sandwiches, fried shrimp, and mint juleps in the shape of a mammy holding a plate of ribs, despite a kitchen full of white cooks and bakers and a white organist pumping melodies in its Julep Room bar.

The Plantation Café, a massive faux plantation house that Fatty Arbuckle put in the middle of Culver City in 1928, was designed by M-G-M studio artists and was a quick Hollywood magnet. Sonny Clay and High Hat Sam provided "continuous entertainment," and Arbuckle served whole squab chicken dinners to Charlie Chaplin and Buster Keaton. The 1940s menu for Carl's Viewpark, a stately drive-in at Crenshaw and Vernon (back when the Crenshaw District was still predominantly white), was perhaps the most elaborately designed plantation fantasy. Its cover, promising "delicious food delightfully served in pleasant surroundings," was a

Old Dixie • 4267 S. Western Ave., Los Angeles • 1950

cutout of a Southern mansion complete with a black butler peering out from the door. Open the doors to the menu and you are in "the home of the sizzling steak" where you can also find Tom Turkey, Italian Spaghetti, Broiled Lamb Loin, Old-Fashioned Mince Pie and the occasional side dish of Black Southern minstrel dialect. "From the Old South comes the new Carl's," the menu announced, two pages over from a drawing of a black female servant in a red head-wrap and red polka dot dress delivering bowls of food to a smartly dressed blond couple. "The gayety, hospitality and good cooking of this land, rich in romance, has been our inspiration. We bring you a bit of the happy showboat days."

Restaurants openly trafficked in antebellum nostalgia, while openly ignoring the realities of Black Los Angeles. Black-owned restaurants serving food to black customers, however, were nearly as old as the L.A. restaurant itself. Their menus are scarce. Few appear in the Library's collection and few L.A. menus are held in African-American archives (local and national alike). The closest we get are mentions in newspaper ads, articles, and lifestyle columns. In 1888, Frank Blackburn opened a coffee and chophouse on First Street and was an early advocate of black culinary entrepreneurism. "If our people would only learn to patronize each other," he told the local black newspaper, the *Weekly Observer*, "we could do a great deal of food." The community listened. A year later, J.R. Walker had a place on San Pedro, and in 1903, A.J. Jones—"one of the most successful restaurant men in the city"—opened an eatery in his hotel. Soon there was Biscuit Jones downtown, the Stapler Brothers' "Dog City" street carts, and a trio of upscale options in downtown and South L.A.: the Blue Lantern Café on Jefferson, Chez Norman in the Hotel Somerville on Central, and Thistle's Café on Ninth.

Black-owned restaurants regularly advertised in the *California Eagle* throughout the 1920s whether it was Wilson Bros. Quick Service with its barbecue meats and "tables for Ladies" or Café Ben-A-Dele and its "special business lunch" for forty cents. "Why stop to cook home?" one restaurant on Central that billed itself as a "rendezvous for young people" asked, "when Stella Ross makes and serves such lovely pies, sandwiches, soft drinks of all kinds, and cigars." On Thirty-eighth and Compton, across the street from the ballpark of the Los Angeles White Sox, the city's Negro League team, was the White Sox Café and Chile Parlor that served up barbecue,

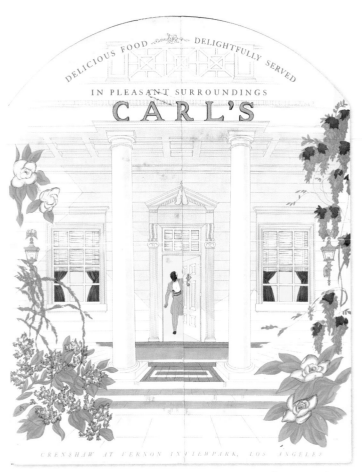

Carl's • Crenshaw Boulevard at Vernon Avenue in Viewpark, Los Angeles
1930s

waffles, homemade pie, hotcakes, and thirty-five cent lunch plates. By the 1940s, L.A. restaurants safe for black patrons like Pig n' Pat, Zombie, and the Fawn were regularly listed in *The Negro Green Book Travel Guides*. A frequent *Green Book* mention was Jordan's Café, which opened in 1942 on Wilmington and served the local community for nearly seventy years. A culinary witness to the neighborhood's transformation from a working-class black neighborhood to a working-class Latino neighborhood, Jordan's was for many years one of the only sit-down restaurants in Watts, and its soul food menu never changed: pork chops and catfish, collard greens and chitterlings, peach cobbler, and more peach cobbler.

Heavyweight boxing great Jack Johnson opened Jack's Basket Room on Central, and just south on Vernon, jazz singer Ivie Anderson helmed her own Ivie's Chicken Shack. In his autobiography, Duke Ellington left us with maybe the best version of her menu: "hot biscuits with honey and very fine chicken-liver omelets." Another celeb of 1940s Black Los Angeles, the spiritual and civil rights magnate Father Divine, also had his own eponymous restaurant on Central, where he made the waitresses dress like nurses. Thirteen cents got you a full chicken dinner most nights, and for two cents extra, you could dive into what musician Phil Moore remembered as "a trowel-sized hunk of hot deep-dish multi-fruit cobbler called the Mixed Multitude."

Contemporary South Los Angeles might now be best known to food insecurity experts as a "food desert"—under-nourished, over-liquor-stored, fast food dominant—but three restaurants with long histories in the area still have menus worth reading. The Watts Coffee House was born out of the ashes of the 1960s Watts Happening Coffee House, the epicenter of the Watts Writers Workshop and a gathering place for neighborhood artists, activists, and musicians to regroup and rebuild after the uprisings of 1965. Those memories still adorn the coffeehouse walls, and traditional soul food—ham steaks with fried apples, various country biscuit concoctions—still defines the menu, even if it keeps it current with its "On the 1 Gangsta Breakfast" (1 chicken wing, 1 salmon croquette, 1 pork chop, 1 hot link).

Sandwiches

Shrimp Po-Boy	$6.00
Add home-cut golden French fries	$7.50
New Orleans marinated & breaded	
w/Popcorn Shrimp on a grilled buttered	
roll, mayonnaise, & lettuce.	
Cajun Chicken Breast $4.00	$4.00
Deep fried- sesame seed bun, lettuce,	
tomato, honey mustard dressing.	
Chicken Sausage $4.25	$4.25
Add an egg, any style	$5.00
Wheat, white or sesame seed bun.	
Philly Cheese Steak $6.75	$6.75
W/green Bellpepper, onion, roll	
w/melted provolone cheese.	
Beef Tri-Tip $5.00	$5.00
Add home-cut golden French fries	$6.50
w/garlic mashed potatoes, steamed	
vegetables, wheat or white bread.	
Smoked Mesquite Turkey Sandwich	$5.00
Baby Swiss Cheese, Lettuce, Tomato,	
Flaky Croissant & Fresh Sliced Fruit.	
BBQ Beef $7.25	$7.25
Complete w/Potato Salad or Home-Cut	
Golden French Fries.	
Funky Blues Favorite	$4.00
1/4 lb., Wisconsin Cheddar or	
Jalapeno Jack, fresh home-cut French	
fries & Lemony Lemonade.	
Fried Bologna "Sammidge"	$4.00
Beef bologna w/melted American	
Cheese & a bag of chips.	
Center Cut Pork Chop $5.50	$5.50
Chicken Cheese Steak $6.25	$6.25
Country Bacon & Eggs	$4.25
Tuna Melt	$4.00
Ground Beef Pattie Melt	$4.00

à la carte

Desserts du jour	$2.00	Soup du jour-	
Fresh Smoothies	$3.00	Garlic Parmesan	
Soft Drink	$1.00	Bread	$5.00
Pink Lemonade	$1.00	Black-eyed Peas	$2.25
- Medium	$2.00	Red Beans	$2.25
- Jumbo	$3.00	Rice	$1.50
Coffee	$2.00	Parsley 'taters	$2.00
- Large to go	$2.25	Cornbread Muffin	$ .50
Mocha Coffee	$3.00	Gravy	$ .50
- Small	$1.50	Hot Link	
Glass of Milk	$1.50	Sandwich	$5.00
- Large	$2.50	Urbia	
Orange Juice	$1.50	"Smo-tatos"	$2.00
- Large	$2.50	Green Salad	$3.00
Fresh Smoothies	$3.00	Garlic Mashed	$1.50
Pink Lemonade	$1.00	Chicken Wing	$1.25
- Medium	$2.00	Chicken	
- Jumbo	$3.00	Drumstick	$1.00
Hot Chocolate	$2.00	Chicken Thigh	$1.25
Cheese Omelet	$2.75	Chicken Breast	$3.50
Chicken		Cajun	$3.50
Sausage Omelet	$4.00	Pork Chop (1)	$2.25
Chicken		Steamed Cabbage	$2.00
Sausage	$3.00	Yams	$2.00
Eggs – 2 Large		String Beans	$2.00
Biscuit	$1.00	Steamed Spinach	$2.00
Toast	$ .75	Steak/Chicken	
Bacon	$3.00	Taco	$2.00
Grits	$2.00	Beef Taco	$1.50
Oatmeal	$2.00	Mac 'n cheese	$2.75
French Toast	$4.00	Rice 'n gravy	$2.00
English Muffin	$1.00	Chicken Wing	$1.50
Bagel w/cream		Chili Fritos	$1.50
cheese	$1.25	Chili Cheese Fries	$3.75
Extra cheese	$ .25	Chili Dog	$2.50

Refills are 50¢

GIFT CERTIFICATES AVAILABLE

The soulful music you hear is on the house — "Watts Coffee House."

Watts Coffee House

Menu

Where we prepare our food with Lots of Love

1827 E. 103rd Street
Los Angeles, CA 90002
Phone: (323) 249-4343
FAX: 323.249.4344
Monday-Friday
8 AM— 3 PM
Saturday
8 AM—1 PM

Watts Coffee House • 1827 E. 103rd St., Los Angeles • ca. 1997

Hawkins House of Burgers has been serving burgers and pastrami between the 105 freeway and the Nickerson Gardens housing project since the 1980s, but its roots took hold when James Hawkins left Arkansas and arrived in South Central in 1939. His neighborhood grocery store became his neighborhood burger joint, equally built on the premise of fresh ingredients for low prices. Like the "On the 1," Hawkins House of Burgers isn't afraid to pile on ingredients in the name of community building. Its relish-and-cheese-soaked Whipper Burger tops two Angus beef patties with a pile of pastrami and a chunky hot link. James Hawkins's daughter Cynthia, who now commands the grill seven days a week, has never failed to recommend a milk shake to help it go down. Zelma and James Stennis opened their first Golden Bird fried chicken restaurant on West Adams in 1957, but it quickly grew into one of the most successful black-owned restaurant chains in the city, with locations in Compton, Inglewood, and Pasadena (perhaps second only to Fatburger, launched by Lovie Yancey in 1947 on Western). Despite the Golden Bird menu's stylized midcentury design, the dishes were kept straightforward (chicken lunches, chicken dinners, individual pieces, a handful of sides), and the prices were kept low. On the Library's copy, a manager's price-increases are scribbled in the margins of most dishes, but even in the 1960s, the half-chicken with fries, hot roll, and a pickle was immune to inflation. You could still get it for under $1.60.

GOLDEN BIRD

FRIED CHICKEN

Los Angeles Area:
1734 West Adams Blvd.—733-9721

Crenshaw Shopping Area:
3767 Santa Rosalia Ave.—296-4466

Compton Area:
12823 So. Central Ave.—632-2054

Pasadena Area:
635 No. Fair Oaks—793-2212

Golden Bird • (various locations) • 1970s

Since the 1980s, the Mexican and Central American transformation of South Los Angeles has also meant a shift in the neighborhood's culinary options. Taquerias are the new soul shacks. As in previous decades, Mexican restaurants serving both nationally and regionally themed specialties have appeared wherever Mexican immigrants and Mexican-Americans have called home. It's a food history that dates back to the founding of Los Angeles as a Spanish pueblo and its earliest days as a young Mexican town.

There were certainly places to eat Mexican food before Casa Verdugo showed up in 1905, but none of them so perfectly predicted the cultural tightrope act that would come to define the business of Mexican restaurants for the next century. The romantic culinary getaway run by the Californio chef and entrepreneur Piedad Yorba de Sowl, Casa Verdugo was a restored nineteenth-century adobe home on the grounds of the former Rancho San Rafael in the Glendale foothills. The building's owners, developer Leslie C. Brand and railroad titan Henry C. Huntington, were after maximum historical nostalgia, so they claimed that the adobe was actually from the eighteenth century, all part of their plan to make Casa Verdugo into a tourist destination for culinary time-travel back to "Old California." The restaurant's Days-of-the-Dons theme-park approach to dining would be reborn again and again over the next century, in both the strolling mariachis and sour cream tortilla casseroles of Lawry's California Center in the

Casa Verdugo • 736 S. Spring St., Los Angeles • 1913

Scenes from the *Modern* Casa de Rosas, *Now Serving You ~*

Although Spanish in atmosphere and tradition the Casa features only the finest of Real American Food. Connoisseurs from far and wide have acclaimed the wide variety of tempting dishes and wholesome goodness offered.

The problem of dining out during the warm weather, ceases to be a problem here. Typically reminiscent of the days of the Dons, is the Spanish Patio, where one may relax amid the beautiful surroundings of shaded arches and clinging wall vines.

ABOVE IS THE OUTSIDE VIEW OF THE CASA
Facing on Hoover Street — Serene in its atmosphere of restfulness that lends so much to the enjoyment of peaceful dining.

The Wishing Well

The visitor will find much of interest here to fascinate and intrigue them, with the atmosphere of old Spain predominating. Feel at liberty at all times to browse through the grounds or patio.

The Spanish Patio

To those romantically inclined, the "Old Wishing Well" is one of the interesting spots. Tradition tells us that a penny dropped in its mystic depth brings good fortune to the donor.

During the warm weather many enjoy dining in the cool outdoors of the patio. Pictured above is a small portion of the patio, accommodating over one hundred persons.

Scene of Banquet Room Now Available

The Casa specializes in Banquets of all sizes. Many ladies find it convenient to hold their Bridge luncheons here or let us arrange the Birthday party.

Pictured on the left is a portion of the large Banquet room. Social gatherings of any group up to 150 can be handled by reservations in advance.

Casa de Rosas • 2600 S. Hoover St., Los Angeles • 1940s

1970s (in Cypress Park, not far from Charles Lummis's Old California headquarters) and in the "romantic casa" of the Casa de Rosas restaurant in West Adams (a 1925 fairytale where the only thing "Mexican" was its "early California" ambiance, not its "Real American food."

Casa Verdugo pioneered the Californio dining experience. It was rooted both in the Spanish and Mexican pasts of Southern California and in the booster fever and cultural mythology that fueled its early twentieth-century growth. Huntington extended his Pacific Electric Railway line so that the train dropped customers right at the restaurant's door, where they were served Mexican dishes that were still being called "Spanish" on a menu shaped like a *tamal*. Yorba de Sowl balanced it all, until a fight with executives at the railway led her to leave the adobe and open her own Casa Verdugo nearby. She kept the name and turned it into a brand, eventually moving away from the rustic charm of Glendale and onto the streets of downtown, where she opened Casa Verdugo (Segundo) and continued to serve both "real Mexican tamales" and "genuine Spanish cooking." As culinary historian Charles Perry has written, the "proprietress of the nation's first upscale Mexican restaurant" had become "Los Angeles's first female celebrity chef."

Mexican restaurants like El Progreso and El Veracruzano thrived along the original city, but few had a big, bankable personality running the show. Los Angeles's second female celebrity chef was the Mexico-born, Boyle Heights-raised Consuelo Castillo de Bonzo. After opening La Misión Café in 1924, she took over the oldest brick building in the city six years later to launch La Golondrina Café, the flagship restaurant on the newly developed Olvera Street. Mov-

ing away from the Californio romances of "Spanish cooking," Castillo de Bonzo, who the *Times* called "the spirit of Mexico" and "the patron saint of Olvera Street" in a 1932 profile, proudly and explicitly advertised La Golondrina as a "Mexican Restaurant" that served Mexican, not Spanish, dishes. As Sidney Hoedemaks, then president of the National Restaurant Men's Association said of La Golondrina, "here you teach people history and Mexican customs, as well as serve them Mexican food." And yet the custom that she might have been most responsible for would have been hard to find in Mexico: the "combination plate" that is still standard on many of L.A.'s Mexican restaurant menus. A World War II menu from the restaurant even offered seventy-five cent "victory combination plates" that starred *chile con carne*, taco *de carne*, and enchilada *con carne*. When Castillo de Bonzo passed away in 1977, the restaurant issued a commemorative menu with her regal portrait towering over gringo-friendly descriptions of

La Golondrina • 17 Olvera St., Los Angeles • ca. 1980

tacos, *chile colorado*, and *arroz con pollo* and, set aside in its own box, a "Truth in Menus . . ." poultry confessional: when La Golondrina sells you a dish with *pollo*, it's really turkey breast.

Castillo de Bonzo and other pioneering L.A. Mexican restaurant families like the Borquezes of El Cholo (which opened in 1925) provided an early model for what would quickly become a chips-salsa-margarita template of the L.A. restaurant industry. Whether at work in citywide taco shops or the Encino-born El Torito, L.A. has been a prime incubator for Mexican-owned restaurants that balanced tourist expectation and mild midwestern palates with regionally nourished Mexican cooking styles and techniques. The Red Onion chain, for example, began in Inglewood serving Sonoran dishes, and then gradually evolved into one of the city's most popular, and most reliably generic and accessible, Mexican-American destinations. Nati Cano, the legendary mariachi musician, first began his career playing at the Granada Restaurant downtown, but quickly saw the value of running his own place. Cano's La Fonda, which he opened in 1967 near MacArthur Park as a mariachi showcase with upscale Mexican and Mexican-American cuisine, was another prime example of a self-made Mexican food empire born at the crossroads of community life and tourist voyeurism.

Ever since El Cholo first put a customer's crude drawing of its namesake on its menu cover—a skinny Mexican laborer in a floppy sombrero tugging on a cigarette—Mexican food rarely appeared on menus without an accompanying visual lexicon of caricatures. Stock graphics of men

The Red Onion • 307 E. Hillcrest Blvd., Inglewood • 1950s

El Cholo • (various locations) • 2006

in sombreros, colorful serapes, and smiling señoritas with flowers in their hair were the Mexican cousins of the Mammies and bandanna-crowned servants who were never far from fried chicken and buttermilk biscuits. The familiar trope of the "sleeping Mexican"—seen everywhere from front-lawn statues and motel signs to margarita glasses and refrigerator magnets—made its way onto menus as well (he's there sleeping on the 1950s menu of La Fonda in Glendale), but usually in slightly modified guises: the singing Mexican, the strumming Mexican, and the cooking Mexican, sombrero-clad all. "The cooking Mexican" shows up on the Henry's menu next to the Chili and Beans, "the strumming Mexican" plays guitar beneath the palm trees on the cover of Olivera's Spanish Café, and he's there next to a hyper-racialized Mexican couple who introduce us to La Olvera's otherwise sophisticated 1930s menu of avocado tacos, tostadas, *refritos*, veal steak *à la Mexicana*, and Mexican cookies with quince jam. On the cover of the 1976 menu of Señor Pico, he becomes a cartoonish waiter whose front teeth, mustache, and sombrero are all super-sized, and he was so popular with the Hotel Figueroa restaurant that he appeared on the front of its menu when the restaurant didn't even serve Mexican food. In some cases—when

La Olvera • 111 E. Macy St., Los Angeles • 1940s • Anonymous Donor   Señor Pico • Century City • 1976

FROM OUR Sandwich Bar

De Luxe Toasted 3-Deckers

A.—Tuna Salad, Deviled Egg, Sliced Tomato,
Lettuce, Mayonnaise 35
B.—Pimiento Cheese, Minced Ham, Lettuce,
and Mayonnaise 32
Y.—Peanut Butter, Sliced Avocado,
Crisp Bacon, Lettuce 35
Z.—Sliced Roast Beef, Swiss Cheese,
Lettuce, Mayonnaise 40

Hamburger	20	Liverwurst	15
Roast Beef	25	Domestic Cheese	20
Fried Ham	25	Pimiento Cheese	20
Corned Beef	25	Ham and Cheese	30
Fried Ham or Bacon and Egg	30	Deviled Egg	20
		Bacon and Tomato	25
Buttercrust	25	Lettuce and Tomato	15
Tuna Salad	25	Peanut Butter	
Salami	15	and Bacon	25

CHOPPED STEER STEAK SANDWICH
Freshly Chopped Steer Steak
Sandwich on a Buttered Toasted
Bun with Mustard, Relish, French
Fried Onion Rings and
Chili Con Carne **30c**

from Thrifty's Spanish Kitchen

LARGE SPANISH TAMALE
with Real Chili con Carne and
Spanish Beans, Saltines **35c**

**BOWL OF PIPING HOT CHILI
CON CARNE** and Spanish
Beans, Salted Wafers **25c**

HAMBURGER SIZE—Hamburger
Steak Covered with Real Chili
con Carne and Spanish Beans
Served with Diced Onions and
Buttered Toasted Bun **49c**

BUTTERED SPAGHETTI
Covered with Piping Hot Chili
con Carne, Salted Wafers **36c**

**LARGE SPANISH
TAMALE
35c**

All prices are our ceiling prices or below. The ceiling is based on prices charged by us from April 4th to April 10th, 1943, or as adjusted by an order of the O. P. A., Los Angeles District Office, dated February 9, 1943. A copy of this order and our current or price list for that week are here for your inspection.

Thrifty's • (various locations) • 1945

you were hungering "for that chili feeling" at the Clock Broiler or a large Spanish "tamale" at Thrifty's Spanish Kitchen—he vanished altogether, leaving only a phantom sombrero or a serape as a trace.

All of this menu minstrelsy took advantage of food's role as a cultural boundary: fried chicken-and-taco combo plates connected communities virtually while keeping them apart physically. Culinary integration and social segregation lived side by side. For Chinese-Americans, no dish bore this out more than the stir-fried hodgepodge called chop suey. A U.S.-tweaked dish born in working-class immigrant Chinatowns, chop suey was arguably the first ethnically specific food craze to become a multi-ethnic menu staple. It was used to both define the Chinese as "other" and to cross Chinese cooking over onto the menus of greater Los Angeles. And when its chopped vegetables, beef, and fish joined forces with the gummy noodles of chow mein (and in many cases merged into a single dish, often dubbed "American chop suey"), its power as both cultural fence-jumper and cultural fence was hard to stop.

Chop suey and chow mein started making their way onto L.A. menus in nineteenth-century Chinese restaurants in part to appeal to the less adventurous palates of non-Chinese customers. The racial love and hate inspired by chop suey was quickly apparent. In 1904, the *Los Angeles Times* ran a story titled "Who is the Noodle Lady of Chinatown?" about an elite white woman dressed for a night at the opera who repeatedly slums it in "a dirty chop suey joint" to binge on bowls of noodles close to midnight. The clientele consists of "outcast negroes and white damsels of no reputation," "blear-eyed hobos" eating chop suey with chopsticks, and "a negro girl" high on opium begging a man for "so 'mo suey." The scene is typical of the caricatures and stereotypes that were chop suey's side dishes, but also typical of just how beloved the dish had become beyond the Alameda corridor that had long been home to Chinese, Mexican, and black Angelenos.

By the 1920s, Far East Café on First was advertising its menu as "Famous Chinese Food" in English and Chinese, the Culver City Chop Suey Café was already open ("American dishes also served"), and in Glendale there was Kin-Chu Café, which claimed it was "the only place on the West Coast making and delivering real Chinese dishes." All the way at the beach, in the dance pavilion on the Venice Pier, you could even find a Chop Suey Sundae (which, according to one

1901 recipe, consisted of ice cream covered in a syrup of figs, dates, and walnuts) on the menu of the Chocolate Garden ice cream shop. In 1931, there were five different chop suey dishes and two chow mein specialties at the Nanking Café on Central and Washington. It had become such a common part of the L.A. palate that in 1937, S.J. Perelman joked that chow mein was an official ingredient of Los Angeles water.

Chop suey and chow mein dominate virtually all of the Chinese restaurant menus in the Library's collection. But just how many dishes each menu offers is a good indicator of how the restaurant was imagining its customer. Chinese food newbies and tourists were undoubtedly more comfortable with the sixteen chop suey dishes on a Tommy Wong's menu from the 1940s than with the mere two appearing on

Tommy Wong's Restaurant • 110 W. Macy St., Los Angeles • 1940s

the menu of Man Jen Low, the first officially documented restaurant in Chinatown (their menu suggested an alternative, "specialties for an adventurous mood into the realm of the Chinese epicurean"). Language was another key factor, both in targeting customers and in using the menu to negotiate Chinese identity against the backdrop of American-ness. Do you opt for an

Chocolate Garden • Venice Dance Pavilion, Venice • 1920s

Man Jen Low • 475 Gin Ling Way, Los Angeles • 1950s

Forbidden Palace · 451 Gin Ling Way, Los Angeles · 1940s

all-English menu like Forbidden Palace did in the 1940s? Do you offer dishes in transliteration? Or do you include both English and Chinese characters like Manshu Low's bilingual 1950s bill of fare?

The all-English 1964 menu for Grandview Gardens went to great lengths to offer non-tourist specialties as proof of its Chinese-ness while announcing its American-ness at every turn. There were in-season-only dishes like Lee Suon Gnow Yuk (asparagus with beef) and dishes like Siu Aup (barbecue duck) that required a full day's advance notice. To keep things simpler, though, you could opt for multi-course meals that played into exotic expectations ("The Imperial," "The Dynasty," "The Cathay") or just abandon Chinese food altogether and order chicken livers and New York steak from the "American Dishes" page. Loretta Mouling Hung put a photograph of herself on the cover of her Mouling restaurant menu—which mixed burgers and Shrimp Louie with Cha Chiang Mien and Spring Cakes (she billed them as "Chinese tortillas")—with a personalized cordial invitation to "patronize her Chinese-American cuisine." In the Mandarin Market in Hollywood—a drive-in grocery store complex that put a faux pagoda on Vine Street in 1929—L.A. hybridity was the main course at the Chilitown Café. There were "Chinese dishes and Chinese tea," accompanied by drawings of cartoonish Chinese men riding rickshaws in rice hats, but they were served alongside chili *con carne*.

Mouling Restaurant • 6530 Sunset Blvd., Hollywood • 1960s

Yet as outwardly directed as many Chinese restaurants and menus were for most of the twentieth century, they remained core building blocks of Chinese community, identity, and politics. The original Los Angeles Chinatown—a working-class, immigrant neighborhood—grew up around the small, informal "chow-chow" eateries that served mostly Cantonese railroad workers and vegetable farmers. Restaurants were at the center of Chinatown's business and employment life up through the 1930s when the city announced it would be razed—and all of its residents relocated—to make room for a new Los Angeles Union Station. It's no coincidence that when Chinese merchants and community leaders met to develop plans for a new Chinatown, they did it at a restaurant, Tuey Far Low. Their plan, hatched at the dinner table, resulted in the city's first modern Chinese-American commercial and residential district that was designed and managed wholly by Chinese-Americans.

New Chinatown, as it was referred to on restaurant menus in the 1940s, was in part the Chinese rebuttal to China City, the short-lived Far East fantasyland invented by white developer Christine Sterling to be the Old Orient version of her previous venture: the Old Mexico of Olvera Street. Instead of New Chinatown's parking lots, contemporary restaurants, and businesses, China City had rickshaws, junk shops, a Great Wall of China replica donated by Cecil B. DeMille, and a "House of Wang" film set used in *The Good Earth* (1937). Its restaurants were all designed for maximum exotic effect: Wong-a-Loo's, the Fong-Fung Café, and Chinaburger. In other words, there was plenty for New Chinatown's advocates to critique, to which Sterling responded: "What do they want? An Oriental Westwood Village? Let them build [their own Chinatown] if they think they can get away with it, but I think it will fail."

Beginning with the chop suey-and-noodle heavy menu of Yee Hung Guey, restaurants were at the heart of New Chinatown ever since it opened for business in 1938. "The cooks and waiters make up one-fourth of the Chinese population in New Chinatown," wrote Garding Lui in his 1948 tour of the neighborhood. Lui even included a section titled "Meaning of Menus" that explained the specifically Cantonese background of most of New Chinatown's earliest restaurants, and the Cantonese dialect of most of New Chinatown's residents. Liu closes his menu discussion with a five-page bill of fare from an unnamed "high-class Chinese restaurant" that he translates dish by dish. "A patron makes his selections from the English," Liu explains, "he picks it out from the Chinese words which begin each line. The waiter smiles at the knowledge of Chinese manifested by the patron and takes pains to give the best of service and quality."

Yet for all of the original commitment to being a modern district, New Chinatown wasn't afraid of catering to tourist fantasies. Streets named Bamboo Lane and Chung King Road and businesses dressed in pagoda facades—presumably not aimed at Chinese locals—had their corollary in restaurant menus, like the one that put a publicity still of Warner Orland as Charlie Chan on its cover (and a "Charlie Chan Special Dish" inside). Throughout the 1940s and 1950s, Chinatown menus didn't necessarily shy away from Hollywood romances of "Old Cathay" and were often rife with self-exoticism and orientalist flair. The Phoenix Bakery and Confectionery mixed what its menu touted as "the good old Chinese traditional ways" with anything but good old traditional fountain drinks like

Yee Hung Guey • Old Chinatown, Los Angeles • ca. 1925

the "Oriental Rubies" and the "Chinese Fruit Basket." The menu provided its own mythology of its namesake birds that "glide merrily around Old Cathay in anticipation of peace, happiness, and matrimony," a legacy of grace and tradition that has made its way into the "Pagoda Sandwich" and the "Chinatown Malted Milk." The only Chinese on the menu appeared in a promotional poem on the back flap that managed to mention Buddha's Wishing Well, fruit ale, ice cream, and Kung Yung, a "Chinese scholar and pastry originator." Other Phoenix menus focused instead on the bakery's knowingly named mascot, Sing Song, a demure Chinese boy in traditional dress who welcomed visitors with an ancient Chinese pastry greeting: "Sing Song says, don't take my sweet package away from me. You, too, can

Sing Song Says...

Don't take my Sweet Package away from me. You, too, can get one at

The Phoenix
409 GIN LING WAY
Chinatown, Los Angeles

MUtual 4642

Many Good Things You Go See!

VISIT
The Phoenix

Chinese Bakery, Confectionery, Tea and Soda Fountain Service In Enchanting New Chinatown (10th Year, Serving Los Angeles)

Open All Year Round 10:00 A.M. to 11:00 P.M.

IT'S . . .
DISTINCTIVE
BEAUTIFUL
DELIGHTFUL

FEATURING
Famous Almond Cookies
Peanut and Sesame Butter Brittles
Sugar Butterflies
Chinese Ice Cream
Glamorous Sundaes and
Banana Splits
Birthday and Wedding Cakes
Ice Cream Party Moulds
Chinese Peanuts Salted in Shells
Various Kinds of Chinese Tea
and Ginger
Chocolate with Chinese Nuts
and Cream Centers

Delicious and Attractive Things For Your Desserts, Parties and Gifts

The Phoenix · 409 Gin Ling Way, Chinatown, Los Angeles · 1948

get one at The Phoenix."

The ultimate Chinatown spectacle for these ancient-meets-modern, authentic-meets-fabricated, historical-meets-pop mash-ups was the Rice Bowl, which billed itself as the "Outstanding Oriental Café." Boasting that it was built of green tile imported from China, the Rice Bowl was "where East meets West across the bridge of centuries," or more accurately across a dance floor and stage where three nightly floor shows kept diners busy between courses of Hot Bar-B-Q Spareribs, Fried Squab snacks, Bird's Nest and Chicken Lotus Berrie Soup, with Gum Quots and Lichee Nuts for dessert. The back of a 1946 menu also explained that its Temple

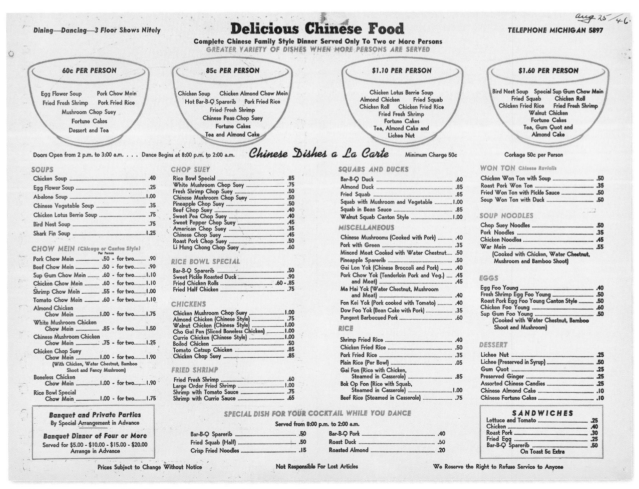

Rice Bowl • 949 Sun Mun Way, Los Angeles • 1950s • Anonymous Donor

of Heaven cocktail lounge doubled as a museum of "Great Chinese Civilization," full of rare, treasured relics—gold-embossed carvings, an eight-foot teakwood and gold-leaf rendering of the goddess Guanyin. The restaurant's walls were doubly extravagant, made of gold and covered in Chinese murals that, as the menu was sure to boast, were tellingly created not by a Chinese artist, but by a "foremost American authority on Chinese mural art." Not all New Chinatown menus took the route of opulent touristic spectacle. With its name, the Celestial connected itself directly to nineteenth-century Chinese immigrant history and with its building and menu—both stylish plays on streamlined modernism—it chose mid-century aesthetics over Old Cathay orientalism. New Moon, on South San Pedro, put a painting by Chinese brushwork expert Professor Huang Chun-Pi on its menu cover (with Chinese characters it didn't translate), and though you could order Egg Spring Rolls and Sweet and Sour Won-Ton, you could also get Sharkfin Soup ("a necessary experience for the true gourmet") and tender Westlake Duck prepared with Black Flower Mushrooms, Bamboo Shoots, and Chinese Parsley.

Charlie Chan • 5570 N. Figueroa St., Los Angeles • 1989

The reign of Cantonese cuisine, and its accompanying outsider lures, extended far beyond Old and New Chinatown. The menu for Kowloon, which opened in 1950 at Pico and La Cienega, begins with two full pages of restaurant history and lore penned by food writer Richard Sharpe to make sure the presumed non-Chinese diners understood just how authentic the meal they were about to eat was. Sharpe makes the case for the restaurant's namesake as the most Californian of Chinese cities, the home of many of the state's first gold miners and railroad workers. We're told that its Kowloon-born owner George Lim abandoned a post in a French restaurant downtown to return home in search of Kowloon's greatest chef. He finds him in Joe Ho, and brings Ho back to L.A. to man Kowloon's kitchen. Together, Sharpe declares, "they are the culmination of 5,000 years of civilization." Five thousand years that include not only the restaurant's secret recipes, marble statue of the goddess Guanyin, and a Pak-Chee miniature garden, but a "Foreign Correspondent's Room" painted "peacock, lacquer red, and corn yellow" where you could order the "Foreign Correspondent's Special." You could also graze across nearly a dozen plates of paper-wrapped chicken, bacon-wrapped shrimp, cubed Mo Kow steak, Cantonese lobster, and more (five bucks a person in 1959).

By the 1960s, when the Hart-Cellar Immigration Act helped open the door to an influx of immigrants from across China, the dominance of Cantonese cooking began to give way to an array of regional Chinese styles (Szechwan, Hunan, Shanghai, Mandarin). It's a shift we see registered across Chinese restaurant menus of the time, and often, as in the case of Chinatown mainstay General Lee's Man Jen Low, within a single restaurant menu. In the 1940s, Man Jen Low was purely Cantonese but by the 1960s it morphed into the Mandarin Room at General Lee's, and its menu included both Cantonese dishes and "Mandarin Supper" selections. In the decades that followed, the rise of Monterey Park and the San Gabriel Valley as the new hubs of Chinese life and Chinese dining put dumplings, dandan noodles, and toothpick lamb into the Angeleno food vernacular. The assumed Cantonese of the "Chinese Restaurant" would become a relic of the culinary past.

In the post-World War II years, Japanese restaurant menus often struggled with similar questions of representation. Back when Charles Hama opened the Kame Restaurant on East First Street

Kowloon • 6124 W. Pico Blvd., Los Angeles • 1959

in 1885, the neighborhood, not yet known as Little Tokyo, was still a small Issei community that mostly consisted of former railroad workers. Over the next four years, fifteen more Japanese-owned restaurants would open, many of them serving "American" meals to ethnically diverse working-class diners who lived, and punched the clock, nearby. As the community grew and Los Angeles became home to the largest population of first- and second-generation Japanese Americans in the continental U.S., restaurants grew into important sites of Japanese identity and community.

In the 1920s and 1930s Little Tokyo restaurants like Tengen and the Nisei Grill increasingly served a mix of generations and a mix of Japanese and non-Japanese customers that would become standard in the post-World War II years. At the New Ginza on East First, the English-language menu was mostly loaded with cocktails like "Japanese Grasshopper" and "Geisha Girl." After 9 p.m., once the floor shows got going, you could order sashimi and cubed abalone to go along with the "colorful entertainment from Tokyo." In 1964, they hosted a Thanksgiving dinner that didn't make patrons choose between "authentic Japanese" and "American": Roast Turkey with Rice and Chestnut Soy Sauce, Baked Ham with a Tofu Turkey Roll, and a Teriyaki Ham. Outside of Little Tokyo, the Cherry Blossom restaurant served Akadashi Beancake

Soup alongside more familiar suki-yaki and teriyaki dinner combinations, but their menu seemed more interested in hyping the restaurant's zashiki, private Japanese rooms where customers "are received and attended to as Japanese Lords of olden times." You could eat sukiyaki from a solid 20-karat gold stew pan while wearing a traditional Japanese gown. The menu also advertised for its neighbor, the Toho Theatre,

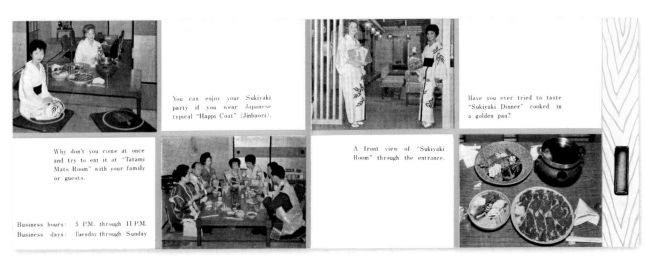

Cherry Blossom • 855 S. La Brea Ave., Los Angeles • 1960s

where after a "traditional and modern" meal, you could catch a first-run Japanese movie.

Of course, for many L.A. restaurants, "Asian" cuisine—a mix-and-match mélange of Cantonese, Japanese, and Hawaiian—was really just an excuse to go to "Polynesia." Chinese restaurants like Ah Fong's in Beverly Hills and the Outrigger in Long Beach explicitly served Cantonese food but used their cocktail menus, or Grog Lists, to reinvigorate the South Seas fantasies that had been part of Southern California restaurant culture since the 1930s. At the Outrigger, you could drink a Singapore Gin Sling or a Lapu-Lapu with your Chicken Canton and Water Chestnut Pork. Ah Fong served Tahitian Punch, Cobra's Fang, and something called a Missionary Downfall. Perhaps most questionably for a Chinese restaurant that explicitly told diners that chopsticks were provided only upon request, you could also order an Ah Fong's Coolie Cup (because nothing is as refreshing as indentured labor). At both restaurants you could get a drink called the Zombie, which by the 1970s was already a South Seas throwback. Its ambitious swirl of rums, citrus juices, falernum, Pernod, cinnamon syrup, grenadine, and bitters was invented by former Prohibition bootlegger Don Gantt in 1934 and was a beloved highlight of his menu at Don the Beachcomber, the McCadden Place source of the soon-to-be-national tiki craze. Here too, despite its Mandarin Duck in Wild Plum Sauce and its rumaki—the Häagen-Dazs of Polynesian appetizers—the food was Cantonese in inspiration and reminded you as much whenever possible (Cantonese Chicken, Cantonese Pork, Cantonese Soups).

Yet China is nowhere to be found on the menu's illustrated maps that charted travel itineraries between Hollywood and Hawaii, Samoa, Tahiti, and the Caribbean. Don the Beachcomber's fantasy geography, given free-libation reign once Prohibition was repealed, opened up the post-World War II floodgates for restaurants like the Luau, Tonga Lei, Bahooka, and the Bali Room, that turned the island locations of U.S. military outposts into tropical fodder for culinary amusement parks. Disneyland's Tahitian Terrace was the craze's most honest simulation, and Kelbo's on Pico Boulevard was its most honest and sexually shady end-point (the block-long hedonistic hub of Hawaiian BBQ is now a "gentleman's club"). The slick primitivism of their menu designs—graphic lookbooks of palm trees, totem statues, jungle spears, and topless island women in grass skirts—was as important to the fantasy as the faux authenticity of the actual food, which the menus nearly always spelled out in a bamboo typeface. Maybe Bertolt Brecht was right about Los Angeles: "This is Tahiti in the form of a big city."

The enduring industry of South Seas-theme restaurants and tiki rooms is an example of what L.A. does best: commodify the fantasy of something instead of dealing with its reality. Immigrants from across Asia and the South Pacific were already domestic actors in the urban culinary culture of L.A. As early as 1938, Filipino restaurants run by Filipinos like Bernie's Teriyaki, LVM Café (named for its owners, the Luzon, Visayas, and Mindanao families), and the Universal Café on Second Street, were already racial sanctuaries and community safehouses where local Filipinos could eat *ampalayang manok* (chicken with bitter melon) and *escabecheng isda* (fish with peppers and tomatoes). As Filipino writer Manuel Buaken described Universal Café in his 1948 memoir, "Here is a place where the pressure of racial differences is relaxed. . . . Here is a place where one hears and speaks one's own dialect without hostile or curious glances. . . . Here

The Luau • 427 N. Rodeo Dr., Beverly Hills • 1953

Don the Beachcomber • 1727 N. McCadden Pl., Hollywood • 1941

is a place to feed your body and relax your mind and feel at home." Beginning in the 1960s, a new wave of immigrants from China, Thailand, Korea, Samoa, and the Philippines arrived in Los Angeles, followed a decade later by the first generation of Cambodian and Vietnamese refugees. But Tonga Lei and Trader Vic's kept serving their pupu platters and scorpion bowls as if Asian and Pacific Islander life in L.A. was just a SoCal version of the "Hawaii Bound" episode of *The Brady Bunch*. During the very same years that Los Angeles was transforming into a bustling Asian metropole and Pacific Rim junction, white chefs were still teaching Thai cooking to white housewives in Santa Monica who had already worn out their fondue sets. Elite banquets and brunch menus were still featuring "Oriental" as a theme, and the *Times* was still printing headlines like "She's Gung Ho for Oriental Cookery" (yes, in 1967!).

Malihinis . . . .

IN ORDER to serve our Cantonese cuisine in the finest way possible, we cook all our dishes to order. This policy permits us to serve a large variety of Beachcomber dishes —in fact, more than forty. However, we suggest that until you become familiar with our menu, it is better to consult with your waiter who will recommend not only entrees that complement each other, but also quantities that will assure a satisfying dinner for you and your guests. This is only a suggestion, of course, but a great majority of our old-time Beachcombers prefer this procedure, and we thought you would like to know about it.

BEACHCOMBER APPETIZERS

FRIED SHRIMP (Cantonese) Cooked in Peanut Oil	1.75	RUMAKI Spiced Chicken Liver, Water Chestnuts wrapped in crisp Bacon	1.35
Half Order	.90	HAWAIIAN-CHINESE BARBECUED SPARERIBS	1.75
CHINESE BARBECUED TENDERLOIN OF PORK	1.60	BARBECUED CHICKEN (Canton Style) Disjointed and served with Seaweed Salt	2.25
EGG ROLL Stuffed with minced Crab Meat, Pork, Bamboo Shoots and Water Chestnuts	1.35		

BABY SQUAB (Canton Style) Disjointed and served with Seaweed Salt........ 2.25

CANTONESE SOUPS

(All prepared with Chicken Broth)

CHINESE WONTON	.70	MINCED BREAST OF CHICKEN WITH RICE	.85
HEART OF CHINESE GREENS	.60	EGG FLOWER WITH SHERRY	.75
CHINESE EGG NOODLES with Pork and Chinese Greens	.85	CHINESE EGG NOODLES with Breast of Chicken and Chinese Greens	.85

ENTREES

MANDARIN DUCK Boned, molded, crisped in Peanut Oil and served with Wild Plum Sauce	2.50	MIXED GREENS Pea Pods, Chinese Greens, Onions, Water Chestnuts, Celery, Bean Sprouts, Green Peppers and Pork	1.75
Half Order	1.30	WATER CHESTNUTS Imported Chinese Water Chestnuts sliced and cooked with Pork	2.00
BEACHCOMBER CHICKEN Strips of Chicken cooked with whole Soya Beans, Ginger, Garlic and other Spices	2.50	CHOW DUN Chinese Water Chestnuts, Green Peas, sauted and scrambled with eggs.	
BEACHCOMBER LOBSTER Prepared Cantonese style with Black Bean sauce, Eggs, and Chinese spices	2.75	With Pork. 1.60 With Shrimp. 1.60 With Chicken. 1.75	
CHICKEN ALMOND Tender Chicken cooked with Mushrooms, Bamboo Shoots, Celery and Water Chestnuts	2.10	SEA BASS BEACHCOMBER Pacific Sea Bass browned, then cooked with sliced Vegetables and Chinese Spices	2.25
CHICKEN MUSHROOM Thinly-sliced Chicken cooked with whole, Black Chinese Mushrooms	2.10	SHRIMP CANTONESE Fresh Shrimps rolled in Egg Batter then sauted with Pineapple and Green Peppers	2.00
CHICKEN PINEAPPLE Chicken sauted with Pineapple and Green Peppers	2.10	SHRIMP VEGETABLE Fresh Shrimps cooked with hearts of Chinese Greens, Onions and Celery	2.00
CHICKEN MANUU Strips of Breast of Chicken with fine cut Chinese Vegetables and Mushrooms	2.10	CHUNGKING SHRIMP Shredded Shrimps cooked with Pork, Water Chestnuts, Eggs and Green Onions	2.25
CANTONESE CHICKEN Thinly sliced Chicken rolled in Egg Batter and sauted with Pineapple and Green Peppers	2.10	Half Order	1.25
CHICKEN SOYO Tender Chicken cooked in Soyo Sauce with Water Chestnuts, Onions, and Bamboo Shoots	2.10	LOBSTER CHUNGKING New Zealand Lobster tails cooked in a Chungking sauce with Water Chestnuts, Eggs, and Green Onions	2.50
CHICKEN TOMATO Tender Chicken cooked with fresh Tomatoes.	2.10	FRIED WONTON Crisped and served with sauce of fresh Tomatoes, Green Peppers, Onions and Barbecued Pork	1.25
BEEF SOYO Tenderloin of Beef sauted in Soyo Sauce with Water Chestnuts, Onions, and Bamboo Shoots	2.00	CANTONESE PORK Thinly sliced Tenderloin of Pork rolled in batter and sauted with Pineapple and Green Peppers	2.00
BEEF TOMATO Beef Tenderloin cubes cooked with fresh Tomatoes	1.90	PORK SOYO Pork Tenderloin sauted in Soyo Sauce with Water Chestnuts, Onions and Bamboo Shoots	2.00
BEEF VEGETABLE Fine cut Filet of Beef with sliced Chinese Vegetables	1.90	PEAS & CHESTNUTS Pea Pods, sliced Pork cooked with Imported Chinese Black Mushrooms and Water Chestnuts	2.00
INDIVIDUAL NOODLES Fried Crisp in Peanut Oil	.50	**CHINESE FRIED RICE**	
CHINESE PEA PODS Young tender Chinese Pea Pods cooked with Celery and Pork	1.75	RICE with minced Roast Pork, Water Chestnuts and Green Onions	.35
CHINESE GREENS Hearts of Chinese Greens cooked with Pork..	1.75	(Also served with either Chicken or Shrimp)	
		(Above prices are for individual servings)	

DESSERTS

FRESH HAWAIIAN SUGAR LOAF PINEAPPLE	1.50	ASSORTED FRUITS IN SEASON served on snow ice	1.50
Half Order	.85	Half Order	.85
JALAPA TREE RIPENED MANGOES (individual serving)	.50	ALMOND COOKIES .... each	.10

Don the Beachcomber • 1727 N. McCadden Pl., Hollywood • 1941

Your Hosts, Tom Kelley & Jack Bouck — Kelbos

PIT BARBECUED SANDWICHES

"Specialty of the House"

Child Orders — Under 12
Ribs, $1.35 — Others, $1.10

Custom Barbecuing

Take Home Service

Combination Sandwich
Beef, Pork, or Ham
85¢

Hawaiian Combination Sandwich
95¢

Kelbo's Famous

Yams, Beans, or Fries

Egg Roll
Full, $1.00—Half, 60¢

Hawaiian Style Spareribs, $1.85

Ala Carte $1.60

Chopped Sandwich
Beef, Pork, or Ham
65¢

Hawaiian Chopped Sandwich
75¢

Ham, Beef, Pork and Ribs

Yams, Beans or Fries

Salad, Beans, Fries, Yams, Pickles
20¢

Soft Drinks 10¢
Coffee & Milk 10¢

Malts   Beers

Tropical Fruit Punches & Drinks
(Non-Alcoholic)

Diamond Head Platter, $2.25

Pit Bar-B-Q Sandwich
45¢

Hawaiian Pit Bar-B-Q Sand. 55¢

Beef, $1.35   Pork, $1.45   Ham, $1.45
Bar-B-Q Plates — Salad, Choice (Yams, Beans, Fries)

Shrimp Plate $1.35

Fish Stix Plate $1.35

Ala Carte $1.00

Ala Carte $1.00

Kelbo's • 11434 W. Pico, West Los Angeles • 1950s

Meanwhile immigrants from Thailand chose East Hollywood to open L.A.'s first Thai restaurant in 1969, as did Luoing Thi Sinh, who opened the city's pioneering Vietnamese restaurant that left no mystery of its national provenance in its name: Vietnam (soon changed to Vietnam Pearl). Cambodian refugees who landed in L.A. and La Habra in the mid-1970s were busy going "gung ho for American cookery"—doughnuts to be exact. By 1980, the Southern California doughnut trade was virtually saved by an extensive network of Cambodian refugees, starting with former gas station attendant Ted Ngoy who led the way with his fifty Christy's Donuts stores.

The exotic Asia of "over there"—villages, luaus, tropics, islands, pagodas—that had for so long hogged the spotlight of pricey L.A. restaurants (men needed a blazer to eat spare ribs at Trader Vic's), was now being replaced with the deep culinary variety and immigrant complexities of a multi-faceted and multi-national Asia "right here" that was equally working-class and upwardly mobile. It would never earn the moniker of a "food revolution" but that's exactly what it was, more than one diaspora inching its way, plate by plate, towards the center. Throw in the latest Mexican and Central American immigration booms, and by the time the 1970s were over, the attempt to define L.A. cooking in a single cultural or national stroke had become a New Yorker's fool's errand—more deliciously and transnationally impossible to do than ever before.

From our wood-burning pizza ovens . . .

WOLFGANG PUCK, Spago menu, 1983

What did get called a revolution happened above the tax bracket of most of the city's immigrant and post-immigrant restaurants: the California food revolution of the 1970s and 1980s. Out with sauté stations and in with grills. Replace old-school Continental cuisine with new-school "local" and "regional," and turn all things "haute" into comfort food, served not in the weighty, ornate establishments Calvin Trillin famously derided in 1975 as "purple palaces," but in a restored breezy beach bungalow with an open kitchen. "I'm afraid that fine dining may be dying in Los Angeles," chef Joachim Splichal told the *Los Angeles Times* in 1987 when he closed his nouvelle cuisine French restaurant Max au Triangle in Beverly Hills. "Here in L.A. the trend is more towards accessible dining than toward a dining experience."

Nearly a decade earlier, the paper's restaurant critic Lois Dwan had already felt the quake coming: "We have crossed a barrier, climbed a mountain, steadied to a direction." She may have written those words after sitting in a patio chair atop Astroturf at Ma Maison and certainly felt vindicated after being served recently picked farmer's market lettuces or a salad that had both duck legs and blueberries by a waiter in a pink Ralph Lauren oxford at Michael's. By the time Wolfgang Puck put cold smoked salmon on a pizza baked in a wood-fire oven at Spago, not only did relaxed and fresh "California cuisine" now have an official L.A. home (a satellite campus of Chez Panisse up north in Berkeley), but a new approach to locally sourced ingredients and a new awareness of industrial global food politics had made their way into local dining consciousness. Experimental nouvelle cuisine restaurants with steeper price tags and Gallic tendencies like L'Ermitage and Orange-

Spago • 8795 Sunset Blvd., West Hollywood • 1983

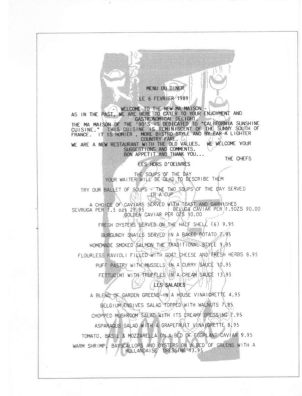

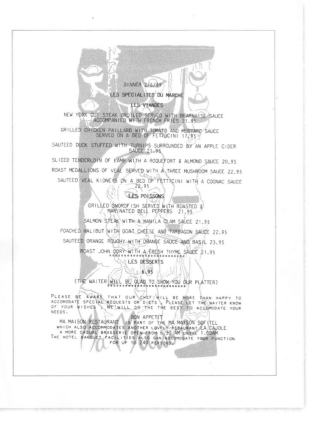

Ma Maison • 8555 Beverly Blvd., Los Angeles • 1989

Michael's • 1147 3rd St., Santa Monica • 1988

rie might have helped kick-start the menu makeovers by Puck, Michael McCarty at Michael's, Michael Roberts at Trumps, Michel Richard at Citrus, and others—it was, after all, L'Ermitage that first used local growers to harvest its ingredients in 1975—but in the age of open kitchens and wood-fire pizza ovens, their newness got musty, and socially passé, real quick.

Though California cuisine was ready for its spotlight in the 1980s, the notion of a cuisine specific to the California lifestyle and the California landscape was nearly as old as L.A.'s restaurant business. When travel writer Ruth Wood visited Los Angeles in 1914 for her book *The Tourist's California*, she visited restaurants in Glendale, Pasadena, Chinatown, and downtown where she ate local delicacies like cheese dipped in egg batter and fried in smoldering fat, ostrich-egg omelettes, the heads of pigs and ducks alongside haloti steaks and pork dumplings, and *nopales* that had been breaded, boiled, and fried. California cuisine, she mused, had come a long way from its Native American and mission roots: "from mush of acorn-meal and ground barley soup to terrapin dressed with cognac and truffles; from chicken, the *gallina* of the Spaniard, fried with cinnamon and nuts, to King Pompano in a *papiotte* ruff, and to frosted sweets served with grapefruit and beaten cream."

Seventy years later, the sentiment was back for a second bow: California cuisine had arrived once again, and once again it could be found in L.A. The trick was convincing food critics, and of course New York epicures, that there was anything to offer here at all. "Los Angeles?" Lois Dwan asked in 1978, "The home of the theme? Where gastronomy has aroused the least of passion?" Four years earlier, food writer Caroline Bates had already expressed a similar

appetizers — *Dinner*

mixed greens 5
marinated seafood & salsa 11
smoked chicken, shrimp, endive & walnut salad 8
buffalo milk mozzarella, red & green tomatoes 9
vegetable & pine terrine 7
salmon tartar 10
smoked salmon 12
plantains & caviar 11
potato pancakes, goat cheese, sautéed apples 9

soups — our daily selection

eggs & pastas
smoked salmon & scrambled eggs 14
fettucine, fresh vegetables 14
fried cornmeal cakes, chicken & clams 14
corn risotto, shiitake mushrooms, chicken livers & okra 14

seafood
grilled swordfish* 17
grilled sea scallops* 17
bay scallops sautéed with pine nuts* 16
steamed fish, tomatillo, & cilantro-priced daily
pan fried catfish, hushpuppies, capers & grapefruit 15
cold lobster-pesto-priced daily
grilled lobster-priced daily   *when available

meats & poultry
rack of lamb 13
new york steak & steak fries 22
roast veal chop, apples, pearl onions, & bacon 21
braised sweetbreads & greek olives 17
double crispy finger duck, vanilla, & sassafras 17
sautéed chicken, roast garlic, & candy lemon 16
grilled chicken 14

late supper after 10:30pm
french toast, sautéed bananas, & bacon 8
herb omelette 8
tomato, cilantro, shredded beef, avocado & potato omelette 12
swedish pancakes, fruit preserves, sour cream, nuts, vanilla sugar, & almond syrup 12

desserts & our daily selection
chocolate cake-pecan pie-bread pudding 5
ice cream trumpettes - 5.50
fruit doughnuts & ice cream - banana split 6.50

beverages
coffee-tea-herb tea-brewed, decaf 1.50
espresso-cafe au lait decaf espresso 2

Afternoon Tea 3:30 to 5:30 daily

L'Ermitage • 730 N. La Cienega Blvd., West Hollywood • 1980s

Trumps • 8764 Melrose Ave., West Hollywood • 1983

prejudice on the pages of the nation's flagship food and wine magazine *Gourmet* when she called L.A. "a city where experimental new restaurants come and go with the inevitability of Capistrano swallows, and sometimes more value attaches to gimmickry than good food."

In what many believe was a media tipping point in the California food revolution, Bates was given control of a new monthly column dedicated solely to reviews of California restaurants (joining columns about New York and Paris). Every other month she devoted thousands of words to the latest in upscale L.A. dining and ended up finding more good food than gimmickry. At Scandia, where chef Kenneth Hansen was a three-time award winner with the Los Angeles Food and Wine Society, she ate the famed Kalv-filet Oskar and praised the menu's seasonal offerings of imported Baltic salmon and Norwegian snow grouse. The natural and the seasonal were also the stars at La Grange, where vegetables were reinvented as sculptural garnishes. "Food is not heaped on a dish," she wrote, "it is composed." The warning shots had been fired on the pages of *Gourmet*: Los Angeles was worth paying attention to. A seasonal, fresh-vegetable and presentation-conscious revolution was in the works and, by the time Trumps and Michael's opened their doors at the end of the 1970s, it was in full bloom.

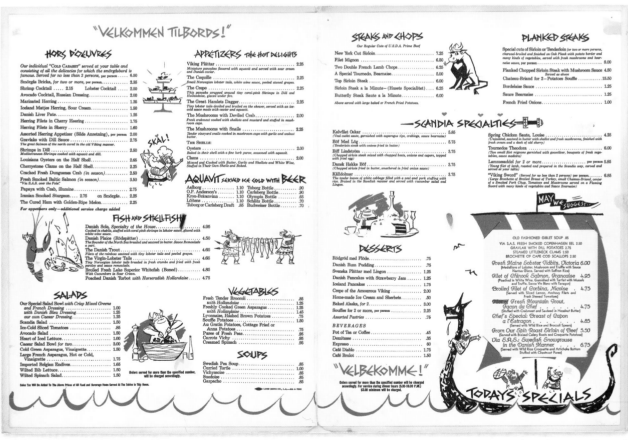

Scandia • Sunset Boulevard, West Hollywood

Menus were the revolution's manifestos, and they were changed daily. As Joyce Goldstein observes in her history of the period, *Inside the California Food Revolution*, shifts in food politics and food tastes were accompanied by the rise of desktop publishing, so menus no longer had to be formally printed and delivered to restaurants but could be written, designed, and modified all in-house and on the fly (even in the middle of a meal when the kitchen runs out of sea urchin or shredded pickled ginger). These farm-to-table missives of the goat cheese avant-garde were necessarily free of the purple prose that was once the house style of Trillin's purple palaces. Instead of his despised "twenty-thousand word menu" at "La Maison de la Casa House," menus at Michael's, Trumps, and West Beach Café tried, for the most part, to be like a Sunday morning freeway: clear, easy, direct, and full of signs showing you where you've come from and where you're heading. If there was French, it was translated with little pretense, as in the *California nouvelle* vernacular that Patrick Terrail made the hallmark of Ma Maison. His famous Brochettes of Boeuf were "brochettes of beef marinated for twenty-four hours in my grandmother's recipe," and the Assiette De Terrines et Pates was just that, "A plate of assorted pates." If there was preparation description, it was either simple, accessible, and to the point (Spago served "Grilled Chicken with garlic and Italian parsley" and "Crab ravioli with fresh tarragon") or a laundry list ingredient roll call ("comma cuisine," to borrow Northern California chef David Kinch's phrase). The restaurant's logo may have been designed by French painter and Picasso muse Francois Gilot, but its menu covers were mostly left to contemporary U.S. and California artists like Futzie Nutzle, Stephen Verona, Joan Worth, and most famously David Hockney who customized an off-kilter portrait of a set restaurant table—cosmopolitan, modern, and cool, yet unmistakably local.

Menus were now also maps of food provenance. Following the lead of Alice Waters up north, L.A. chefs like Michael McCarty and Michael Roberts made sourcing ingredients from local farmers a top priority, and their menus made sure that customers knew it, a trend that still dominates local menu vernaculars (and episodes of *Portlandia*). Yet reading "California cuisine" menus in the context of the Library's full collection is a reminder that listing provenance and working with local small farms were revolutionary moves only in that they were a return to the small-farm ethos that defined food production and restaurant culture in the nineteenth and early twentieth centuries. Back then, nobody was calling it farm-to-table because where else did food come from? The 1913 Christmas menu at Casa Verdugo's downtown branch proudly featured "Young Turkey From Casa Verdugo Hacienda" with its Spanish meatballs and fried green chiles. In 1929, downtown restaurant Oaks Tavern, known for its fried chicken dinners in the summertime, alerted the *Los Angeles Times* that all of its chickens come directly from its owner's ranch. In the 1930s, a menu from the Brown Derby in Beverly Hills specified Catalina sand dabs "caught especially for the Brown Derby this morning," the fried chicken served at McDonnell's Rancho came from McDonnell's own chicken ranch, and the Wasco Malt Shop menu put a picture of its dairy cows grazing at the Wasco Creamery Dairy Farm on its cover.

When jazz bandleader Horace Heidt bought Eaton's steakhouse in 1945 to open his own,

McDonnell's Rancho
San Fernando Boulevard, Glendale • 1950s

Horace Heidt's Steak House
9060 Wilshire Blvd., Beverly Hills • 1940s

the menu tried to be farm-to-table but was honest about its failed ambitions: only "some of the farm products" Heidt served were "brought direct" from Horace Heidt Ranch in the San Fernando Valley. Thrifty's Fount 'n Grill insisted that all of their doughnuts, pastries, and cakes were made in their own "sanitary bakery" and "delivered to our stores fresh daily with the morning sunrise." Even Ships Coffee Shop, home of the Hot Cake Sandwich, went to great lengths on the back of a 1960s menu to address the provenance, freshness, and quality of its ingredients, even if little of it was local (even the ham from Cudahy was Eastern). "In our opinion," the menu pledged, "the products and the brands listed below represent the highest standard of quality obtainable," and offered an explanatory list:

- Jones Link Sausage and Bacon (From Wisconsin)
- Huggins Young Coffee (Pure Cream)
- Four S Bakery Products (Baked For Restaurants Only)
- Heinz Ketchup, Mustard, Relish, & Steak Sauce
- U.S. Choice Beef For Hamburger (We Grind Our Own)
- Cudahy's Eastern Ham
- Edgemar AA Fresh Large Eggs and Dairy Products
- Chicken Pot Pie (100% Meat with Natural Gravy)
- Foremost-Golden State Ice Cream
- We Bake Our Own Deep Dish Fruit Pies
- Nesbitt's Sundae Toppings and Flavors
- California Oranges Squeezed To Order

Wasco Malt Shops • (various locations) • 1940s

Ships Coffee Shop • Washington Boulevard at Overland Avenue, Culver City • 1971

Of course, some restaurants flaunted just how un-local their products were, still worshipping at the throne of the non-local (the "farther the distance the fancier the food" motto). At King's on Santa Monica Boulevard, the menu was a map to everywhere but L.A. The lobster and scallops were "Eastern," the Riesling was from Johannesburg, the steaks were from Kansas City, and the chicken was from Rhode Island.

During the culinary shifts of the 1970s and 1980s, though, provenance went far beyond tracing an ingredient trail. It was about rethinking the food system. Menus quickly emerged into farm-to-table Star Maps, sneaky political tracts for food change and organic farming that boasted of sustainable ingredients and proudly name-dropped local farms. As Waters put it, "We are in a position to cause people to make important connections between what they are eating and a host of critical environmental, social, and health issues." Menu writing became willful political interventions; menus were thoughtful critiques

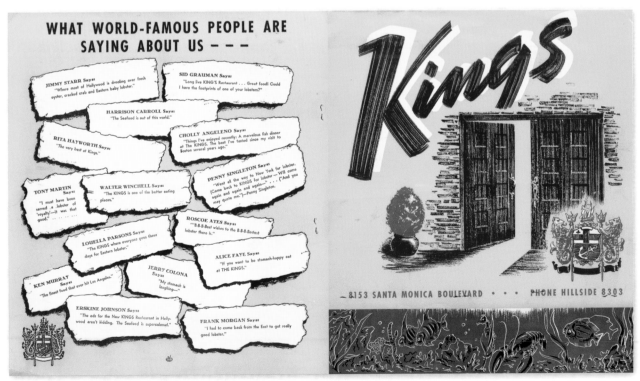

King's Tropical Inn • Washington Boulevard at Adams, Los Angeles and 8153 Santa Monica Blvd., West Hollywood • 1941

of the industrialized farming and corpo-
rate agribusiness that had come to dominate food production and distribution in
the U.S. since the 1950s heyday of frozen
foods, refrigerated long-distance ship-
ping, and grocery store behemoths.

The new focus on locavorism by
so many L.A. chefs led them not only
to farms and ranches, but also to local,
ethnically specific city markets—Indian, Mexican, Japanese, Korean. Duck
sourced from Chinatown markets and
butcher shops started making its way
into Westside kitchens and Wolfgang
Puck's visits to Little Tokyo famously
influenced him to add tuna sashimi to
Spago's menu (likewise, his Chinatown
visits helped birth the Cali-Asian fusions
of Chinois). Susan Feniger worked as a
line chef under Puck at Ma Maison before opening City restaurant on Melrose
with Mary Sue Milliken in 1985. At City,
there was warm goat cheese and avocado but there was also Thai melon salad,

City Restaurant • La Brea Avenue and Second Street, Los Angeles • 1987

tandoori steaks, and short ribs slathered with Chinese barbecue sauce next to cold spicy soba
noodles. It was perhaps the perfect example of post-1965 California food revolutions meeting
post-1965 California immigrant revolutions. While the high price points listed on these new
menus meant that they may only have been dining guides to a small percentage of the city's
population, they direct us to the long history of food change, community change, and cultural
change that helped fuel their politically minded approach to ingredients and food production.

All restaurants are built on the bones of other restaurants, all new cooking riffs on traditions
that we may not even taste. All menus are citations of menus past. In that way, the best
of L.A. restaurants and the best of L.A. menus—whether lunch counter or coffee shop, whether
purple palace or artisanal pop-up—return us to the city that inspired them, while helping us to
see it anew.

The city is entangled in our meals, but the meals are always at risk of extinction. In Los
Angeles, restaurants have the turnover rate of tween stars, boot camps, and juice cleanses.

They rise and fall like flash empires, in a constant cycle of hype and ruins, renovations and rubble. Most of the time, after the kitchens are gutted, the LED lights are hung, and the dining room gets new industrial flooring, the only thing that's left of the original pyramid besides memories and saved web bookmarks of favorable reviews are its holy scrolls and culinary codices, those artifacts of a lost civilization that—here and elsewhere—we've been calling "menus" with far too much humility.

As I began working on this book, two iconic L.A. restaurants saw their civilizations toppled, both by urban renewal tsunamis they couldn't stop. By the time you read this, what was once left of their cross beams and dry wall, the remains of their bones, will already have been bulldozed and dumped and replaced with new foundations growing tall behind shields of scaffolding. Their menus, however, are safe and sound, resting next to all the menus in this book, in folders stacked in file cabinets in the rare book room of the Central Library under constant care from librarian guardian angels.

Little Joe's • 904 N. Broadway, Los Angeles • 1980s

The bulldozers got to work on Little Joe's in early 2014. There was plenty past to knock through. It opened at the corner of Broadway and College in 1927 as the Italian-American Grocery Company in the heart of what was then an Italian-American enclave. It was a grocery store that sold sandwiches, sliced meats, and pastas that were popular with local Italian-American housewives who made its deli counter part of their daily tour of duty. Once construction began on nearby Union Station—which was itself built atop the bones of the old Chinatown—Italian-American male labors started making the grocery their lunch break headquarters. There was too much co-ed around too many cold cuts, so they opened Little Joe's as an adjacent restaurant mostly for the men. And there it stood, family run, for the next five decades, even as working-class Italians became the working-class Chinese of the Chinatown corridor that Little Joe's was now smack in the middle of. There are three Little Joe's menus in the Library's collection just waiting for someone to find them, search for clues, and read between the lines of the Pickled Brook Trout and Eastside Ale it served in 1935 and the Scallopini of Veal with Mushrooms that it served in 1962.

But not even the menus could have prepared people for the true history buried within the bones of Little Joe's. Once demolition began, excavators found that deep beneath the ground floors of Little Joe's was a piece of the original Zanja Madre pipeline. The deli known for salami that became a restaurant known for its Half and Half Pasta combos was built on the bones of the city's original, indigenous water supply: the water that allowed Los Angeles to exist. It might be the most profound example of a restaurant as a historic vessel, a literal part of L.A.'s ancient urban infrastructure: no water, no city, no restaurant, no menu. Little Joe's was the restaurant as city history.

Down at the other end of Broadway is another restaurant tomb, this one in the process of getting a second life. Clifton's Brookdale opened in 1935 and up until just a few years ago, its oddball mix of cafeteria, soup kitchen, theme park, and spiritual sanctuary was still standing, its tables still full of *L.A. Times* reporters, domestic workers just off a downtown bus, and homeless regulars from nearby Skid Row, all stacking the same trays with soup, coffee, and Jell-O. As the gentrification of downtown began to hit full stride, Clifton's was an ideological holdout in the face of developer bottom-lines and hipster up-pricing: a place for food democracy and community sustenance that appeared to defy the gravity of artist lofts. It was finally sold in 2010 and underwent years of remodeling and refurbishing—with the promise that its old bones would be cared for and preserved, and what's new will be an homage to what's old. But who will eat there? Who will be *allowed* to eat there? Will "Clifton's Golden Rule"—nobody is turned away for lack of funds—still apply to kale salads and harissa quinoa fritters? Will its history guide the way it thinks about the city around it, a city where feverish foodie culture and devastating food insecurity are the two most prominent features of the local food landscape? What can we learn from menus past to help us write better menus for the future?

In her 1974 review of Kavkaz, the restaurant that once stood where Spago once stood, Caroline Bates didn't just comment on the menu's Armenian and Georgian dishes and its Sunday night folk music jams that attracted local Russians, Armenians, and Ukrainians. She also commented on the view: "Situated high on a hill, Kavkaz commands a long view of Los Angeles spread south and a couple of picturesque billboards that could only be found on Sunset Strip, and as night falls the scene has a smoggy charm."

This is what restaurants and their menus can do, no matter where they are perched—a Sunset foothill, a Venice alley, a San Gabriel Valley mini-mall, a Boyle Heights boulevard, a Crenshaw mall. They give us a singular view of our city. They frame it for us. They both give the city back to us, but also help us imagine a city yet to come. Their menus write the script for what we see and what we taste but also for what we never thought could be possible. The stories that they tell—as real as they are fantasy, as literal as they are figurative—can stay with us long after we've stopped ordering from them. They have the potential to become transformative urban blueprints that change the way we think about what we eat and how we feed each other, designs for a new approach to food, culture, and community in the modern city.

In 1974, The Los Angeles Women's Saloon and Parlor opened on Fountain in East Hollywood. It was the first, and last, feminist restaurant in the city. It didn't allow male diners, let you work off a meal you couldn't pay for by helping in the kitchen, and was supported by the Feminist Research and Reading Society. On its sidewalk menu board, instead of listing daily specials, it only advertised its motto: "a way to invade society and create a place that reinforces what feminists believe." The Saloon and Parlor was the ultimate model of the restaurant as a social utopia and an experiment in social change. Its menus were hand-written in calligraphy and never included grapes or lettuce (in support of the United Farmworkers Union) and never advertised diet meals (in support of women of all shapes and sizes). They served tofu and homemade mayonnaise.

That's all that's known. The rest of the menu is a mystery. It's not in the Library's collection, and after months of hunting, no copies have turned up. Which is why it makes for a good ending. It's a reminder, one among thousands, that this book is just the start. The full Los Angeles Menu, the complete menu history of the modern city, is still being written.

Ollie Hammond's • (various locations) • 1946

MENU

SUNSET
INN

H·A·Gonden
MANAGER

SANTA MONICA — CALIFORNIA

Sunset Inn • Ocean Avenue and Colorado Avenue, Santa Monica • 1920

Hollywood Palladium · 6215 Sunset Blvd., Hollywood · 1947

House of Murphy · 410 S. San Vicente Blvd., Los Angeles · 1941

Earl Carroll · 6230 Sunset Blvd., Hollywood · 1944

Dancing nightly..

to the Music
of the
Best Dance Bands
Procurable —

Smooth, Spacious
Dance Floor

ORCHIDS FOR EVERY OCCASION

Order your Orchids from Vivian Laird's

The lovely blooms displayed in the lobby are from the finest Orchid plants obtainable.

Because growing orchids is our hobby, our prices are unbelievably low for such blooms.

Orchids in corsage or vase.
$2.00 - $5.00

Songs in the Jungle Room

SEE INSIDE
COVER

Plan a party

For two — or Two Hundred

And let us solve your entertainment problems. At a cost no greater than serving in your own home, we offer you delicious food, excellent service, and the best in entertainment.

The simplest party takes on the air of a Special Occasion in the beautiful, gay and informal atmosphere of Vivian Laird's. Birthdays, Anniversaries, and special events celebrated here become treasured memories.

A private dining room, overlooking the main room and separated from it by a disappearing wall when privacy is required, is available to groups of 25 to 100.

NO COVER / NO MINIMUM

TURN THE PAGE---

IN DOWNTOWN LONG BEACH

Vivian Laird's

Vivian Laird's

DELICIOUS FOOD • DANCING

First and Alamitos
Long Beach, California
Phone Long Beach 6-1974

Vivian Laird's • First and Alamitos, Long Beach • 1950s

PAUL'S
DUCK PRESS
RESTAURANT

PAUL DELLA MAGGIORA

Fred Harvey • Santa Fe Dining Car Menu, Los Angeles • 1950s

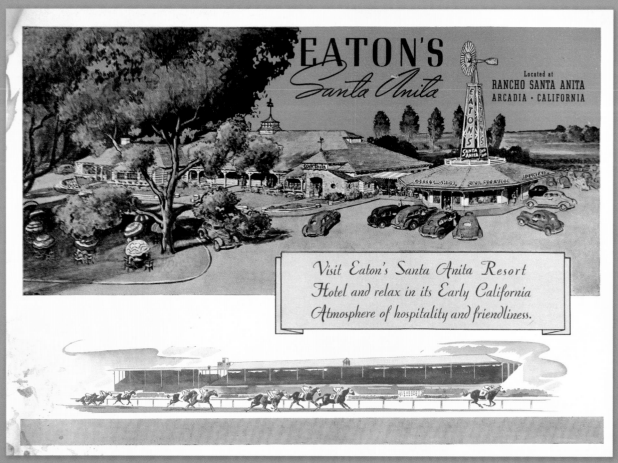

Eaton's • 1150 W. Colorado Blvd., Arcadia • 1960

TO LIVE AND DINE IN L.A.

Robinson's Tea Room · Seventh Street and Grand Avenue, Los Angeles · 1948

Frank Sennes' Moulin Rouge · 6230 Sunset Blvd., Hollywood · 1950s · Anonymous Donor

The Vista del Arroyo - Pasadena, Cal.

BREAKFAST

Sliced Oranges   Baked Apples   Grapefruit
Stewed Rhubarb   Stewed Prunes
Whole Figs in Syrup   Orange Juice   Clam Broth
Comb Honey   Marmalade   Jam

Wheatena   Cracked Wheat   Rolled Oats

Corn Flakes   Bran Flakes   Triscuits
Puffed Rice   Puffed Wheat   Health Bran
Grape - Nuts   Shredded Wheat Biscuits

Eggs to Order

Calves' Liver and Bacon

Broiled Ham or Bacon   Jones Sausages
Lamb Chops   Sirloin Steak

Broiled or Fried Fresh Fish

Broiled Kippered Herring

Baked Potatoes   Potatoes Saute

Flannel Griddle Cakes   Hot Cornbread
Buttered Toast   Assorted Hot Rolls
Popovers   Bran Muffins

Coffee   Postum   Buttermilk   Tea   Cocoa
Certified Milk   Malted Milk

February 4, 1927

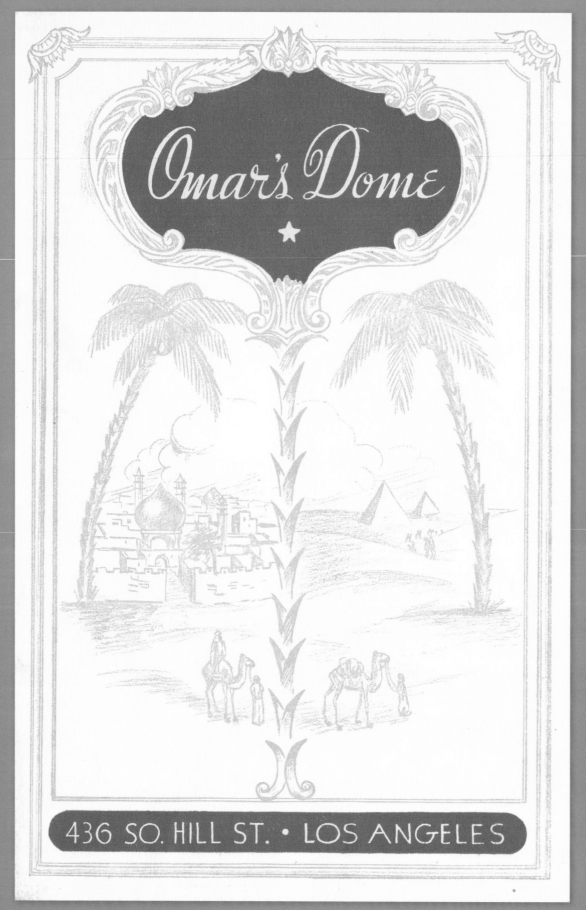

Omar's Dome • 436 S. Hill St., Los Angeles • 1936

ESSAYS

THE VICTOR HUGO INN   LAGUNA BEACH, CALIF.

PRICES OF ENTREE DETERMINES COMPLETE MEAL

D I N N E R

* * * * * *

On tonight's menu a rare selection
of delicious small plates:

JONATHAN GOLD time-travels back to St. Estèphe

BRICIA LOPEZ follows her family's flavors
from Koreatown into Oaxacatown

and STACI STEINBERGER visits the Bali Room,
the Cocoanut Grove, and the Burger That Ate L.A.

POTATO AND VEGETABLE SERVED WITH ENTREE

DESSERTS

Hot Mince Pie
CHEESE CAKE VICTOR HUGO - FRENCH APPLE TURNOVER -
ALMOND CREAM SLICE - BANANA CREME SLICE -
ASSORTED PETITS FOURS - MONT BLANC CAKE -
BOYSENBERRY COBBLER - NAPOLEON SLICE - CREAM PUFF -
CHOCOLATE ECLAIR - FUDGE CAKE A LA MODE -
MARQUISE SALAMBO - CARAMEL CUSTARD - BABA AU RHUM -
MOCA LAYER CAKE - FRESH FRUIT COMPOTE -
JELLO WITH WHIPPED CREAM - NEAPOLITAN ICE CREAM -
CHOCOLATE OR STRAWBERRY ICE CREAM - ROMAN PUNCH -
PINEAPPLE SHERBET - BLUE CHEESE AND CRACKERS

TEA   COFFEE   MILK

WINES - BURGUNDY HALF $1.25 FULL $2.25
CABERNET " 1.00 " 1.75
SAUTER NE " 1.00 " 1.75
MUMM'S CORDON ROUGE " 12.50
MERCIER " 10.50

If you had visited Saint Estèphe in the mid-1980s, a bleached-white dining room near a Coco's in a Manhattan Beach mall, you probably ordered the chile relleno with goat cheese, the restaurant's most famous dish. This was a different L.A. then, with Depeche Mode on the radio and *Less Than Zero* on the bestsellers list; the internationalist good vibes and the turquoise-magenta palette from the 1984 Olympics just beginning to fade. Spago was the dominant restaurant, not just in Los Angeles, but in the United States then, and casual, highly flavored Spago-style grill cuisine was in its ascendency.

But Saint Estèphe, you could tell in an instant, was something else entirely. That chile relleno, for example, was listed on the menu as "chile relleno, *farci avec une duxelle et servi avec un sauce de chevre et d'ail,*" and the crispness of both the service and the dining room also hewed to the original French. The roasted, peeled chile, when it came, was in the precise center of a very large plate, atop a pil-

Saint Estèphe · 2640 N. Sepulveda Blvd., Manhattan Beach · 1984

low of cream sauce flavored with Laura Chenel's fresh goat cheese from Sonoma, that was as ubiquitous in a certain kind of restaurant then as uni is now, and stuffed with *duxelles*, a rich preparation of minced mushrooms cooked down in butter that has been a part of haute cuisine since at least the time of La Varenne. This was not smoky, crisp, herbaceous California cuisine; this was classic French cooking with New World ingredients, and, in fact, the same *duxelles* had stuffed a steamed chicken breast at Saint Estèphe just a few years before when the restaurant was purely French. It was the birth of something—but of what, it was hard to tell.

John Sedlar, who was chef at Rivera and who was the young auteur of Saint Estèphe then, is one of the most innovative chefs ever to wield a whisk in Los Angeles, a veteran of Jean Bertranou's great La Cienega French restaurant L'Ermitage who created the institution of Modern Southwestern Cuisine at Saint Estèphe out of classical technique and the earthy ingredients he'd grown up eating as a boy in Abiquiu, New Mexico, not far from the studio of Georgia O'Keeffe.

The first blue-corn tortilla chip came out of Saint Estèphe, as a single, crunchy star served as an amuse-bouche of three corn kernels and a swirly stripe of chile puree, and Sedlar may also have been the first French-trained chef to play with chile-rubbed meat. He arranged American caviar, which was then considered vulgar, into abstracted rattlesnakes or into fierce-eyed kachina heads, like something out of a Hopi weaving. He raised the then-new art of plate-painting to new, squirt bottle–driven heights. (The Painted Desert salmon was plated on something like a Frederic Remington sunset drawn entirely in flavored sauce.)

Saint Estèphe • 2640 N. Sepulveda Blvd., Manhattan Beach • 1984

Twenty-five years later, when Sedlar served the 1986 Saint Estèphe menu at his downtown restaurant Rivera, it was a fascinating look at the food at an important moment in Los Angeles culinary history, like a set by Led Zeppelin tucked into the context of a Robert Plant show. That chile relleno, that interplay between the goat cheese and suave chile heat, the impossible butterfat bomb of the cream sauce and the *duxelles*, was as precise an evocation of a specific historical moment as anything I've ever encountered: an old menu made flesh.

Saint Estèphe had been a restaurant in a constant state of evolution, from classic nouvelle cuisine to what it had become by 1986 or so: still a French restaurant but transformed, so that the squab was served with a buttery puree of pinto beans instead of sorrel sauce; the red-wine sauce with the duck breast, formerly in the style of Bertranou, was spiked with hominy; and the *jus* on the saddle of lamb was amped up with tiny, spicy *chiles piquins*. In just a couple of years, the sauteed sweetbreads in the style of the Parisian chef Alain Dutournier, with turnips, pistachios, and orange zest, had become sweetbreads with chile con queso, the favorite guilty pleasure of every Tex-Mex aficionado, although I suspect that Sedlar's version contained neither Velveeta nor Ro-Tel tomatoes.

But as the Don Quixote written by a twentieth-century Frenchman in the Borges story was not the Don Quixote written by the sixteenth-century Cervantes—in the context of Rivera, Saint Estèphe became something radically different. In the 1980s, diners may have recognized a dish of eggs scrambled with goat cheese, cream, and jalapenos, then put back in their shells, as a Southwest challenge to the nouvelle cuisine standard of soft-scrambled eggs with caviar. Twenty-five years later, the preparation read as nostalgic comfort food.

A plate of ravioli stuffed with *carne adobada*, a dish that had worked its way through the Cheesecake Factories of the world by the end of the Reagan administration, was less revolutionary than it was delicious. I loved that Painted Desert salmon, and the frieze of squirted cream sauces that framed the small piece of steamed fish—I once compared the pattern to an EKG chart—and Sedlar's seared-scallop nachos with Roquefort. The slouchy blue-corn crepes were exactly as I remembered, down to the half-melted scoop of pumpkin ice cream. The prices on the menu were even pretty much unchanged—we were spending a lot more for nice meals in the 1980s.

But could the same menu cooked by the same chef, with the same ingredients from the same farmers possibly be the same as it was in that Manhattan Beach dining room? Clearly, it could not.

MY LOS ANGELES MENU

was ten when I moved to Los Angeles. Before Los Angeles, my world was Oaxaca, a small city-state on the south side of Mexico. I was born in the small village of Mitla, teeth and all. Yes, I was born with teeth, ready to eat everything the world would hand me.

My father was a mezcal man, and because of him, I learned how to hustle at a real early stage of my life. He opened his first *mezcaleria* in *El Tule*, a small town thirty minutes drive from the city. My sister was ten and I was seven when we joined the family mezcal business. Our jobs were loud and clear, because my sister was the oldest and knew how to add and subtract, she would take care of the register. *I* would have to go out by the *El Arbol de Tule*, the biggest (and only) attraction *El Tule* had to offer and hustle tourists to go into my dads place and get a sip of what I said "was the best mezcal Oaxaca had to offer."

I loved my days at the *mezcaleria*. I made a lot of friends and began to develop a taste for agave. My father never allowed my sister and I to drink, but the smell of the barrels and tubs will never leave my memory. Soon enough, the economic instability of Mexico led my father to take a different course in life. In 1994, Mexico had its biggest currency crisis of all time. My family woke up flat broke and my dad, left with no other option, took the little savings we had and bought one one-way ticket to Los Angeles.

My dad tells me those first few months in Los Angeles were the hardest of his life. His family was thousands of miles away, he had no money, and for the first time in his life, he felt what real hunger was like. His sister had moved to L.A. some years before him and took him in at her Mar Vista apartment. She had made her living like a lot of Mexican women did back then, cleaning the homes of the wealthy *gringos* on the hills. She also had a little side business. My aunt had figured out the value her fellow Oaxaqueños had put on Oaxacan goods like *quesillo, tazajo, chiles de agua, tlayudas, chapulines,* chocolate, and *mole* and begun selling these goods with my dad to other *paisanos* in the area. Shortly after partnering with his sister, my father discovered that hundreds of other Oaxaqueños had also fled Mexico's crisis in search of a better life, and had not only settled in Mar Vista, but in other pockets across California. He discovered towns like Santa Ana, Oxnard, Santa Barbara, Santa Maria, Madera, and Fresno, but most importantly, Koreatown in Los Angeles.

Koreatown became *his* hub, and he would set-up shop there every night after his long daytrips, right on the corner of 8th Street and Irolo. There would be a line of people waiting for him when he arrived. He'd pull out the grill, and the smell of grilling *tlayudas, tazajo,* and *quesillo* wafted through the streets of Koreatown. After months of this routine and saving up, he realized it was time to bring his family to him; after all, he had also just opened Guelaguetza, his first restaurant on that same Koreatown corner.

When I turned fifteen, my dad opened the second Guelaguetza on the corner of Olympic and Normandie. It was a gigantic white building with Korean architecture, home to one of Koreatown's first Korean buffets. Our grand opening was my dad's dream come true. He always envisioned a restaurant with a stage where live music would play every night, where the Guelaguetza dances could be performed on weekends, and a banquet hall where families could hold their *quinceañeras* and wedding celebrations. And

Guelaguetza • 3014 W. Olympic Blvd., Los Angeles • 2002

OAXACAN FOOD TERMS

CECINA
Chile paste- marinated leg of pork. Thinly sliced and fried.

CHORIZO
Small, round pork sausages flavored with chile and herbs. Grilled or fried.

CLAYUDA
Large, thin corn tortilla. Handmade and cooked on a clay cooking disc.

MOLE
Sauce or mixture. Most often refers to a rich chile, nut and seed sauce mixed together.

TASAJO
Salted beef round. Thinly sliced and grilled.

MEMELA
Thick handmade corn tortilla

QUESILLO
Oaxacan string cheese.

DESAYUNOS · BREAKFAST

1. HUEVOS RANCHEROS
(servido con arroz y frijoles negros)
Fried eggs on crispy tortillas covered with spicy
tomato sauce. Served with rice and black beans $6.00

2. HUEVOS REVUELTOS CON JAMON
(servidos con arroz y frijoles negros)
Scrambled eggs with ham. Served with rice and black beans $6.00

3. HUEVOS REVUELTOS CON CHORIZO
Scrambled eggs with chorizo. Served with rice and black beans $6.50

4. HUEVOS A LA MEXICANA
Scrambled eggs with chopped tomato, onion and
jalapeña chile. Served with rice and black beans $5.50

5. SALSA DE HUEVOS
Huevos en torta, en salsa de jitomate y jalapeño.
Servido con frijoles negros.
Scrambled eggs covered with spicy tomato sauce.
Served with black beans $6.00

6. SALSA DE CHORIZO
Chorizo en salsa de jitomate y jalapeño. Servido con frijoles negros
Chorizo covered with spicy tomato sauce.
Served with blck beans $7.50

7. SALSA DE QUESO
Queso fresco con salsa de jitomate y jalapeño.
Servido con frijoles negros
Fresh cheese covered with spicy tomato sauce.
Served with black beans $7.50

8. SALSA DE CHICHARRON
Chicharrón en salsa de jitomate y jalapeño.
Servido con frijoles negros
Fried pork skin covered with spicy tomato sauce.
Served with black beans $7.00

that was exactly what Guelaguetza on Olympic became. It was the gathering place of every Oaxacan family across California.

My dad became a little adventurous and created new dishes when this location opened. He added new items he created himself, like the *Nopal Zapoteco*, the *Tuxtepecana* and our most popular mezcal cocktail to date, *Garra de Tigre*, as well as old traditional dishes like Milanesa, Alambres, Molotes, and about fifteen new seafood dishes. Today, our menu has over seventy dishes to offer all day, every day. When going through this new menu transition, people had hundreds of suggestions for him. At some point, someone suggested he added fajitas to the menu.

People said the restaurant was too big to continue being profitable just by selling Oaxacan dishes. My dad always said he always wanted to sell food to and for *Oaxaqueños*. "If a Oaxaqueño likes it, then that's all I need" he would reply proudly. Fajitas never made it to our menu.

We have always stuck to traditional recipes, and always will. Oaxacan cuisine has hundreds of years of history, and we don't intend to alter any of the sacred dishes. The only thing we can do is to keep doing what our ancestors have done for years, use the best of ingredients and pay homage to our food to the best of our ability.

From the day I turned fifteen, every day after school and every weekend thereafter was spent at the new restaurant. My older sister had moved to Mexico City for college, my brother was still too young to have a management position, and my baby sister was seven. So it was just me, running around the restaurant acting like the lady boss I eventually grew up to be. Late nights after closing were mostly spent at El Taurino on Olympic and Hoover. My family and I would go in there and always order the same twelve tacos *al pastor*, two burritos and four *atoles*. Sometimes when our restaurant closed later than usual, we'd pull up to their truck parked out back and order curbside. I remember saving the small cups of salsa they packed with our to-go orders. After chowing down four tacos before bedtime, I would go to bed thinking about the breakfast I was to have the next morning—scrambled eggs with ham and the Taurino's red salsa on the side.

After our lunch rushes, we'd head across the street to Gam Ja Goi and have "Korean soup," as my dad always called it. My dad has always noticed the similarities the two cultures have to one another when it comes to food. He would go on and on at lunch time about how the soup was the exact same as the "*caldo de espinazo*" my mom would make for him back in Oaxaca.

Maybe the food is what originally attracted so many *Oaxaqueños* to settle in Koreatown, one of the similarities in our cultures, we didn't even know were there. It is as if all of us spoke the same "language." We just somehow felt those same family and cultural values rooted deep down within us. It is that same energy that originally brought us together, and I believe still keeps us together today.

When I drive through the streets of K-town today, I can't help but get emotional and think of just how incredible this city was to open its arms to a man who had nothing to offer but his food and some bottles of mezcal.

DESIGNING THE L.A. MENU

On October 8, 1924, the *Los Angeles Times* heralded the completion of a new "FilmLand" hot spot, Paulais Confectaurant in Hollywood. Praising its "exemplification of unusual completeness and moderness," the reporter lauded both its "old-world palace" decor and remarkable refrigeration system. This combination of make-believe and modernity carried over onto the café's luxurious gold-cord-bound menu. Though its cover depicted a fairytale castle towering over a European countryside, its simplified, abstracted style tied the illustration firmly to the twentieth century. The name "Paulais," scrolled across the bottom corner in elegant script matched the establishment's prominent signage. Despite its historical appearance, Paulais's consistent branding provided a subtle hint of new design practices.

Illustrated menus are, in themselves, artifacts of modern life. When menus first appeared in France in the late eighteenth century, they were densely packed, newspaper-like lists. A century later, many had taken on a new format with lavishly decorated covers that imitated the popular lithographed posters of Jules Cheret and Henri Toulouse-Lautrec. The connection isn't intuitive—posters lured patrons into theaters and expositions, while menus greeted customers who had already chosen where to eat. Though most relied on stock borders and basic layouts, the best examples were integrated with their settings, drawing on culinary themes and elements of the decor. By unifying the graphics with interiors, restaurant owners invoked (intentionally or not), the *Gesamtkustwerk* or total work of art, a central tenet of modern design, transforming dinner into an artistic experience.

In some cases, like Saul Bass's late 1950s logo for Lawry's the Prime Rib, this took the form of a simple, iconic mark. The solitary bullseye "L" was repeated throughout the restaurant, from exterior signage, matchboxes, and flatware, to doggy bags and a widely distributed product line. It put the pride of place on menu covers, where its familiar form was enough to alert visitors they had finally arrived at the storied steakhouse. But earlier menu covers, like advertisements, often elaborated on a brand, creating a narrative context for names and trademarks. The Pig'n Whistle, a confectionery café chain that opened in 1908, reproduced a simple line drawing of its eponymous mascot on signs, advertisements, and candy displays.

Bali Room at The Beverly Hilton • 9876 Wilshire Blvd., Beverly Hills • 1955

This version of the pig dances across several corners of a 1919 menu, and on others, painter and Hollywood artist Duncan Gleason brought the character to life in a fairyland tableaux, appealing to the shop's youthful audience by mimicking the delicately stylized naturalism of contemporary picture books.

Though Gleason signed his illustrations, most commercial artists worked anonymously. In the early twentieth century, graphic design was largely the purview of printers. Even after the rise of consultant design firms in the mid-twentieth century, many restaurant owners continued to work directly with their publishers. At Los Angeles's Lord Printing Company, the largest specialty menu publisher in the country, the in-house staff devised most of the designs. As a 1967 *Los Angeles Times* article by its future restaurant critic Lois Dwan noted, this "at times became the theme of the restaurant." Lord's 1950s menu for Burl's diner showcased one of the company's innovations—glamorized color images of menu items—adding an element of Technicolor realism to the space-age fantasy of the cover.

Burl's dynamic red triangle and atomic starbursts capture the energetic optimism of post-war Los Angeles. Some of the most appealing menu covers signal their owners' aspirations to be *au courant*, representing the best version of the present, rather than idealizing a romantic past. The tightly tracked speed lines and precise, machine-age typography of the 1930s Pucci Café menu evoke moderne glamor. While it's difficult to ascertain whether the long-forgotten restaurant matched the elegance of the design, one can easily imagine picking the card off of the low-slung streamlined bar on a Golden Age Hollywood set.

Other restaurateurs used design to transport patrons out of their ordinary lives, adding to the illusion that a local joint could substitute for a tropical escape. When the much-anticipated Beverly Hilton opened in 1955, each of its entertainment spaces, such as the elite L'Escoffier restaurant and Red Lion bar, had

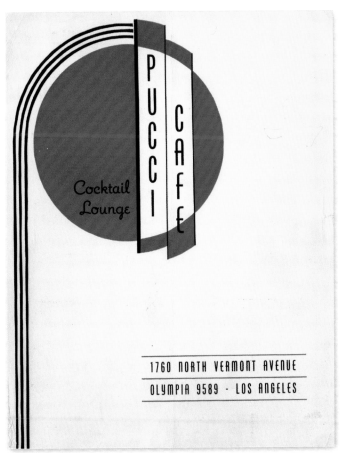

Pucci Café • 1760 N. Vermont Ave., Los Angeles • 1930s

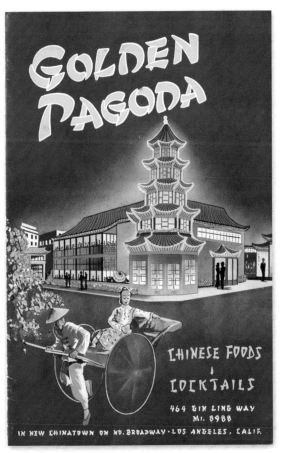

Golden Pagoda • 464 Gin Ling Way, Los Angeles • 1943

its own thematic style. Hilton designer Don May integrated the alluring pink-and-turquoise color scheme of the Bali Room into the menu, capturing the club's exotic atmosphere. As befitting a conventional chain hotel, he embellished the vivid sunset with a montage of floating Balinese dancers but contained the spectacle within an orderly geometric screen. Two years later, May updated the menu of the Ambassador Hotel's Cocoanut Grove restaurant to coincide with the 1957 renovation of the storied nightclub. Like the interior, May's cover (still in use in 1960), maintained the restaurant's Moorish overtones, layering abstracted bulbous domes into a colorful contemporary pattern.

In a tourist stronghold such as Chinatown, proprietors used different aesthetic strategies for marketing their own cultures to expectant outsiders. The collaged 1943 cover of the Golden Pagoda menu juxtaposes images of the restaurant's stage-set architecture with familiar images of Chinese rickshaw travelers. The gold lettering mimics calligraphic brushstrokes, further invoking Western stereotypes of Asian culture. In contrast, designer Frederick Usher's 1960s menu for the popular General Lee's Mandarin Room used understated blocks of color to project an upscale image, maintaining the modern aesthetic through pages of lowercase, sans serif entrees.

As the meaning of fine dining and design evolved, menus changed as well. The signed Wolfgang Puck sketch on Spago's *carte* implied that true artistry underpinned the celebrity chef's creations; the labeled ingredients reminded diners of the high-quality foodstuffs that were central to his brand of California cuisine. This postmodern self-consciousness took on a very different form in the 1989 menu for the Burger That Ate L.A., a hamburger-shaped eatery on Melrose. The restaurant's kitschy pastiche of the mid-century burger joint is reflected in illustrator Charles White III's blend of vintage B-movie hyperbole and New Wave collage (mustard and ketchup stand in for the style's characteristic squiggles). Like so many of its predecessors, the menu epitomizes design as entertainment, promising a theatrical immersion that goes far beyond a list of entrees.

General Lee's The Mandarin Room • 418 Bamboo Ln., Los Angeles • 1960s

COCOANUT GROVE

Ambassador Hotel / Cocoanut Grove • 3400 Wilshire Blvd., Los Angeles • 1960

FREE INFORMATION FOLDER AT FRONT DESK

TAP GLASS FOR DINING ROOM SERVICE

Clifton's

POLICIES

(SEE OVER FOR SERVICES)

Pay what you wish—Dine free unless delighted.

No guest shall go hungry for lack of funds.

Larger portions of divisible items on request.

On over 75 million meals, profits average less
than one-half cent per meal.

Food for the soul is important too.

Associates receive top wages; free medical and
surgical service, hospitalization, sick pay; group
insurance; vacations; etc.

No person on earth need starve if research in which Clifton's
participates is applied. *Meals for Millions*, a Clifton's
sponsored foundation, works for this goal.

Clifton's makes continuing contributions for better local,
state and national government.

Life, Time, Reader's Digest, Fortune, Collier's, American and
many others have reported on Clifton's.

CLIFTON'S

Pacific Seas • 618 South Olive Street
Brookdale in the Redwoods • 648 South Broadway
Los Angeles

Clifton's • 648 S. Broadway, Los Angeles • 1937

Counter Service

WALT DISNEY'S STUDIO RESTAURANT

BURBANK CALIFORNIA

Walt Disney's Studio Restaurant · Burbank · 1958

the *Broadway*

DINING FOR

YOUNG CUBS

Under 12

GOLDILOCKS

GRILLED HAMBURGER
with Potato Chips,
Sliced Tomato, Dill Pickles,
Milk or Pepsi-Cola

.75

BABY BEAR

PEANUT BUTTER AND JELLY SANDWICH

with Fruit Jello,
Milk or Pepsi-Cola

.60

PAPA BEAR

FRENCH FRIED SHRIMP

Slim Jim Potatoes,
Fruit Jello,
Milk or Pepsi-Cola

$1.15

JUNIOR BEAR

GRILLED HOT DOG on a Bun
with Potato Chips,
Sherbet or Ice Cream,
Milk or Pepsi-Cola

.75

MAMA BEAR

**ITALIAN SPAGHETTI
AND MEAT SAUCE**

with Garlic Toast,
Milk or Pepsi-Cola

$1.00

The Broadway · Broadway and Fourth Streets, Los Angeles

John's Café Avalon · Santa Catalina Island · 1940s

Carl's at the Beach • Roosevelt Highway (later 15145 Pacific Coast Hwy.), Los Angeles • 1939

VOYAGE 102   EN ROUTE: LOS ANGELES TO HONOLULU

S. S. "City of Los Angeles"

F. I. Hamma, U. S. N. R., Commander

SATURDAY, MARCH 28th, 1931

Luncheon

Grapefruit Cocktail

Spring Onions   Garden Radishes

———

Puree Split Peas au Crouton   Consomme Vermicelli
(Cold) Jellied Consomme

———

Broiled Fresh Mackerel, Anchovy Butter

———

Fricasse of Spring Lamb a la Parisienne
Fried Jumbo Scallops, Bacon, Shoestring Potatoes
Boiled Brisket of Corned Beef and Cabbage
Omelette Plain, or with Fresh Mushrooms
TO ORDER:
Broiled Sirloin Steak, Bordelaise

———

Baked Potatoes   Hawaiian Poi   Brown Potatoes
Italian Squash   Boiled Rice   Cauliflower au Gratin

COLD BUFFET
—

Prime Roast Beef   Salami   Hormel Ham
Head Cheese   Bologna
Potato Salad Served with All Cold Meat Orders

———

Salad: Sliced Tomatoes, French Dressing

"A BIT OF SWEET MAKES THE MEAL COMPLETE"
—

Grape Nut Custard Pudding, Orange Sauce
Chocolate Ice Cream
Lemon Cream Pie
Golden Pound Cake

———

Fresh Hawaiian Pineapple

———

American, Pineapple and Edam Cheese

———

Tea, Milk, Iced Tea and Coffee

MENU No. 6

S.S. *City of Los Angeles* · (Los Angeles Steamship Company) · 1931

DINNER

LOS ANGELES, CAL., MARCH 2, 1911

OYSTERS   California 35   Cocktail 30   Alexandria 75   Toke Points 40   Eastern 40
Blue Points 40   Cocktail 40   Clams 40   Cocktail 35

HORS D'OEUVRE   Radishes 15   Lyon Sausage 50   Caviar Imperiale d'Astrachan 80-150
Marinierter Herring 40   Boneless Sardines 60   Mackerel in Oil 50
Canape of Caviar 50   Pim Olas 25   Salted Almonds 40   Salted Pecans 40
Pickled Walnuts 30   Mixed Pickles 20   Anchovies in Oil 50   Tomato, Mirabeau 60
Chow-chow 25   Cal. Ripe or Green Olives 20   Queen Olives 25
Spiced Pineapples 35   Dill Pickles 20   Orange, Pepper and Cucumber Mangoes 35
Individual Pate de Foie-gras 60   Young Onions 15   Celery 30
Royans 50   Antispastis 60   Thon Marine 50   Buffet Russe 75

Alexandria Assorted Relishes 15c per Piece

SOUP   Consomme Fleury 20   Potage Parmentiere 20
Cream of Peas 20   Hot or Cold, (Cup) Strained Okra 25   Cream of Tomatoes 20
Chicken Broth in Cup 25   Puree of Tomatoes with Rice 20

Cold Soup   Consomme Frappe 20   Rhine Wine 30   Tomato Bouillon 20

FISH   Pompano or Sand Dabs, Meuniere 50, Papillotes 60   Broiled Shad 50
Shadroe with Bacon 60   Fried Scallops with Bacon 75
Terrapin a la Maryland 90-175   Broiled Salmon Steak 50
Planked Striped Bass, Alexandria 75   Broiled Barracuda 40   Mussels, Bordelaise Style 60
Fried Filet of Sole, Tartare Sauce 60   Broiled Boneless Smelts 60
Crab Flakes au Gratin 75
Broiled Live Lobster Butter Sauce, half 80, whole 150
Cold Lobster Mayonaise, half 80, whole 150
Brochette of Lobster, Colbert 85   Baked Barracuda a l'Italienne 60

HOT ENTREES
Vol-au-vent of Shrimp, Cardinal 75
Salmi of Domestic Duck, Bigarad 85
Sweetbread en Cocotte, Chasseur 80
Small Tenderloin Steak en Casserole, Parisienne 90
Rack of Lamb, Bouquetiere 75
Pineapple Fritters, Brandy Sauce 40

BROILED   Corn-fed Turkey or Capon for Parties   Fresh Mushrooms on Toast 90

ROAST   Beef 50   Lamb 50   Turkey 75
Fricandeau of Veal with Peaches 75

COLD   Pate de Foie-gras in Jelly 60   Assorted Buffet, piece 60
Boned Squab en Aspic 75   Galantine of Guinea Chicken 75   Corned Beef 40
Kalter Aufschnit 70   Assorted Meats 60   Roast Beef 50   Tongue 50
Pickled Lambs' Tongue or Pigs' Feet 40   Eel in Jelly 60   Chicken 75   Turkey 75

VEGETABLES   Spinach in Cream or Anglaise 25   Boiled Rice 20   Brussels Sprouts 30
French Whole Artichokes 60   Artichokes 40, Hollandaise 50   Stringless Beans 25
Cauliflower 40, Hollandaise 50   New Green Peas 25   French Peas 40
Stuffed Green Peppers 40   Hubbard Squash 25   Stuffed Tomatoes 40   Lima Beans 25
Teltauer Rubchen 40   Succotash 25   Stewed Corn 20   Butter Beets 20
French Carrots in Cream 40   Fried Egg Plant 40   Boiled Onions 25
Fried or Stewed Parsnips 30

Asparagus: French Colossal 80   German 140   California 40   Hollandaise 50
Potatoes: Baked or Mashed 15   New in Cream 20   au Gratin 25   a la Reichl 40
Long Branch 30   Lorette 30   Fondante 30   Sweet Potatoes, Southern Style 40

SALADS   Chiffonade 50   Head Lettuce 25   Cucumber 30   Potato 25
Romaine 25   Chicken 70   Lobster 60   Tomato 40
Shrimp 60   Crab 60   Alexandria 40   Tomato Princess 50   Alligator Pear 100
Combination 40, Special 50   Chicory 30   Marguerite 60   Escarole 30
California 50   Mexicain 50

ENTREMETS   Coccanut Custard Pudding, Maraschino Sauce 20   Strawberry Shortcake 35
Napoleon Slices 20   Orange Custard Pie 15   Bombe Glace 35
Rhubarb Pie 15   Apple Pie 15   Hot Mince Pie 15   Charlotte Russe 30
Brandied Peaches 75 or Cherries 50
Meringue a la Chantilly 30   French Pastry (1) 15 (2) 25
Stewed Rhubarb 25   Stewed Fresh Strawberries 30   Apple Sauce 25
Confitures de Bar-le-Duc Individual White and Red Strawberries
Currant, Raspberry, Gooseberry 25-40
Cup Custard 20   Spiced or Preserved Figs 40   Cal. Grape Fruit Marmalade 30
Individual Jellies: Crab Apple, Currant, Guava, Quince, Apple, Satsuma 25
Wine Jelly 20

ICE CREAM, Etc.   Neapolitan 25   Vanilla 20   Chocolate 20   Strawberry 20
Alexandria Special Souvenir Ice Cream 75
Sorbet, Roman or Maraschino 25   Nesselrode Pudding 35   Peach Melba 60
Lemon Ice 20   Pineapple Ice 25   Sultana Roll, Claret Sauce 25   Lady Fingers 20
Sponge Cake 20   Macaroons 20   Petit Fours Glace 25   Cafe Parfait 35
Fruit Cake 20   Pound Cake 20   Chocolate Eclairs (1) 15, (2) 25

FRUIT   Oranges [1] 15, [2] 25   Apples 25   Tangerines 25   Smyrna Figs 25
Strawberries 30   Fresh Grapes 30   Bananas 25
Assorted Fruit 40   Assorted Nuts and Raisins 35

CHEESE—Imported   Camembert 25-40   Brie 25-40   Stilton 25-40   Roquefort 20-30
Edam 15-25   Swiss 20-30   Gorgonzola 50
Domestic   Oregon Cream 20-30   Neufchatel 20-30   McLaren's Club 20-35
Sierra 20-30   American 15-25

TEA, COFFEE, Etc.   Tea or Coffee 15-25   Special Alexandria 25
Cocoa or Chocolate 20-35   Demi Tasse 10   Bottle of Milk 10   Horlick's Malted Milk 20

One portion served to one person only.   Room Service 25c per person extra.

DRAUGHT BEER   Domestic Beer, Glass 10, Stein 20
Imported Pilsner Hoffbrau, Glass 15, Stein 25   Wurzburger, Glass 15, Stein 25

Mission Indian Grill (at the Alexandria Hotel) • Fifth and Spring Streets, Los Angeles • 1911

JB's

Little Bali
House of the Authentic Indonesian Dinner

217 EAST NUTWOOD STREET
DOWNTOWN INGLEWOOD, CALIFORNIA
OR. 4-9835 — PHONES — OR. 4-1378

YOUR HOSTS JIKKY & BOB GOEY

— *The Indonesian Dinner (Rijsttafel) Rice-Table* —

A delightful combination of 13 gourmet dishes and condiments served with fluffy steamed
white rice.   A must for the "EPICURE"! $5.00

Salad
GADO-GADO   * An Indonesian salad of stewed vegetables (broccoli, bean sprouts, green cut beans and cabbage), sliced cucumber, sliced potatoes, sliced hard boiled egg and topped with an exotic flavored peanut base sauce and imported shrimp crackers.

Entree
NASI PUTIH   * Fluffy steamed white rice.

KAREE AJAM   * Chicken specially cooked in coconutmilk and deliciously seasoned with curry.

DAGING BUMBU RUDJAK   * Marinated beef cooked in coconutmilk and chile.

SATEE DAGING   * Bbqd marinated chunks of top grade filet mignon on a skewer and topped with a delicious sauce.

SAMBAL GORENG TELOR   * Sliced hard boiled egg in a tasty coconutmilk sauce.

UDANG GORENG   * Fried selected jumbo shrimps specially prepared with a delightful flavor.

SAJUR   * Broccoli, cabbage and cut beans cooked in coconutmilk.

KRUPUK UDANG   * Imported shrimp crackers.

Condiments
SAMBAL GORENG KENTANG   * Special prepared fried shoestring potatoes.

SAMBAL GORENG EBI   * Delightfully flavored ground shrimps.

SRUNDENG KELAPA   * Fried grated coconut mixed with fried peanuts.

ATJAR   * Home-made vegetable pickles.

SAMBAL BADJAK   * A blend of red peppers, spices, onion and vegetable oil.

Dessert
JB's ICE-CAKE   * A delicious home-made combination of ice-cream and chocolate rum cake.

Beverages   * Java Coffee   or   Chinese Jasmin Tea.

Also available and highly recommended for this dinner - imported from Holland

"HEINEKEN's" BEER on draft ....50 cents a big mug

 LET US CATER YOUR PARTY BIG OR SMALL!

OPEN: Wednesday through Sunday ~ 5 p.m. - 10 p.m.

CLOSED: Monday and Tuesday

FOR RESERVATIONS CALL: OR 4-9835

JB's Little Bali • 217 E. Nutwood St., Inglewood • 1970s

BREAKFAST AT...
Coffee Dan's

**WILSHIRE
BOULEVARD
AT
CAMDEN**
Beverly Hills

•

**HOLLYWOOD
BOULEVARD
AT
HIGHLAND**
Hollywood

•

**VINE AT
SUNSET**
Hollywood

•

**BROADWAY
AT FIFTH**
Los Angeles

•

**EIGHTH
AT HILL**
Los Angeles

Gloria De Haven and Robert Maxwell a winsome twosome at Coffee Dan's.

Luscious Gloria De Haven is currently starring in 20th Century-Fox's "I'll Get By". Robert Maxwell is the noted young swing harpist whose music will soon be heard in the same studio's "For Heaven's Sake".

Coffee Dan's • (various locations) • 1950

The Hot Dog Show • 450 S. La Cienega Blvd., Los Angeles • 1949

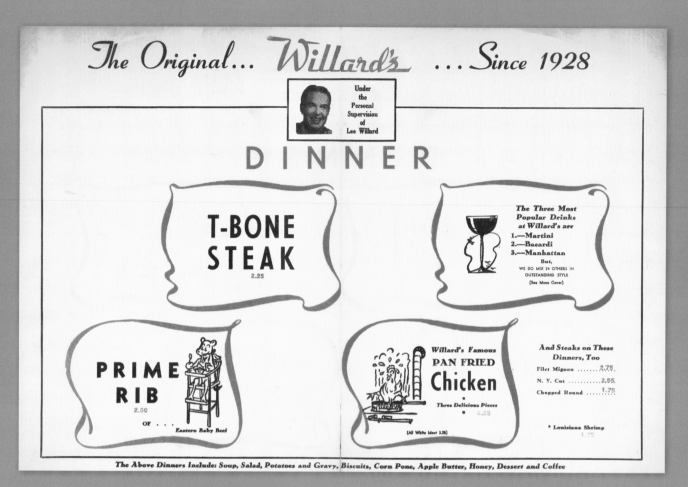

Willard's • 9625 W. Pico Blvd., Los Angeles • 1930s

Los Angeles UNION STATION *Restaurant*

TELEPHONE MUTUAL 5753

600 NORTH ALAMEDA

By Fred Harvey
3000 MILES OF HOSPITALITY
FROM CLEVELAND TO THE PACIFIC COAST

From Our
Cocktail Room

Glass of California Wine (Your Choice) 25

Manhattan Cocktail 55

Martini Cocktail, Very Dry 50

Supper Menu
NINE - TO - TWELVE SUPPER SPECIALS

APPETIZERS

Chilled Tomato Juice 20   Orange Juice 25

Special Shrimp Cocktail 60

SPECIAL SUGGESTIONS

For Today's supper special we have Menus a la Remix, eight dishes all born from vintage menus reinterpreted and reconsidered by contemporary L.A. chefs.
NANCY SILVERTON on mock turtle soup, RICARDO DIAZ on Roasted Pig's Feet, JAZZ SINGSANONG on Hamburger Steak Tropics Style, and so much more.
Your tasting menu awaits.

SANDWICHES

Special Hamburger De Luxe on Toasted Bun, Served with
    French Fried Potatoes, Sliced Tomato, Dill Pickle 60

Baked Ham 50	Lettuce and Tomato 35
American Cheese 35	Smoked Tongue 35
Swiss Cheese 40	Fried Egg 30

Smoked Liver Sausage 35

Special Club House (Bacon, Turkey, Tomato, Mayonnaise) 1.00

Sliced White Meat of Chicken 70

SALADS

Chicken (White Meat Only), Melba Toast 1.10

Fresh Jumbo Shrimp, Mayonnaise Dressing 95

DESSERTS AND BEVERAGES

Ice Cream 20	Sherbet 20	Layer Cake 20
Coffee 10	Milk 12	Buttermilk 12	Pot of Tea 15

IN ADDITION TO PRICES
LISTED, APPROXIMATELY
2½% STATE AND ½% CITY
SALES TAX WILL BE
COLLECTED

*Sorry, We Are Not Responsible
for Loss or Exchange of
Wearing Apparel*

**OPEN DAILY
9 A. M. UNTIL
MIDNIGHT**

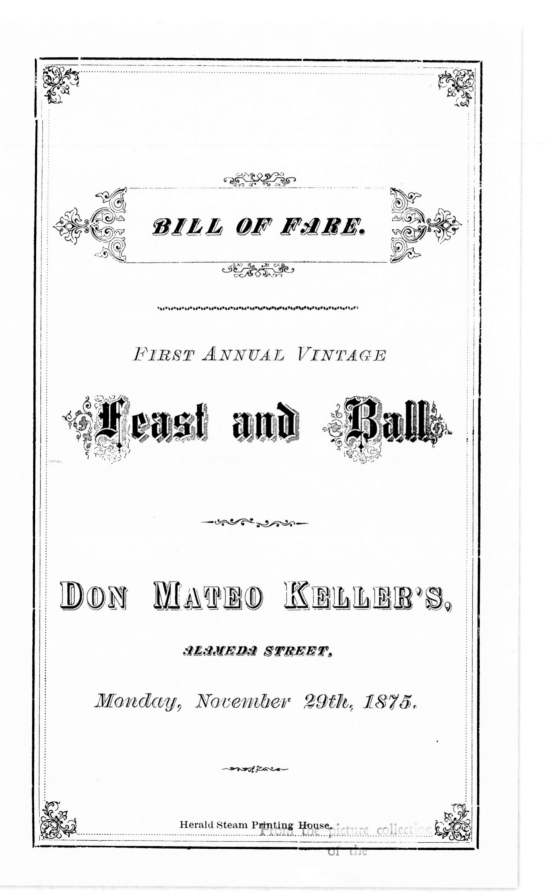

Don Mateo Keller's • Alameda Street, Los Angeles • 1875

1875 Bill of Fare from Don Mateo Keller's downtown vineyard

When I first looked at this, even though no prices were listed, I thought it was odd that it was coursed out for a banquet event. He definitely had choices at this party. Maybe you had to pay a certain amount of money first and then you got choices. So I knew that if I were to recreate this my own way, it was going to have to be coursed.

No chef today who does a dinner like this would do anything with this kind of variety. For instance, you wouldn't have a choice between roast chicken, kidney pie, veal, lamb, and cold joints, and then a variety of meat dishes, and then a tremendous amount of dessert offerings. You would never have meat entrees and roasted meats and boiled meats. And poor fish was barely there, just the soup and the oyster patties, but I would never do a fish soup and follow it with oyster patties. No vegan. No gluten-free. No sauces were listed.

I didn't see any vegetables, so I added a cauliflower wedge in the boiled course, which is almost an entrée in itself—a blanched cauliflower that you then warm up in the oven to give it a little color, and then it gets a bagna cauda and anchovy sauce, and I put some grated egg over it. It's a knife-and-fork kind of course, because it's hefty. If I did a roasted meat like he did, it would have been just too heavy, so I did three roasted vegetables instead.

The descriptions were not very appealing; they were real cut-to-the-chase. In those days, nobody tried to fancify menu descriptions. They were not highlighting the farm they bought it from or the sustainability of it.

I wanted to do something traditional with it, something that is prepared very basically. You could do modern techniques and use modern methods, but I wanted to celebrate the intentions of Don Mateo Keller, do just one menu for one meal, and make it real traditional. I followed his categories, but I had to do a little bit better with the wine pairings. I love fried oyster sandwiches, but I went with crab cakes as a first course because they are easier to pick up. For the entree, I didn't want to do kidneys—I hate kidneys—so I did a dish we do at Chi Spacca. It's a delicious pie I had in Australia a few years ago, but ours is made with beef cheek, onions, mushrooms, with a giant marrow bone that's cooked in the middle. We serve it with a potato puree. For dessert, I thought candies would be really terrific. I had to do something about that coffee and add some tea, and say something about it.

I wanted to keep it simple and traditional, while modernizing the sourcing and preparations, and reducing the general heaviness of the meal. This is my contemporary spin.

DINNER.

SOUPS.

Mock Turtle,   Oyster.

FISH.

Oyster Patties.

BOILED.

Rump Beef, (Corned), with Cabbage.

Leg of Mutton, Caper Sauce.

ROAST.

Beef.   Mutton.   Lamb.   Pork, with Sage and Onions.

Pig, with Apple Sauce.

ENTREES.

Blanquette of Chicken.

Veal Cutlets, breaded.

Steak and Kidney Pudding.

Curried Pig's Feet, with Rice.

Maccaroni and Cheese.

DESSERT.

English Plum Pudding.   Mince Pie.   Blackberry Pie.

Apricot Pie.   Green Gage Pie.

FRUIT, &C.

Apples.   Pears.   Grapes.   Nuts.   Raisins.

Mixed Candies.

COFFEE.   TEA.

Claret.   White Wine.

Eldorado.   Sherry.

Madeira.   Port.

Angelica.

Don Mateo Keller's • Alameda Street, Los Angeles • 1875

SOUP
Mock Mock Turtle Soup: with Milk-Fed Veal Tripe and Hen of the Woods Mushrooms
WINE 2010 Domaine Roulot Bourgogne Rouge

FISH
Peekytoe Crab Cakes with Celery Root Slaw and Charred Lemon Aioli
WINE 2012 Bastianich Friulano

BOILED
Chino Farms Cauliflower Wedge with Bagna Cauda and Sieved Egg
WINE 2011 Pietracupa Fiano di Avellino

ROASTED
(Served Family Style)
Cumin-Roasted Rainbow Carrots from Weiser Farms
Delicata Squash with Brown Butter and Fried Sage Leaves
Charred Broccoli with Chilies and Vinegar
(Veggies go with the ENTREE so no additional wine)

ENTREE
Beef Cheek and Bone Marrow Pie with Pureed Potatoes
Market Lettuce with Soft Herbs and Lemon Vinaigrette
WINE 2001 Giacomo Conterno "Cascina Francia" Barolo

DESSERT
Apple Borsellini with Tahitian Vanilla Bean Gelato
DESSERT WINE Domaine Dupont Pommeau de Normandie

Concord Grapes
Valrhona Chocolate-Covered Candies
Hazelnut Clusters with Gold Leaf
Honeycomb
LIQUEUR Averna Amaro

COFFEE
Stumptown Coffee Roasters: Espresso, Cappuccino, or Pour-Over
A Selection of Loose-Leaf Teas from T Project, Portland, Oregon

Don Mateo Keller's 1875 banquet menu, revisited and remixed by Chef Silverton · 2015

Banquet

tendered to

Honor Our Distinguished Visitors

Professor and Mrs. Albert Einstein

by the

Jewish Community of Los Angeles

at the

HOTEL AMBASSADOR

February the sixteenth,

Nineteen Hundred and Thirty-one

Ambassador Hotel / Einstein banquet • 3400 Wilshire Blvd., Los Angeles • 1931

1931 Ambassador Hotel Banquet for Albert Einstein Menu

I've always had a thing for Einstein ever since I was assigned to write about him for an assignment in third grade. So when I saw a menu celebrating him at the Ambassador, with Rabbi this and Rabbi that as guests, all sponsored by B'nai Brith—I couldn't resist. Hotel menus like this one tend to have nondescript dishes with names like Chicken Sauté Ambassador. What is that? A protein plus the name of a hotel doesn't tell you much about what it actually is. What is a Salad Beaudry? I started researching this menu in order to rewrite it the same way I researched historic menus for my To Live and Dine in L.A. meal series. I dig deep on Google, I follow clues, and I look for a voice of a certain recipe until it gets louder and louder. When I start imagining how to approach it anew, my eye is focused on history and tradition. I don't want a complete departure. My first approach: what is the dish in its most classic sense? And then I start to break it down, keeping some elements, adding others. For example, on the original menu they served Olives and Celery Hearts, probably a simple mix of canned and raw vegetables. I started to think about Einstein, a Jew, a Zionist, and started to think about olive branches. I would do stuffed fried olives, but when I plated them, I would use an actual olive branch. It's about going beyond the food itself. I like to go into the history of the individual, the history of the place.

1931 banquet menu, reconsidered by Chef Wexler • 2015

1st

Cali Fruit Salad

Green zebra tomato,
serpent cucumber, avocado,
almond crunch,
caviar vinaigrette

2nd

The Olive Branch

Fried olives stuffed with
celery pipérade, ibérico ham

3rd

Chicken and Dumplings

Chicken consommé,
gnocchi *Parisienne*,
black truffle, herb salad

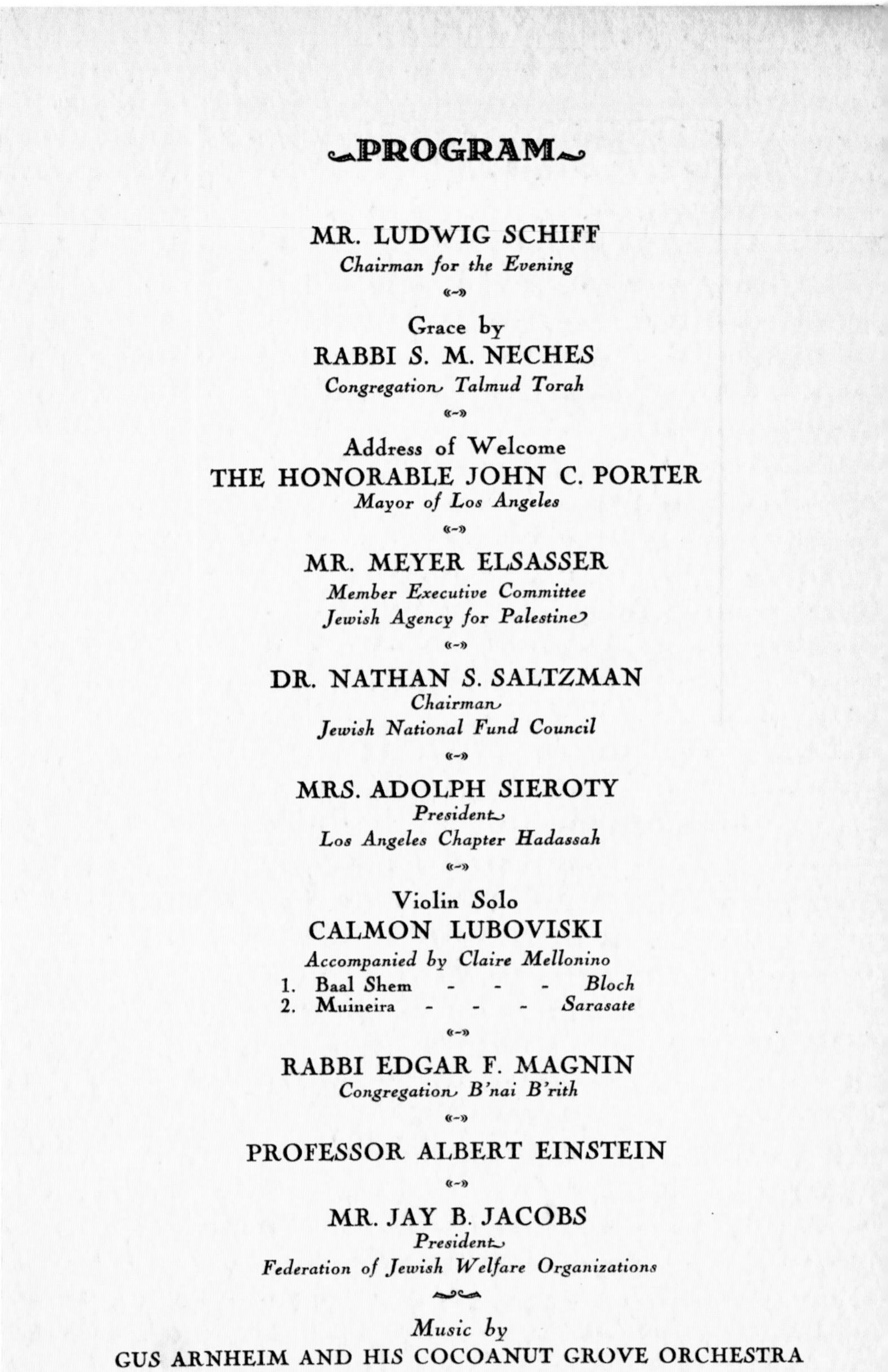

⌒PROGRAM⌒

MR. LUDWIG SCHIFF
Chairman for the Evening

Grace by
RABBI S. M. NECHES
Congregation Talmud Torah

Address of Welcome
THE HONORABLE JOHN C. PORTER
Mayor of Los Angeles

MR. MEYER ELSASSER
*Member Executive Committee
Jewish Agency for Palestine*

DR. NATHAN S. SALTZMAN
*Chairman
Jewish National Fund Council*

MRS. ADOLPH SIEROTY
*President
Los Angeles Chapter Hadassah*

Violin Solo
CALMON LUBOVISKI
Accompanied by Claire Mellonino
1. Baal Shem - - - Bloch
2. Muineira - - - Sarasate

RABBI EDGAR F. MAGNIN
Congregation B'nai B'rith

PROFESSOR ALBERT EINSTEIN

MR. JAY B. JACOBS
*President
Federation of Jewish Welfare Organizations*

Music by
GUS ARNHEIM AND HIS COCOANUT GROVE ORCHESTRA
and
JOSEF ROSENFELT AND HIS AMBASSADOR TRIO

Ambassador Hotel / Einstein banquet • 3400 Wilshire Blvd., Los Angeles • 1931

~MENU~

FRESH FRUIT SUPREME CALIFORNIA

HEARTS OF CELERY   RIPE OLIVES

ESSENCE OF CHICKEN AUX QUENELLES

HALF SPRING CHICKEN SAUTE AMBASSADOR

NEW PEAS IN BUTTER   POTATOES RISSOLE

SALAD BEAUDRY, FRENCH DRESSING

FANCY FORM ICE CREAM

PETIT FOURS

DEMI TASSE

4th
Chicken all dressed up
Butter-poached
guinea hen breast,
brioche herb crust,
English pea *fourchette*,
charred shallot chimichurri

5th
Salad Beaudry
Watercress, heart of palm,
mint, French dressing

6th
Ice Cream Sandwich
feuilletine cookie,
vanilla bean ice cream,
chocolate crumb

On both sides of the original 1881 banquet menu is the re-envisioned version by Chef Wexler • 2015

Tait's Menu

Throughout the years, communities have evolved with the migration of different cultures that have brought their language, customs, beliefs, and, most of all, their exquisite cuisine. With the arrival of the Spaniards in Mexico during the 1500s, the local Mexican cuisine, which relied mainly on a non-meat diet, was revolutionized. Many centuries and generations later, Americans can still enjoy exquisite Mexican dishes such as the *Mole poblano* and the *Chili en Nogada*.

Inspired by the menu from Tait's, we have decided to create our own version. We have incorporated many of the traditional ingredients that were used by Mexican natives such as chili peppers, grains, avocado, cactus, herbs, and spices. Influenced by the traditional cuisine that our grandmothers and mothers taught us, we have given a twist to this menu, adding spices, color, and succulent herbs that make it a delightful dish today.

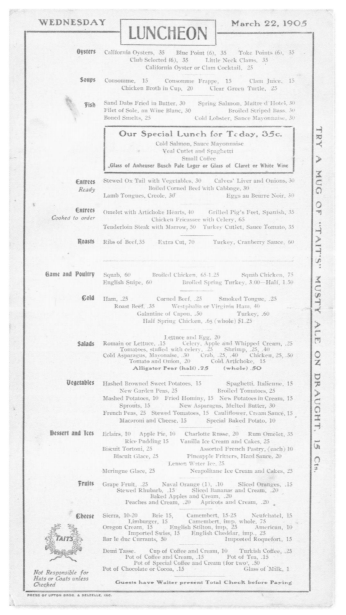

Tait's • 520 S. Broadway, Los Angeles • 1905

Oysters

BLUE POINT OYSTERS
grilled with cotija cheese, tomatoes, onion, cilantro and fresh jalapeño peppers

LITTLE NECK CLAMS with green tomatillo sauce, steamed with beer

Soups

CONSOMME OF AVOCADO with shredded chicken,
morita chile sauce, green beans, and chickpeas.

COLD CLAM JUICE with cucumber, cilantro, serrano pepper and lime juice

Fish

GRILLED SALMON with achiote paste and bitter orange juice marinade

FILLET OF SOLE breaded with pumpkin seeds
and served with a cilantro sauce infused with tequila.

STRIPED GREEN CEVICHE marinated with lime juice/orange juice
and flavored with onions, *epazote* and the green tomatillo.

COLD LOBSTER CRISPY TOSTADA served with a chipotle mayonnaise

Entrees

OXTAIL *MOLE DE OLLA* made with potatoes,
Mexican zucchinis, green beans, and *xoconostles*

CALF'S LIVER AND ONIONS with cilantro and Serrano peppers

LAMB TONGUE TACOS *BARBACOA*
served with freshly made tortillas, onion, cilantro, and a chile ancho sauce

OMELET WITH ARTICHOKE HEARTS AND CACTUS
smothered with a light tomatoes sauce

TENDERLOIN STEAK *MIXIOTE* wrapped in a cactus-leaf skin
and marinated with achiote, avocado leaves, potatoes, and onions

TURKEY CUTLETS MILANESA TORTA

Roasts

RIBS OF BEEF *AL PASTOR* (in the style of the shepherd)

Poultry

SQUAB CHICKEN IN RED SAUCE

Cold

PICKLED PIG'S FEET with marinated onions and carrots

Salad

ALLIGATOR PEAR SALAD (CHAYOTE SQUASH SALAD) with aromatic vinaigrette

Vegetables

BREADED CAULIFLOWER with a sweet tomatoes sauce

Desert

RICE PUDDING with goat's milk caramel

Fruits

APRICOTS WITH KAHLUA CREAM

Cheese

MEXICAN CHEESE PLATTER cotija, *queso fresco, queso Oaxaca*, enchilada de *queso panela*

POT OF CAFÉ DE OLLA with cinnamon, cloves and lemon zest

POT OF MEXICAN CHOCOLATE infused with vanilla

HIBISCUS FLOWER HOT TEA sweetened with agave nectar

Tait's 1905 luncheon menu, reinterpreted by Chefs Arvizu and Martin del Campo • 2015

Mme. Portier's French Restaurant • 5122 E. Olympic Blvd., Los Angeles • 1930s

Mme. Portier's French Restaurant

After my family moved to Montebello from Highland Park in 1975, I became aware of the only French restaurant I knew, Marcel and Jeanne's French Café. It always seemed so foreign to me, so intriguing. The architecture was very European, the essence of what I thought chateaus must be like. Unfortunately, I never got the opportunity to eat there. By the time I was old enough to drive and make my own dining decisions, the restaurant had been closed several years.

Coming upon the menu for Mme. Portier's French Restaurant, I was immediately interested in the fact that it was another French locale in East Los Angeles, an area that now is predominantly Hispanic. In fact, the building where it was located still stands, but now as a Tacos Mexico and Rental Hall called Salon Fiesta Mexico. Seeing past migratory patterns of cultures move through different areas—whether the Jewish in Boyle Heights, Russians along the L.A. River, or the later Armenian influx in Montebello—has always been fascinating to me. I don't know of any large French culture in Los Angeles, so becoming aware of French restaurants is a treat.

Interestingly, I feel that though Los Angeles has a varied and rich food tradition, the fact that it is not based on the French culinary model like many renowned restaurant cities—New York, Barcelona, and, of course Paris—has defined it as the dining mecca it is. Of course those of us who have grown up here and live here, know different.

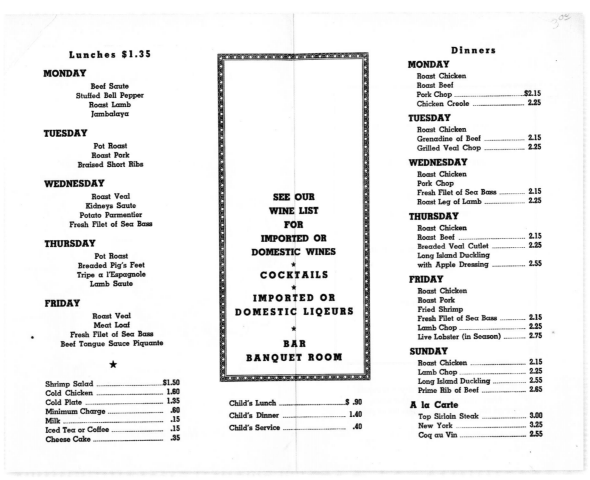

Lunches $1.35

MONDAY
Beef Saute
Stuffed Bell Pepper
Roast Lamb
Jambalaya

TUESDAY
Pot Roast
Roast Pork
Braised Short Ribs

WEDNESDAY
Roast Veal
Kidneys Saute
Potato Parmentier
Fresh Filet of Sea Bass

THURSDAY
Pot Roast
Breaded Pig's Feet
Tripe a l'Espagnole
Lamb Saute

FRIDAY
Roast Veal
Meat Loaf
Fresh Filet of Sea Bass
Beef Tongue Sauce Piquante

★

Shrimp Salad $1.50
Cold Chicken 1.60
Cold Plate 1.35
Minimum Charge .... .60
Milk .... .15
Iced Tea or Coffee .... .15
Cheese Cake .... .35

SEE OUR
WINE LIST
FOR
IMPORTED OR
DOMESTIC WINES
★
COCKTAILS
★
IMPORTED OR
DOMESTIC LIQEURS
★
BAR
BANQUET ROOM

Child's Lunch ....$ .90
Child's Dinner 1.40
Child's Service .... .40

Dinners

MONDAY
Roast Chicken
Roast Beef
Pork Chop $2.15
Chicken Creole 2.25

TUESDAY
Roast Chicken
Grenadine of Beef 2.15
Grilled Veal Chop 2.25

WEDNESDAY
Roast Chicken
Pork Chop
Fresh Filet of Sea Bass 2.15
Roast Leg of Lamb 2.25

THURSDAY
Roast Chicken
Roast Beef 2.15
Breaded Veal Cutlet 2.25
Long Island Duckling
with Apple Dressing 2.55

FRIDAY
Roast Chicken
Roast Pork
Fried Shrimp
Fresh Filet of Sea Bass 2.15
Lamb Chop 2.25
Live Lobster (in Season) 2.75

SUNDAY
Roast Chicken 2.15
Lamb Chop 2.25
Long Island Duckling 2.55
Prime Rib of Beef 2.65

A la Carte
Top Sirloin Steak 3.00
New York 3.25
Coq au Vin 2.55

Mme. Portier's French Restaurant • 5122 E. Olympic Blvd., Los Angeles • 1930s

Lunches $1.35

MONDAY
- Beef Saute
- Stuffed Bell Pepper
- Roast Lamb
- Jambalaya

TUESDAY
- Pot Roast
- Roast Pork
- Braised Short Ribs

WEDNESDAY
- Roast Veal
- Kidneys Saute
- Potato Parmentier
- Fresh Filet of Sea Bass

THURSDAY
- Pot Roast
- Breaded Pig's Feet
- Tripe a l'Espagnole
- Lamb Saute

FRIDAY
- Roast Veal
- Meat Loaf
- Fresh Filet of Sea Bass
- Beef Tongue Sauce Piquante

★

Shrimp Salad	$1.50
Cold Chicken	1.60
Cold Plate	1.35
Minimum Charge	.60
Milk	.15
Iced Tea or Coffee	.15
Cheese Cake	.35

handwritten notes: Latin Styles; Cod!; lengua Salsa; Milk!

SEE OUR WINE LIST FOR IMPORTED OR DOMESTIC WINES

COCKTAILS

IMPORTED OR DOMESTIC LIQEURS

BAR
BANQUET ROOM

Child's Lunch	$ .90
Child's Dinner	1.40
Child's Service	.40

Dinners

MONDAY
Roast Chicken	
Roast Beef	
Pork Chop	$2.15
Chicken Creole	2.25

TUESDAY
Roast Chicken	
Grenadine of Beef	2.15
Grilled Veal Chop	2.25

WEDNESDAY
Roast Chicken	
Pork Chop	
Fresh Filet of Sea Bass	2.15
Roast Leg of Lamb	2.25

THURSDAY
Roast Chicken	
Roast Beef	2.15
Breaded Veal Cutlet	2.25
Long Island Duckling with Apple Dressing	2.55

FRIDAY
Roast Chicken	
Roast Pork	
Fried Shrimp	
Fresh Filet of Sea Bass	2.15
Lamb Chop	2.25
Live Lobster (in Season)	2.75

SUNDAY
Roast Chicken	2.15
Lamb Chop	2.25
Long Island Duckling	2.55
Prime Rib of Beef	2.65

A la Carte
Top Sirloin Steak	3.00
New York	3.25
Coq au Vin	2.55

handwritten notes: Farm to table?; Seafood on Friday! Catholic offerings; ...mmmm!

handwritten notes: Cold Chicken? ; Southern French Jambalaya & Chicken Creole ; Extra charge for children or Allowing kids to eat off of Mom's Plate.

handwritten list: # times/week
Roast Chicken 6
Roast Beef 2
Pork Chop 2
Roast Veal 2
Pot Roast 2
Roast Pork 2
Sea Bass 2
Lamb chop 2

Mme. Portier's 1930s French menu with notes by Chef Ricardo Diaz • 2015

This menu from the 1930s caught my attention for a number of reasons, some amusing. I love the fact that there is a different and limited menu for each day of the week. I am a big fan of keeping menus simple and focused. It allows me to concentrate on what I do best. This is the model for many smorgasbords, but I am sure this was individually plated. More so, the lunch and dinner offerings are different from each other daily. For example: on Monday for lunch there is: Beef Sauté, Stuffed Bell Pepper, Roast Lamb, and Jambalaya. For dinner you have the option of Roast Chicken, Roast Beef, Pork Chop, or Chicken Creole. Some items like Roast Chicken are offered six times throughout the week, almost all other dishes only twice. The daily preparation would be intense, even though there are only about eight different options per day, because every day is different. Also if they were concerned with keeping everything fresh, I'm sure there was a lot of discarded inventory if certain dishes didn't sell that day.

There are also a number of dishes that I would enjoy tasting today. Some seem very Latin, like Breaded Pig's Feet, except that we normally fry them in an egg batter and then sauté them in a red chile sauce. The Beef Tongue Piquante clearly speaks to its Spanish roots. The Tripe a L'Espagnole would be very similar to a dish we call Guisado de Pancita, a very thick and saucy menudo that's eaten in central to southern Mexico. On Monday, they offered a stuffed bell pepper. We have Chile Relleno that can be filled with cheese or more commonly with a ground beef mixture in Mexico.

I don't know how French this menu is but the similarities with Latin cuisine reflect on the commonality of world cuisines, especially central European with American comparisons. The fact that you can see it in a menu from the 1930s before the supposed fusion and melding of recipes that defined the 1990s is beautiful. Just like music and its roots, it is important for people to know that there is nothing new under the sun. Everything is an evolution . . . borrowed, shared, inspired. We all build on each other. We all create for future translations.

Smith's • 226 W. Manchester Ave., Los Angeles • 1950s

Notes on Smith's Wood Barbecue Menu Remix

- Remove SOUVENIR MENU

- Keep LOGO and PICTURE, add BECAUSE AT HAWKINS WE MAKE EATING A JOY

- Include address, phone number, fax number, website and how to order online.

- Use different background; more colorful and vibrant to draw the eye

- Change WOOD BARBEQUE to simply HAWKINS HOUSE OF BURGERS. There is enough space to include a brief history (short, sweet and funny) for the customers to read while they are waiting for their order. I would keep the menu no more than two pages (front and back) because people don't like to read (except on their I-phones). The goal would be for the customer to keep the menu and use it repeatedly, as well as share with others.

I like how specials can be added and highlighted in this menu; as well as presenting in a clean, and clear manner, the food items and costs.

- Omit the NO SERVICE LESS THAN; we want to draw people, not limit them.

- A menu should be precise and clear; I hate menus that are so jumbled with every single item that is served that you don't know what you are really getting, so I've eliminated the last two pages.

If you want to include pictures of the meals, have them posted in the restaurant. Make sure it is realistic and not Photoshopped (how many times I am disappointed with what I received when it looks nothing like what I ordered). A picture will help customers who are not sure of what they want (and really don't want to read), and they will be drawn to order the picture each time.

- Instead of Sandwiches, it should be labeled BURGERS and should list
  1. Jr. Burger, 2. Jr. Burger w/cheese, 3. Fish Burger, 4. Fat Burger,
  5. Fat Cheese Burger, 6. Double Burger, 7. Double Cheese

- Bacon, Egg, Chili or Sausage are EXTRA (centered)

Smith's Wood Barbecue menu from the 1950s, evaluated by Chef Hawkins • 2015

Sandwiches

"LIKE YOU NEVER HAD, AND FRESHLY SLICED"

BAR-B-Q BEEF ....1.05   BAR-B-Q HAM 1.05
BAR-B-Q PORK ....1.05   BAR-B-Q HOT LINK 75
BAR-B-Q TURKEY (all white meat) 1.25
BAR-B-Q BURGER, Cheese or Chili 80
BAR-B-Q VENISON, BEAR, ELK, BUFFALO 1.25

"Served on Toasted Dipped French Roll with Shredded
Cabbage Slaw, Choice of French Fries or Bar-B-Q Beans"

SPECIAL DISHES

ABALONE STEAK 1.75
FROG LEGS FRENCH FRIED 1.85
FRIED LOBSTER TAILS, CUBAN 1.65
BAR-B-Q HEN PHEASANT 1.95

"Consist of Soup, Salad, Choice of
Potatoes or Bar-B-Q Beans"

Side Orders

BAR-B-Q PORK SPARE RIBS 1.35
BAR-B-Q BEEF SHORT RIBS 1.35
BAR-B-Q ½ CHICKEN 1.25
"Each Three Items Above Consist ½ Dipped French Roll"
FRENCH FRIES 30   BAR-B-Q BEANS 30
COLE SLAW 30   BOWL SOUP 20

SPECIAL PIE OR COBBLER 30
JELLO, WHIPPED CREAM 25
STRAWBERRY SHORTCAKE 40

Beverages

Coffee, per Cup 10   Sweet Milk 15
Hot Tea, cup 10   Buttermilk 15
Iced Tea 10   Soft Drinks 10

Carta Blanca, Mexico 50   Frydenlund, Norway 50
Lowenbrau Pale, Germany .50   Gold Star, Spain 50
Orangjeboom, Holland 50   Asahi, Japan 50
Birra Pedavena, Italy 50   Eastside Old Tap Lager 35
Lamot, Belgium 50   Lucky Lager 35

Prices do not Include State Sales Tax
NO SERVICE LESS THAN 25c

Smith's • 226 W. Manchester Ave., Los Angeles • 1950s

Notes on Smith's Wood Barbecue Menu (*continued*)

Keep SPECIALS (in box); no one eats these items (at least not here in Los
Angeles), so I would add perhaps different DAILY SPECIALS, with choice
of sides and beverages. Because people don't cook at home anymore (and
therefore eat out), it is important that they get GOOD, HOMEMADE,
HEALTHY foods at an AFFORDABLE price. I would provide different dinner
meals here (Southern Fried Chicken, BBQ Ribs, Pork Chops, Chicken Curry,
Spaghetti, *et. al* with sides of Collard Greens, Spinach, homemade cole slaw/
potato salad/chicken salad, mac 'n' cheese, etc.)

Sides

1. Fries 2. Onion Rings 3. Chili 4. Peach Cobbler 5. Banana Pudding

Beverages

1. Coffee 2. Can/Bottled Soft Drinks 3. Fountain Drinks 4. Water

SPECIAL EVENTS MENU AVAILABLE (centered, large font)

The main thing to stress in creating a menu is QUALITY FOODS at
AFFORDABLE PRICES! What I put on this menu would be affordable to
everyone.

Robaire's • 348 S. La Brea Ave., Los Angeles • 1960s

Robaire's

Rabbit with Mustard Sauce and Roasted Kale
(Inspired by: *Le Lapin Au Vin Rouge*)

Lobster Risotto with Pink Peppercorn Sauce
(Inspired by: Lobster Thermidor)

Roasted Duck Breast with Dates and Soft Polenta with Sherry Sauce
(Inspired by: *Canard a L'Orange*)

Cioppino
(Inspired by: *Bouillabaisse*)

Squab with Medley of Mini Green Peppers
(Inspired by: Squab Chicken *A La Reine*)

Lobster Couscous with Spicy Harissa Sauce and Poached Organic Vegetables
(Inspired by: Cous Cous *A La Robaire*)

HORS D'OEUVRES

Eggs with Truffle Cream
(Inspired by: *Oeuf Du Mayonnaise Aux Anchovies*)

Layer Cake of Liver Mouse with White Mushroom
(Inspired by: Homemade Chicken Liver Paté)

Asparagus with Frisee, Bacon and Poached Egg
(Inspired by: Asparagus and Tomatoes Vinaigrette)

6 Escargot *En Croute*
(Inspired by: 6 *Escargots De Bourgogne*)

Terrine of Foie Gras with Artichokes and Walnut Salad
(Inspired by: *Pate De Foie Gras Truffe*)

Robaire's daily specials from the 1960s, remixed by Chef Splichal • 2015

SOUPES—SOUPS

Soup of Shallots with Port Wine

(Inspired by: *Soupe A L'Oignon*)

VIVANDE—MEAT

**Steamed Veal Escalope
with Steamed Organic Vegetables
with Tomato Coulis**

(Inspired by:
L'Escalope De Veau Provencale)

**Roasted Rack of Veal
with Roasted Green
and White Asparagus**

(Inspired by:
Le Carre De Veau Au Jambon)

Robaire's FRE[...]

Included with the Entree are Salad, Potatoes Au Gratin, T[...]

Don't add any spice until you taste the fo[...]

Hors d Oeuvres

CANAPE ROBAIRE (for two) 8.00	
Shrimp, Cream Sauce au gratin on Sourdough Toast	
FRESH MUSHROOM SALAD 3.00	
HOUSEMADE PATE AU POIVRE WITH DUCK 4.00	
SIX ESCARGOTS IN SHELL 4.50	
SIX ESCARGOTS IN FRESH MUSHROOM CAPS 4.50	
FRESH ARTICHOKE BOTTOM WITH BAY SHRIMPS 5.00	
SHRIMP COCKTAIL 6.00	
SHRIMPS SAUTE WITH GARLIC AND SHERRY 8.00	
GARLIC BREAD (for two) 1.25	

Soupes

SOUPE A L'OIGNON (Onion Soup) . . . . Bowl
LA GRATINEE (Onion Soup au Gratin) . . . . . . Tureen

Oeufs - Eggs

OMELETTE PROVENCALE . . . .
   Tomato Sauce, Mushrooms
OMELETTE PRINCIERE . . . .
   Cheese, Mushrooms, Chicken Livers
OMELETTE INDOCHINOISE . . . .
   Shrimp and Beef
OMELETTE NANTUA . . . .
   Shrimp in Seafood Sauce

Specialites de la Semaine - Daily Specialties

May we suggest you order these specialties when making your table reservations

Every Tuesday
SPECIALITE DE LA MAISON
   Ask Your Waiter About Tonight's Very Special Dish

Every Wednesday
COTE DE VEAU SUZY 13.50
   Veal Chop Saute with Port Wine and Mushrooms

Every Thursday
FILET DE SOLE MONA 11.00
   Au Gratin with Shrimp, Melted Cheese, Hollandaise Sauce

Every Friday
BOUILLABAISSE 17.50

Every Saturday
CORNISH GAME HEN . . . . 9.0[...]
   Stuffed with Wild Rice, Fresh Mushrooms and
   Chicken Livers

Every Sunday
BOEUF BOURGUIGNON . . . . 8.0[...]
   Tenderloin Tips in Burgundy Sauce with Fresh
   Mushrooms and Egg Noodles

Last Wednesday of Every Month
COUS COUS TUNISIEN . . . . 12.5[...]
   With Tunisian Dessert

Viande - Meat

ROAST BEEF AU JUS 8.00
TENDERLOINS EN BROCHETTES 10.00
MEDAILLONS DE FILET MIGNON 12.00
   Sauce Bearnaise and Sauce Bordelaise
ROAST RACK OF LAMB 13.50
BROILED FILET MIGNON OF LAMB 13.50
   Fresh Garlic and Green Peppercorn

LE CHATEAUBRIAND 1
   Tenderloin, Sauce Bearnaise
NEW YORK CUT STEAK 1
   With Green Peppercorn, Add 1.00 Extra
FILET MIGNON ROSSINI 1
   Topped with Liver Pate
FILET MIGNON A L'AIL 1
   With Fresh Garlic

CHILD'S PLATE (children under 12) - ROAST BEEF or CHICKEN 5.00

TAKE HOME A BOTTLE OF ROBAIRE'S ORIGINAL PURE ALMOND OIL DRESSING

ENJOY A GLASS OF FRENCH WINE (Red, White or Rose) 2.00

White

	SMALL	LARGE
TOURAINE		
VOUVRAY (Chateau Moncontour)		13.00
BORDEAUX		
GRAVES (Armand Roux)		11.00
BOURGOGNE		
PINOT CHARDONNAY (Macon Villages) . .	8.00	15.00
CHABLIS (Armand Roux)		20.00
POUILLY FUISSE (Armand Roux)		20.00
ALSACE		
RIESLING (Gaschy)		12.00

Red

	SMALL	LAR[...]
BORDEAUX		
GRAND VIN SUPERIEUR (Verdillac)		8.0[...]
ST. EMILION (Font Villac)		15.0[...]
BOURGOGNE		
BEAUJOLAIS (Villages) (Armand Roux) . . .	6.00	11.0[...]
NUITS ST. GEORGES		35.0[...]
POMMARD (Barton & Guestier)		40.0[...]
RHONE		
CHATEAUNEUF DU PAPE		20.0[...]
(Chateau de la Gardine)		

Robaire's California Vin Maison

	SMALL	LARGE
CHABLIS (Wente Bros.)	4.00	7.5[...]
ROSE		7.5[...]
BURGUNDY	4.00	7.5[...]
GREY RIESLING (Wente Bros.)		9.0[...]
PINOT NOIR (Wente Bros.)		9.0[...]
CABERNET SAUVIGNON		
(Stephen Zellerbach)		12.0[...]

Pink

	SMALL	LARGE
TAVEL (Domaine des Roches)		12.00
ANJOU ROSE (La Pucelle)	4.00	7.50

MINIMUM CHARGE 3.50 PER PERSON

Robaire's • 348 S. La Brea Ave., Los Angeles • 1960s

**Back From France, Our Chef is Making
a New Special Every Night.
ASK YOUR WAITER ABOUT IT!**

CUISINE
ench Rolls

French Country Style Specialties

L'ESCALOPE DE VEAU PROVENCALE 9.50	FROG LEGS PROVENCALE 10.00
Veal Saute with Cheese, Tomato, Mushroom	With Garlic and Butter
LE CARRE DE VEAU AU JAMBON 9.50	SWEETBREADS ROBAIRE 10.00
Veal with Ham, Olive and Cheese Sauce	Breaded and Sauteed
L'ESCALOPE DE VEAU MAISON GERARD 9.50	SWEETBREADS EN CASSEROLE 10.00
With Orange Sauce and Curacao	In Wine Sauce
LE CASSOULET TOULOUSAIN 12.00	FEUILLETTE OF SWEETBREADS 11.00
White Beans, Lamb, Pork Sausage au Gratin	Champagne and Mushroom Sauce
CANARD A L'ORANGE 12.00	SPECIAL VEGETARIAN PLATE 7.50
Half Duck in Orange Sauce	

Poisson-Fish

> Ask About Our FRESH FISH
> and Other SPECIALS OF THE DAY

T DE SOLE MEUNIERE 9.00	
LLOPS AU PERNOD 12.00	
erved in a Delicious Puff Dough	
LLOPS EN BROCHETTES 12.00	
ith Ham, Mushrooms, Cherry Tomatoes	
IMPS JEAN-JEAN 13.00	
hablis Cream Sauce, Rice Pilaf	
IMPS NICOISE 13.00	
ith Garlic and Sherry	
ILED LOBSTER TAIL 17.50	

Poulet-Chicken

CKEN LIVERS SAUTE AUX CHAMPIGNONS . . . 8.00	
/2) POULET ROTI AU VIN 8.00	
n Wine Sauce	
/2) POULET ROTI A L'AIL 8.00	
n Fresh Garlic Sauce	
OULET MICHELINE 8.00	
oned Chicken, Rice, Ham, Cheese en Casserole	

Desserts

VANILLA ICE CREAM 1.50

> **TRY OUR DELIGHTFUL HOUSEMADE DESSERTS**
> CREME CARAMEL 1.50
> MOUSSE AU CHOCOLAT 2.00
> CHEESE CAKE IN A GLASS (No Crust) 2.00
> PATISSERIE FRANCAISE 2.50
> FRESH STRAWBERRIES 3.00
> Dipped in Chocolate (Creme Chantilly)
> LA SURPRISE DE JODY 3.00
> With Wild Strawberry Liqueur
> FRESH STRAWBERRIES NATHALIE 5.00
> With Grand Marnier, French Vanilla Ice Cream and
> Creme Chantilly
> SOUFFLE AU CHOCOLAT or GRAND MARNIER 5.00
> With Creme Anglaise (Order in Advance)

Beverages

COFFEE, TEA, MILK, ICED TEA or SANKA 75	
IRISH COFFEE 3.00	
IMPORTED PERRIER WATER 1.25	
CAFE EXPRESS 1.25	
CAPPUCCINO AU BRANDY 3.00	

TAKE HOME A BOTTLE OF ROBAIRE'S ORIGINAL PURE ALMOND OIL DRESSING

WINES

*se wines are personally selected
be Vineyards in France
Monsieur Robaire*

Les Fines Bouteilles

S VOUGEOT 40.00	
TEAU MARGAUX 50.00	
TEAU HAUT BRION 50.00	
TEAU MOUTON ROTHSCHILD 45.00	
TEAU LAFITE ROTHSCHILD 75.00	

Champagnes and Sparkling Wines

	SMALL	LARGE
CALIFORNIA CHAMPAGNE		
CHATEAU ROBAIRE	4.50	8.00
DOMAINE CHANDON BRUT		18.00
DOMAINE CHANDON BLANC DE NOIR		18.00
FRENCH CHAMPAGNE		
MUMM'S EXTRA DRY	18.00	35.00
MUMM'S CORDON ROUGE BRUT	21.00	40.00
DOM PERIGNON		90.00

Food to go available

Sales Tax Will Be Added to All Items Served at the Table

NO SUBSTITUTION PLEASE

POULET—CHICKEN

**Roasted Chicken, Baby Carrots
with Lavender and Thyme**
(Inspired by:
Le (1/2) Poulet Roti Au Vin)

**Lasagna of Potatoes and
Chicken Breast
with Black Trumpet Mushrooms**
(Inspired by:
Le Poulet Micheline)

POISSON—FISH

Halibut Nicoise Style
(Inspired by:
Halibut *Saute Au Beurre*)

**Rolls of Filet of Sole
with Yuzu Mousse and
Champagne Sauce**
(Inspired by:
Filet De Sole Meuniere)

**Tournedo of Swordfish
with Pepper Sauce,
Potato Mousse and Bacon**
(Inspired by:
Swordfish *Amandine*)

**Soft Omelette with Bacon,
Chanterelle Mushrooms
and Chive Sauce**
(Inspired by:
Omelette Fines Herbes)

Flanking the original Robaire's menu from the 1980s is reinterpreted fare by Chef Splichal • 2015

Angel's Flight • Hyatt Regency,
Los Angeles • 1970s

First Course
Kaya Toast
A Singaporean "Hangover Cure"
Malaysian *pan de mie* toasted with coconut kaya jam, fried egg and
dark soy

Second Course
The Angel's Kiss
Smoked salmon on buttered black bread with caper cream cheese,
"angry" deviled eggs, heirloom tomato and California avocado

Third Course
The Vegan Reuben
Roasted cauliflower steak Reuben with homemade sauerkraut, gruyere
and Thousand Island Dressing

Fourth Course
Market Salad Bowl
Mexican chopped salad with fresh assorted heirloom beans, Pink Lady
apple, Cabrales blue cheese and cumin vinaigrette

Hot Curried Crab
on muffins with cheddar cheese
sauce, toasted coconut,
fresh pineapple, peach and chutney
3.50

The Angel's Kiss
smoked salmon on buttered black
bread with chopped eggs, scallions,
capers, sliced tomato and Swiss cheese,
fresh fruit
3.25

The Sirloiner
sirloin of beef sandwich au jus
on black bread,
rice pilaf and vegetable
3.75

Market Salad Bowl
mixed greens with fresh
zucchini, cauliflower, mushrooms
and spinach, gouda cheese,
turkey, corned beef, ham,
eggs, cucumbers and tomatoes
3.25

Angel's Flight • Hyatt Regency,
Los Angeles • 1970s

First Course:
Avocado Royale

California avocado and Pea sweet pea spread on toast
with assorted radish salad

Or

Korean Rice salad with daikon, carrots, sunflower sprouts, California avocado,
toasted rice cracker croutons and sesame dressing

Second Course:
Moroccan Lamb Meatballs
Served with chimichurri and fresh tzatziki

Or

Crispy Basmati Rice
Served with curry neem leaf masoor dal and eggplant spinach curry

Third Course:
Cumin & Cilantro Marinated Skirt Steak
With farmers' market corn & poblano relish, quinoa fritters
and Persian cucumbers

Fourth Course:
Mexican Bread Pudding
with Cream Cheese, Apples and Piloncillo
With whipped crema and raspberries

Mexican Dulce de Leche Churros
With homemade chocolate sauce and whipped crema

Meringues with Lime Curd
With graham crackers, blueberries and fresh mint

Mud Hen Tavern • 742 Highland Ave.,
Los Angeles • 2014

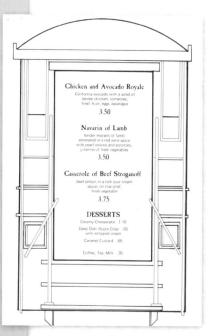

Angel's Flight • Hyatt Regency,
Los Angeles • 1970s

Menus from the 1970s Angel's Flight Restaurant at the Hyatt Regency
were remixed by the Mud Hen Tavern's Chef Feniger • 2015

In Our **9th** Year of Consistently Serving You "THE BEST!"

"Sugie's" DE LUXE DINNER $3.25
SERVED DAILY FROM 5 P.M.

Choice of—
Shrimp Cocktail Supreme
Fresh Fruit Maraschino
Marinated Herring
Chilled Tomato Juice

• Soup du Jour
• Celery Hearts
• Super Colossal Olives
• Relish

CHOICE OF ▼

★ **New York Sirloin Steak, Eastern Beef, Extra Cut**
(Special Steak Sauce made to order, 75¢ extra)
★ **Chicken Curry, Steamed Rice, with Condiments and Chutney**
★ **Roast Tom Turkey, all white meat, Cranberry Sauce**

★ **Roast Prime Ribs of Beef, Au Jus, Extra Cut**
★ **Roast Squab Chicken Farci, Guava Jelly**
★ **Grilled Filet Mignon, Fresh Mushrooms**
(IN SEASON)

★ **French Lamb Chops, Special Double Cut (2)**
★ **Broiled Squab Chicken with Bacon**
★ **Fricassee of Chicken (Tropics Style)**

Fresh Vegetables
(IN SEASON)

Potatoes
BAKED OR FRENCH FRIED
(Choice Until 9:30 P.M.)

★ **Lake Superior White Fish (Chef's Special)**
★ **Fresh Rainbow Trout, Sauted in Butter**

Coffee
Tea
Milk

YOUR CHOICE OF DESSERTS OF THE DAY

☆ CHEF'S SPECIAL SALAD ☆

"FOOD WITHOUT WINE IS LIKE LIFE WITHOUT LAUGHTER!"

The Informal Cocktail Lounge and Dining Rooms of the Motion Picture Industry

★ All prices listed are at or below our ceiling prices. By O.P.A. regulation our ceilings are our highest prices from April 4, 1943 to April 10, 1943. Records of the prices are available for your inspection.

TABLE D'HOTE DINNER

Price of Entree Determines Price of Complete Dinner, Including Dessert

CHOICE OF
Fresh Shrimp Cocktail • Fresh Fruit Cocktail
Marinated Herring • Cold Tomato Juice

Soup-Du-Jour
•
Tropics Choice Super Colossal Olives and Relish

CHOICE OF

Chicken Curry, Steamed Rice (with Condiments) 1.95
Louisiana Shrimp Curry, Steamed Rice 1.65
Broiled or Fried Half Spring Chicken 1.75
Prime Ribs of Beef, Au Jus with Mashed Potatoes 1.95
Half Chicken, Sauted in Butter 1.85
Roast Tom Turkey, Cranberry Sauce 1.65
★ Fish Curry, with Steamed Rice 1.65
Fresh Rainbow Trout, Sauted in Butter 1.65
Broiled Halibut Steak 1.50
Broiled Sword Fish, Tropics Style 1.75

★ Robert Z. Leonard
Famous Motion Picture Director
Says "SENSATIONAL!"

● *Sugie's* **TROPICAL FISH DINNERS**
And MANY TASTY DISHES for a Meatless Friday!
—AS NOTED THROUGHOUT THIS MENU—

Fresh Vegetables • **Potatoes**
(IN SEASON)

Choice of Desserts of the Day

Coffee • Tea • Milk

Sugie's Tropics • 421 N. Rodeo Dr., Beverly Hills • 1940s

AMERICAN - TRADITION

JAZZ Pourger.   ~~Spagetti~~ with Salty FISH.
ANGEL ~~HAIR~~ HAIR w/ green curry. THAI MACCONI
                              STAIR FRIED w/ TOMATO
                                        / Sauce

SANDWICH

~~Spicy~~ TUNA Somwich.
cucumber Ham Samwich WITH SPICY MAYO.

THAI BEEF STEAK (spicy sauce)
3 FLAVOR CHICKEN wing

Salad - Rice Salad , mango Salad   cc
Papaya Salad   BEEF Salad (LABB) ~~BEEF~~ PORK

TAPPIOKA Coconut.
Coconut. Banana (PALM SUGAR)
Mango STICKY Rice.

~~fresh~~
Banana Mango with Coconut Ice cream

Sugie's Tropics 1940s American menu, rethought by Chef Singsanong • 2015

Chinese a-la-Carte Menu

```
Chinese Special Plate —Tropics Style
Chicken Fried Rice, Egg Foyung, Won Tun,        1 95
Chicken Almond, Mandarin Duck
        NO SUBSTITUTIONS ALLOWED
```

CHINESE APPETIZERS

Egg Roll	.75	Won Tun		.85
Fried Shrimp	.75	Mixed Chinese Appetizer		1.00
Barbecued Spare Ribs	.75	Chinese Barbecued Pork		.75

SOUP

No. 1	Gai Min Gong (Chinese Noodle Soup)	.50
No. 2	Gar Choy Gong (Chinese Vegetable Soup)	.50
No. 3	Lin Doo Gai Gong (Chicken and Lotus Nut Soup)	.75
No. 4	Yin War Gai Gong (Chicken and Bird's Nest Soup)	1.00
No. 4X	Egg Flower Soup	.50

NOODLES

No. 5	Char Sue Yetkomein (Pork Noodles)	.75
No. 6	Gai So Yetkomein (Chicken Noodles)	.80

CHOW MEIN

No. 7	Char Sue Chow Mein (Pork Chow Mein)	.95
No. 7X	Ha Chow Mein (Shrimp Chow Mein)	1.00
No. 8	Gai Chow Mein (Chicken Chow Mein)	1.35
EXTRA—Pan Fried Noodles (Canton Style)		.35

EGG FOYUNG

No. 9	Char Sue Foyung Dun (Pork with Eggs and Vegetables)	.90
No. 10	Foyung Ha Dun (Shrimps with Eggs and Vegetables)	.90
No. 11	Gai Foyung Dun (Chicken with Eggs and Vegetables)	.90

(PLEASE ORDER BY NUMBER)

CHOP SUEY
IN VARIOUS MANDARIN STYLES

No. 12	Kna Choy Chow Yuk (Pork and Bean Sprouts)	.85
No. 13	Ha-Chop (Shrimp Chop Suey)	1.00
No. 14	Lun Dao Yuk (Chinese Green Peas with Pork)	1.00
No. 15	Mai Tai Yuk (Water Chestnuts with Pork)	1.10
No. 16	Bo Lo Pai Gwat (Pork Spare Ribs with Pineapple, Vegetables)	.90
No. 17	Lard Du Yuk (Beef Tenderling Chop Suey)	1.10
No. 18	Hun Yun Gai Ding (Chicken, Almond, Mushrooms, Bamboo Shoots)	1.35
No. 19	War Su Ap (Chinese Duck Mandarin Style)	1.35
No. 20	Chow Gai Pan (Chicken Chop Suey—all white meat)	1.35
No. 21	Sub Gum Chop Suey (with Chicken—white meat)	1.35
No. 22	Mow Ko Sai Pen (White Mushroom with Chicken)	1.35
No. 23	Bolo Sai Pan (Chicken with Pineapple)	1.35

FRIED RICE

No. 24	Ha Chow Fan (Shrimp, Fried Rice)	.85
No. 25	Char Sue Chow Fan (Pork, Fried Rice)	.85
No. 26	Gai Chow Fan (Chicken, Fried Rice)	.85
No. 27	Chow Fan (Plain Fried Rice)	.50

A-LA-CARTE

No. 28	Chinese Green Peas (No Meat)	.90
No. 29	Chinese Mixed Greens (Cooked Vegetables—No Meat)	.75

DESSERT

Bo Lo (Chinese Domestic Pineapple)	.40
Chinese Mixed Fruits	.40
Lichee (Preserved Lichee)	.75
Almond (Chinese Almond Cookies)	.40
Tea (Pot) Per Person	.25

(PLEASE ORDER BY NUMBER)

AMERICAN ★ ★ ★ A-LA-CARTE MENU ★ ★ ★ AMERICAN

Appetizers

Seafood Cocktail (Supreme)	.50	Assorted Hors d'Oeuvres		1.00
Fresh Fruit Cocktail (Supreme)	.50	Caviar Canape		1.50
Grapefruit Supreme	.50	Half Avocado on Shell		.50
Shrimp Cocktail (Supreme)	.65	Celery		.35
Avocado Cocktail	.65	Olives		.35
Imp. Fresh Caviar Romanoff	1.50	Marinated Herring		.50
Anchovy Canape	.75	Young Onions		.25
Chopped Chicken Liver	.50	Soup du Jour		.35

Entrees

Curry of Chicken, Steamed Rice, with Condiments—Chutney	1.75
Fried Shrimp, Tropic's Style	.75
Mountain Trout—Sauted in Butter	1.25
Chicken a la King, Shoestring Potatoes	1.25
Half Chicken Saute in Butter, Sweet Potatoes	1.50
Fricasse of Chicken, Rice	2.00
Chicken Liver Saute, French Fried Potatoes	1.35
Fried Half Spring Chicken, Candied Yams	1.25
Shrimps a la Newburg	1.25
Shrimp Curry, Steamed Rice, Chutney Sauce	1.25
Spaghetti, Italian Style	.85
Chili Beans, Tropic's Style	.50
Welsh Rarebit	.75

Roasts

Roast Squab Chicken, Guava Jelly	2.00
Roast Tom Turkey, Cranberry Jelly	1.35
Roast Prime Ribs of Beef Au Jus	1.40

From the Broiler

New York Cut Sirloin Steak, Fresh Mushrooms	1.95
New York Cut Sirloin Steak, Fresh Mushrooms—FOR TWO	4.75
Filet Mignon, Mushroom Sauce	2.25
Spring Lamb Chops, Double Cut (2), Guava Jelly	1.95
Broiled Squab Chicken, Bacon	1.85
Broiled Half Spring Chicken	1.25
Hamburger Steak, Tropic's Style	1.25
French Fried or Mashed Potatoes Included With Above Orders	

Salads

Sugie's Special Health Salad	.75	Stuffed Tomato with Fresh		
Salad Francaise	.85	Jumbo Shrimps		.85
Chiffonade Salad	.85	Shrimp Louie		.85
Stuffed Tomato with		Hearts of Lettuce		.45
Chicken Salad	.85	Avocado Salad		.85
Chicken Salad with Pineapple	.85	Sliced Tomatoes		.45
Chef's Mixed Green Salad		Combination Salad		.85
Julienne of Chicken, Tongue	.85	Fresh Cooked Vegetable Salad		.85
Pineapple and Cottage Cheese	.85	Fresh Fruit Salad		.85

Chicken Salad (all white meat) 1.10

Choice of French, Mayonnaise, or 1,000 Island Dressing

Cold

Assorted Cold Meats	1.25	Sliced Breast of Turkey	1.25
Sugar Cured Ham	.95	Cold Roast Beef	1.00
Smoked Ox Tongue	.95	Sliced Breast of Chicken	1.50

Imported Sardines .75

(All Cold Cuts Served with Sliced Tomatoes and Dill Pickles)

Vegetables In Season

String Beans	.40	French Fried Onions	.60
Fresh Peas	.40	Stewed Tomatoes	.45
Lima Beans	.40	Spinach	.45
Asparagus	.45	Creamed Spinach	.50

Eggs and Omeletts

Ham and Eggs	1.25	Ham Omelette	1.00
Bacon and Eggs	1.00	Spanish Omelette	1.00
Two Eggs, any style	.75	Cheese Omelette	.85
Mushroom Omelette	1.25	Fresh Tomato Omelette	.85
Chicken Liver Omelette	.90	Turkey Omelette	1.25

Sandwiches

Sirloin Steak Sandwich	1.25	Swiss Cheese	.50
Tropics' Special Club Sandwich	1.00	Brisket of Corned Beef	.50
Turkey or Chicken Sandwich	.65	Melted Cheese on Toast	.60
Denver (Open Style)	.65	Combination Ham and Cheese	.85
Deviled Egg	.50	Imported Romanoff Caviar	1.25
Crisp Bacon and Tomato	.65	Cannibal (Tropic's Style)	1.25
Baked Sugar Cured Ham	.50	Hamburger Steak	
Imported Sardine	.65	(Tropic's Style)	.75
Smoked Ox Tongue	.50	Monte Cristo	1.00

Chicken Salad Sandwich .50

Desserts

Crepe Sussette, per order	1.50	Chocolate Sundae	.30
Ice Cream	.25	Butterscotch Sundae	.30
Sherbet	.25	Fresh Fruit Sundae (in season)	.35
Pineapple Upside Down Cake	.25	Melon (in season)	.35
Fresh Sliced Pineapple	.35	Compote of Fresh Fruit	.35

Cheese

Camembert	.35	Philadelphia Cream	.25
Roquefort	.35	American	.25
Imported Swiss	.35	Edam	.35

Hot Beverages

Coffee	cup .10 pot .25	Hot Chocolate (Pot)	.25
Postum	cup .15 pot .25	Green or Black Tea (Pot)	.25
Kaffee Hag	cup .15 pot .25	Milk	.15

Iced Coffee or Tea .20

★ No Service Under 50¢ After 8 P.M. and Persons Not Ordering Will Be Subject to a Charge Not Less Than 50¢ ★

Sugie's Tropics · (Chinese a-la-carte menu) · 421 N. Rodeo Dr., Beverly Hills · 1940s

JAZZ. a-la-Cont.

loco Lotus soup.
pamelo Salad with SHRIMP.
DUCK curry. PINEAPLE / W/R OR BROW Rice
Mango Sticky Rice

APPETIZERS.

CORN WITH BEEF Patfi.   TAPPIOCA BALL WITH. CK.
WONTON WITH SHRIMP.   SEVEN HEVEN.

SOUP.

VEGETABLE SOUP 1.DRY FISH. Pumkin. spinach. GREEN BEAN mucoor.
TOM YUM Salmon. Lemongrass. KAFFIERLIME left. Selmon

Noodle.

GARDEN NOODLE BY. JAZZ.
Spicy BEEF Noodle Soup.

ALL ABOUT EGG.

SON IN LAW EGB.   SHRMP
THAI Scamble egg with meat. PORK CK crab-or 🦐

MY VEGETABLE

STAIR FIRE MORNING glory.
STAIR FINE jICAMA.
ICEBERG WITH FISH sauce.

RICE. DREAM —

TUMARIC FRI RICE WITH WING
Spicy BROWN. FriedRice choice of meat.

Sugie's Tropics 1940s "a-la-carte" menu inspires another by Chef Singsanong • 2015

Bit o' Tokyo · 314 E. 1st St., Los Angeles

El Tepeyac Cafe
Menu

812 No. Evergreen • Los Angeles
(213) 268-1960 • 267-8668

El Tepeyac Café · 812 N. Evergreen, Los Angeles · 1980s

金海

PRIZE WINNING PHOTO BY BOB PLUNKETT R5

Allan Lums'

NEW GRAND EAST CAFE

911 NORTH BROADWAY   LOS ANGELES 12, CALIFORNIA   MAdison 8-4965

Allan Lum's New Grand East Café • 911 N. Broadway, Los Angeles • 1950s

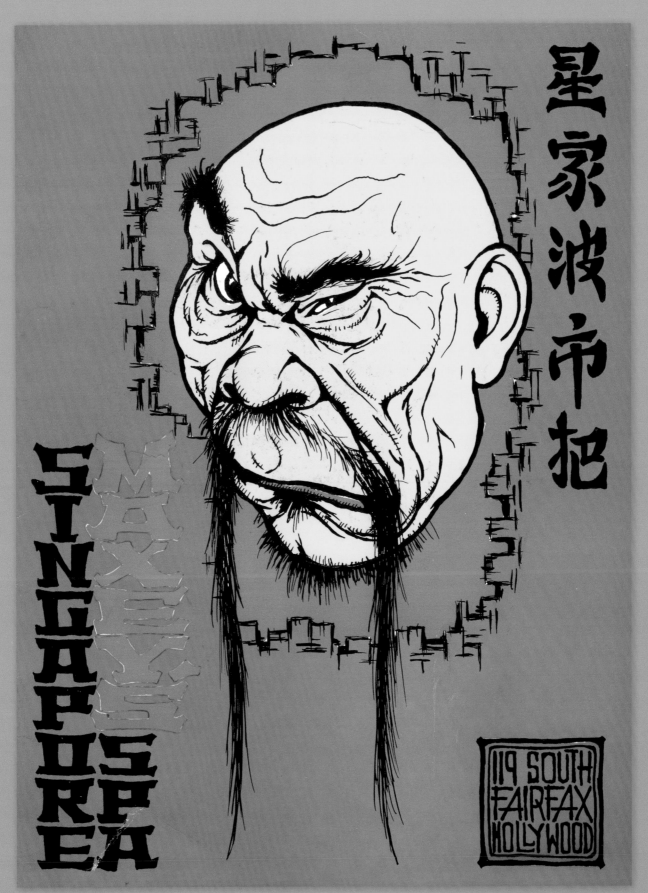

星家波市把

SINGAPORE SPA

119 SOUTH FAIRFAX HOLLYWOOD

Maxey's Singapore Spa • 119 S. Fairfax Ave., Hollywood • 1930s

Bob's Big Boy · 1001 E. Colorado, Glendale · 1950

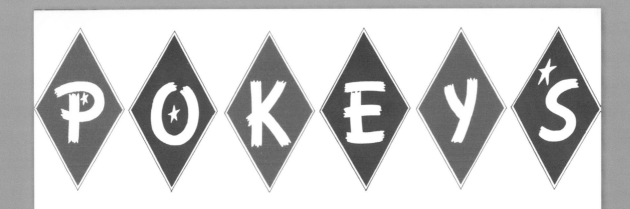

Pokey's · Beverly and Santa Monica Boulevards · 1950s

Tommy's · 6343 Vineland Ave., North Hollywood · 1964

DINO'S LODGE

Dino's Lodge • 8524 Sunset Blvd., West Hollywood • 1959

HERMAN BYRENS'

Dresden Room

Hollywood's New and Smart Rendezous

★ DINNER ★

Shrimp Cocktail Made with Jumbo Louisiana Shrimp
and Served in Our Delicious Cocktail Sauce 60

Our Famous Chef's Salad Bowl

Charcoal Broiled Spring Chicken 1.75
Old Fashioned Beef Stew with Dumplings 1.25
Pot Roast of Beef with Buttered Noodles 1.50
Mixed Seafood Fry 1.25
Grilled Chicken Livers with Bacon 1.25
Fried Jumbo Louisiana Shrimp 1.25
Charcoal Broiled Filet Mignon Steak 2.40
Charcoal Broiled New York Cut Steak 2.40
Charcoal Broiled Ground Sirloin Steak 1.25
Broiled Calf's Liver with Bacon 1.50
Delicious Lake Superior Whitefish 1.00
Broiled Choice Lamb Chops with Bacon 1.75

POTATOES, VEGETABLE, DRINK AND DESSERT
ARE INCLUDED WITH ABOVE ORDERS

Dresden
Dream 75c
•
Zombie 1.25
•
Frozen
Daiquiri 60c

**Our Expertly Prepared Rum Drinks
Are World Famous**

Dresden Room—43—2   Friday, July 13, 1945

Dresden Room · 1760 N. Vermont Ave., Los Angeles · 1945

Toto · 735 S. Figueroa St., Los Angeles · 1960s

TROPICANA

coffee shop

dining room

Tropicana Coffee Shop • 11163 Prairie Ave., Inglewood • 1968

NOTES

In addition to the specific citations listed below, this book relied heavily on general research provided by the following archival sources: *Los Angeles Times, Los Angeles Sentinel, California Eagle, Los Angeles Star, Los Angeles Herald, Pacific Coast Record, The Negro Motorist Green Book*, and the Images of America archival photography book series and its many L.A. titles (among them *Pig'n Whistle, Chinatown in Los Angeles, Historic Hotels of Los Angeles and Hollywood, Los Angeles's Little Tokyo, African Americans in Los Angeles*). The books and research of Jim Heimann were invaluable in providing general history and context, especially *Out With the Stars, California Crazy, May I Take Your Order?*, and *Menu Design in America*, as were the numerous food history articles written by Charles Perry during his time at the *Los Angeles Times*. The recorded lectures of the Culinary Historians of Southern California also provided vital resources and filled in many gaps.

Page 12: In 1949, the historian Arthur M. . . .
Arthur M. Schlesinger, "Food in the Making of America," *Paths to the Present*

Page 12: There's only a century's slice. . .
Soja has written about this over his career, but summarizes it nicely in *My Los Angeles*

Page 14: In his introduction to the 2012 anthology. . .
Jeffrey Pilcher, "Introduction," *Oxford Handbook of Food History*, xvii–xxiii

Page 14: When I was first asked to take a look. . .
Roy Choi, "A Gateway to Feed Hunger: The Promise of Street Food," available at Madfeed.co (http://vimeo.com/75204171). Also see his *L.A. Son*

Page 15: Our first conversations there orbited. . .
For a useful summation of contemporary L.A. food insecurity numbers, see FeedingAmerica.org and Los Angeles Food Policy Council (Goodfoodla.org). See also Mark Vallianatos, "Food Justice and Food Retail in Los Angeles" and Robert Gottlieb, *Reinventing Los Angeles*; Evan Kleiman et al., "How Angelenos Eat Now," Zocalo Public Square talk (http://www. zocalopublicsquare.org/category/events/video-archive/?postId=51713)

Page 26: Before Los Angeles became. . .
Ana Bégué de Packman, *Early California Hospitality*, 13

Page 26: In the eighteenth century, local missions. . .
Gloria Ricci Lothrop, "Los Angeles Originals," 44

Page 26: It was also good land for planting. . .
For a nice summary of early L.A. food culture, see Charles Perry, "Go West, Jean-Francois," *Los Angeles Times*, July 14, 2004

Page 27: In her 1925 memoir *Adobe Days*. . .
Sarah Bixby Smith, *Adobe Days*, 65, 105, 113.

Page 27: The abundance of vegetables, fruit, fish. . .
"Cost of Living in Los Angeles," *Los Angeles Times*, January 1, 1895

Page 27: For those who took the bait. . .
John Moste, "Iowa Picnic in Los Angeles," in Kurlansky, *The Food of a Younger Land*

Page 28: Restaurants in hotels and boarding houses. . .
Harris Newmark, *Sixty Years in Southern California*, 27–28

Page 28: From then on, every year brought more restaurants. . .
All restaurant dates and information culled from early advertisements in the *Los Angeles Times*, the *Los Angeles Herald*, the *Los Angeles Star*, the *California Eagle, El Clamor Público*, and the *Los Angeles Sentinel*.

Page 30: Between the industrializing years of 1880. . .
See Andrew Haley, *Turning the Tables*, 72

Page 32: By 1922, seventy-five percent of the city. . .
Otis M. Wiles, "All Nations Food Served Here," *Los Angeles Times*, January 15, 1922; Lothrop, "Los Angeles Originals;" "Passing of the Kitchen," *Pacific Coast Record*, July 1923, 21; "American Restaurant Publisher Pays Tribute to L.A. Caterers," *Pacific Coast Record*, August 1923, 34

Page 37: The brute function of the menu is obvious. . .
Priscilla Parkhurst Ferguson, *Word of Mouth*, 146-149

Page 37: Instant individualization has been the menu's. . .
Rebecca Spang, *The Invention of the Restaurant*, pages 64–87; "Menus and Their Manufacture," *Caterer and Household Magazine*, March 1885.

Page 37: Chef Jeremiah Tower. . .
Jeremiah Tower, *California Dish*, 55

Page 38: Ruppersberg was riffing on the menu. . .
Robin Lakoff, "Identity a la Carte;" Ann D. Zwicky and Arnold M. Zwicky, "America's National Dish: The Style of Restaurant Menus"

Page 38: The menus on these pages. . .
Arthur Schwartz, "Mangled Menus," 21

Page 38: Menus were early forms of social media. . .
Spang, 86

Page 39: In the broadest sense, menus are media. . .
Roland Barthes, "Toward a Psychosociology of Contemporary Food Consumption;" Georg Simmel, "Sociology of the Meal" in *Simmel on Culture: Selected Writings*; Sidney Mintz, *Tasting Food, Tasting Freedom*, 29–32

Page 46: This all began to change during World War II. . .
James M. Cain, *Mildred Pierce*, 55; Shoson Nagahara, "The Tale of Osato" in *Lament in the Night*, 314–315

Page 47: Women also played key leadership roles in tearooms. . .
Agnes Gleason, "Tea Room Management From The Manager's Point of View;" Jan Whitaker, "Domesticating the Restaurant: Marketing the Anglo-American Home"

Page 47: That was certainly the aim of the Tick Tock. . .
Eleanor Alexander, "The Woman's Place Is in the Tea Room: White Middle-Class American Women as Entrepreneurs and Customers," *Journal of American Culture*; "The Woman Executive," *Restaurant Management*, May 1936

Page 49: The vast majority of Chinese restaurant menus. . .
Hua Hsu, "Wokking the Suburbs"

Page 52: As design historian Jim Heimann has shown. . .
Jim Heimann, *May I Take Your Order?*, 4–6; "Menus and Their Manufacture," *Caterer and Household Magazine*, March 1885

Page 52: When the rise of both urbanization. . .
"Menu Profit-Maker," October 1936

Page 70: Yet these are not the only city maps. . .
Charles Perry, "Dinner in the Exploding City 1830–1930," recorded lecture, Culinary Historians of Southern California;
Erin M. Curtis, "Cambodian Doughnut Shops and the Negotiation of Identity in Los Angeles"

Page 70: Once the Library's collection turns to the 1980s. . .
Charles Jencks, *Heteropolis*; Jonathan Gold, *Counter Intelligence*, vii

Page 71: While the immigrant, working-class restaurants. . .
"Peripatetic Restaurants: One hundred of them in Los Angeles," *Los Angeles Times*, Dec 30, 1901

Page 72: By 1922, the *Los Angeles Times* could run. . .
Otis M. Wiles, "All Nations Food Served Here," *Los Angeles Times*, January 15, 1922; Bertha Anne Houck, "Gastronomic Adventures," *Los Angeles Times*, May 13, 1928

Page 73: Throughout the 1930s, the *Times's*. . .
For example, see "Southland Cafés: World's Choicest Menus Found in Southland," *Los Angeles Times*, April 21, 1937; B.M. Little, "What You Can EAT in Los Angeles," *Los Angeles Times*, September 23, 1934; "Let's Dine Abroad in Los Angeles Metropolitan Area," *The Weekly Publishing Service of Los Angeles*

Page 73: What is now typically used to define. . .
"Who Will Concoct a New Dish To Make Los Angeles Famous," *Los Angeles Times*, May 15, 1910

Page 76: By 1913, the anti-gastronomic smear. . .
Willard Huntington Wright, "Los Angeles—The Chemically Pure," *Smart Set*, March 1913; James M. Cain, "Paradise," *American Mercury*, March 1933

Page 78: The humorist S.J. Perelman picked. . .
S.J. Perelman, "Avocado, or the Future of Eating," *New Yorker*, May 1937; Lois Dwan, "Foreword," *Super Los Angeles Restaurant Guide*

Page 80: Beyond culinary boosterism. . .
Charles Perry, "The Vita-Veg Days," *Los Angeles Times*, March 8, 2000; Elisabeth Webb Herrick, *Curious California Customs*, 111

Page 80: Eating healthy, pure, and raw. . .
Don Dolan, "Food a la Concentrate in Los Angeles," 329; Perelman, "Avocado, or the Future of Eating"

Page 81: An early guru of the L.A. vegetarian menu. . .
Caroline Bates, "Specialities de la Maison: California," *Gourmet*, November 1974

Page 81: In her 1935 tour of Los Angeles restaurants. . .
Elisabeth Webb Herrick, *Curious California Customs*, 34

Page 81: L.A. has always been beefsteak country. . .
Don Dolan, "A Los Angeles Sandwich Called a Taco," 330

Page 87: As was the case with other growing. . .
"Have We Forgotten How To Really Dine?" *Los Angeles Times*, November 26, 1933

Page 88: Perino's had just opened on Wilshire. . .
For a wider context on the history of fine dining in the U.S. see both David Strauss, *Setting the Table for Julia Child: Gourmet Dining in America 1934–1961* and Patric Kuh, *The Last Days of Haute Cuisine: The Coming of Age of American Restaurants*

Page 93: The Ambassador's gourmet sensibilities. . .
See Jim Heimann, *Out With The Stars*

Page 93: In Budd Schulberg's 1942 short story. . .
Budd Schulberg, "A Table at Ciro's," *Some Faces in the Crowd: Short Stories*, 50

Page 94: By the early 1900s menus with middle-class. . .
See Andrew P. Haley, *Turning the Tables*, for a detailed study of this trend and period.

Page 94: In an 1892 feature for the *Los Angeles Times*. . .
Alessandro, "Los Angeles Restaurants," *Los Angeles Times*, April 30, 1892; "Cost of Living in Los Angeles," *Los Angeles Times*, January 1, 1895

Page 95 The democratization of the L.A. restaurant. . .
Charles Perry, "The Cafeteria: An L.A. Original," *Los Angeles Times*, November 5, 2003; Carey McWilliams, *Southern California: An Island on the Land*, 171

Page 96: The lonely had a group home at Clifton's. . .
There have been numerous Clifton's histories, but for a nice primer see Russ Rymer, "The Cafeteria of the Golden Rule,"
Los Angeles magazine, November 1, 2003

Page 98: Working-class and middle-class eating. . .
Raymond Chandler, *The Little Sister*, 79

Page 98: Throughout the 1940s and 1950s, the drive-ins. . .
Kevin Starr, *The Dream Endures: California Enters The 1940s*, 187

Page 99: The rise of the automotive eater. . .
Reyner Banham, *Los Angeles: The Architecture of Four Ecologies*, 95; David Gebhard, "Introduction," *California Crazy: Roadside Vernacular Architecture*, Heimann and Georges, eds.

Page 101: After the white British archivist. . .
Aldous Huxley, *After Many a Summer Dies the Swan*, 9–15

Page 101: The newcomer has stumbled. . .
Duke Ellington, *Music is My Mistress*, 176

Page 103: Many remember the Wich Stand. . .
Josh Sides, *L.A. City Limits*, 133; Buddy Collette, "The Watts Scene," *Central Avenue Sounds*, 160

Page 104: A 1947 menu for Carolina Pines. . .
"Famous Southland Cafés," *Los Angeles Times*, April 19, 1940

Page 106: Heavyweight boxing great Jack Johnson. . .
Richard O. Beyer, "The Hot Bach," *The Duke Ellington Reader*, 226; Donald Bogle, *Bright Boulevards, Bold Dreams*, 139

Page 110: Casa Verdugo pioneered the Californio. . .
Charles Perry, "Piedad Yorba," 52

Page 111: Mexican restaurants like El Progreso. . .
For early histories of L.A. Mexican restaurants, see William Estrada, *The Los Angeles Plaza*, and Gustavo Arellano, *Taco U.S.A.*;
For De Bonzo, see Lee Shippey, "The Lee Side o' L.A.," *Los Angeles Times* November 7, 1932

Page 114: All of this menu minstrelsy. . .
Samantha Barbas, "I'll Take Chop Suey," 670

Page 114: Chop suey and chow mein started. . .
"Who Is the Noodle Lady of Chinatown?" *Los Angeles Times*, September 18, 1904

Page 117: Yet as outwardly directed as many. . .
Charles Perry, "From Chop Suey to Chiu Chow," *Los Angeles Times* February 21, 2007

Page 118: New Chinatown, as it was referred to. . .
Glenna Dunning, "China City—The Busy Little Village North of the Plaza," 5

Page 118: Beginning with the chop suey. . .
Garding Lui, *Inside Los Angeles Chinatown*, 173–184

Page 124: The enduring industry of South Seas-theme restaurants. . .
Dawn Bohulanu Mabalon, "As American As Jackrabbit Adobo," 162

Page 126: Meanwhile immigrants from Thailand . . .
Jean Murphy, "She's Gung Ho for Oriental Cookery," *Los Angeles Times*, August 31, 1967

Page 129: What did get called a revolution. . .
Calvin Trillin, "The Traveling Man's Burden," 456–457; Ruth Reichl, "Dinosaur Under Glass," *Los Angeles Times*, January 4, 1987

Page 129: Nearly a decade earlier. . .
Lois Dwan, "L.A.'s Creative Chefs—The Main Ingredient," *Los Angeles Times*, September 17, 1978

Page 131: Though California cuisine. . .
Ruth Kedzie Wood, *The Tourist's California*, 51

Page 131: Seventy years later, the sentiment was back. . .
Dwan, "L.A.'s Creative Chefs—The Main Ingredient"

Page 132: In what many believe was a media. . .
See Kuh, *The Last Days of Haute Cuisine*; Bates, "*Specialites de la Maison*: California," *Gourmet*, January 1974, 6

Page 134: Menus were the revolution's manifestos. . .
Joyce Goldstein, *Inside the California Food Revolution*, 130–154; Terrail, *A Taste of Hollywood: The Story of Ma Maison*

Page 137: During the culinary shifts of the 1970s and 1980s. . .
Janet A. Flammang, *The Taste for Civilization*, 179

Page 140: In her 1974 review of Kavkaz. . .
Bates, "*Specialites de la Maison*: California," *Gourmet*, 48

Page 141: In 1974, the Los Angeles Women's. . .
Jeanne Cordova, *When We Were Outlaws*, 141–157; Sharon Johnson, "In Los Angeles Saloon, Women Get the Red Carpet,"
Lakeland Ledger, June 1976

CONTRIBUTORS

Ramiro Arvizu and **Jaime Martin del Campo** each learned to cook from their grandmothers when they were growing up in Jalisco, Mexico. In 1998, they opened La Casita Mexicana, their nationally acclaimed restaurant in Bell, and followed it up with the full-service restaurant Mexicano and the fast-casual Flautas, both in the Baldwin Hills Crenshaw Plaza.

Ricardo Jordan Diaz comes from L.A. food royalty. His grandfather started Guadalajara Carnitas in 1968 on Brooklyn Avenue and eight years later launched El 7 Mares on Whittier Boulevard, the original location of what is now a beloved seafood mini-empire across the greater Eastside. As a chef, Diaz has been responsible for the tacos at Guisado's and the tortas at Cook's Tortas, and now runs Tacoteca in Santa Monica, Colonia Taco Lounge in La Puente, and in his hometown of Whittier, Bizarra Capital and Colonia Publica.

Hody's • 3553 S. La Brea Ave., Los Angeles • 1950s

Susan Feniger has been cooking food in the shadow of Bunker Hill since 1998, when she opened Ciudad on a bustling strip of Figueroa with her longtime culinary partner Mary Sue Milliken. It's now a link in their chain of Border Grill restaurants, which began in the bones of their first L.A. creation in 1981, City Café. Feniger, the author of numerous popular cookbooks and a frequent television advocate for the L.A. food scene, now runs Mud Hen Tavern in Hollywood.

Jonathan Gold is the restaurant critic for the *Los Angeles Times*. He won the Pulitzer Prize for criticism in 2007. He is the author of *Counter Intelligence: Where To Eat in Los Angeles* (2000).

Cynthia Hawkins is the proprietor of the legendary Hawkins House of Burgers, the sit-down or takeout institution where she's been the grill guru since the 1980s (her father originally opened it as a food stand). The stacked burgers and piled pastrami that Hawkins makes right across the street from the Nickerson Gardens housing project have made her an L.A. burger-and-sandwich legend, often winning annual Best Of accolades.

Bricia Lopez is co-proprietor of the Guelaguetza restaurant, a 2015 James Beard "American Classics" award winner. She is the co-founder and current president of the Taste of Mexico Association and a frequent blogger and writer on mole, mezcal, and more.

Staci Steinberger is Assistant Curator of Decorative Arts and Design at Los Angeles County Museum of Art (LACMA) and an essayist on twentieth-century design history.

Nancy Silverton won the distinguished James Beard Foundation's Outstanding Chef award in 2014. The debut pastry chef at Spago, Silverton went on to spearhead Campanile, La Brea Bakery, and Osteria and Pizzeria Mozza, all canonical entries into any history of dining out in Los Angeles.

Sarintip "Jazz" Singsanong is the creative force in the kitchen at Jitlada, the beloved East Hollywood restaurant she co-owns that is acclaimed for its spice-spiked Southern Thai cooking. After arriving in L.A. in 1979 from Thailand, she held stints at Emporium and the Biltmore Hotel before she and her brother Suthiporn "Tui" Sungkamee took over Jitlada in 2006. Rousing accolades—everywhere from *L.A. Weekly* to the Food Network—have followed ever since.

Joachim Splichal is co-founder of Patina Restaurant Group, responsible for sixty restaurants and food service operations in performing arts centers throughout the United States. In Los Angeles, where he arrived in 1981 to be executive chef at the Regency Club, his influence as a chef, entrepreneur, and mentor is legendary. His restaurants have included Seventh Street Bistro, Max Au Triangle, and Patina—and no restaurant in L.A. is closer to Los Angeles Central Library than his Café Pinot.

Micah Wexler opened Wexler's Delicatessen in Grand Central Market in 2014 and was quickly anointed the heir apparent of the L.A. pastrami kingdom. His To Live and Dine in L.A. pop-up dining series—which inspired this book's title—was dedicated to L.A. food history. As a restaurant chef, he was behind the stove at Mezze and worked under Joël Robuchon at L'Atelier.

BIBLIOGRAPHY

Alessandro. "Los Angeles Restaurants," *Los Angeles Times*, April 30, 1892.

Alexander, Eleanor. "'Woman's Place Is in the Tea Room': White Middle-Class American Women as Entrepreneurs and Customers." *Journal of American Culture* (32:2) 2009.

Andrews, Colman. "In Celebrations of Restaurants Past." *Los Angeles Times*, September 29, 1994.

Arellano, Gustavo. *Taco USA: How Mexican Food Conquered America*. New York: Simon and Schuster, 2012.

Avins, Mimi. "The Last Days of Spago." *Los Angeles Times*, March 19, 2001.

Azuma, Andrea. "Food Access in Central and South Los Angeles: Mapping Injustice, Agenda for Action." Urban and Environmental Policy Institute, 2007 (http://scholar.oxy.edu/uep_faculty/346).

Banham, Reyner. *Los Angeles: The Architecture of Four Ecologies*. Berkeley: University of California Press, 2009.

Barbas, Samantha. "I'll Take Chop Suey: Restaurants as Agents of Culinary and Cultural Change." *Journal of Popular Culture* (36:4) 2003.

Barthes, Roland. "Toward a Psychosociology of Contemporary Food Consumption." In *Food and Culture*, edited by Carole Counihan and Penny Van Esterik. New York: Routledge, 1997.

Bates, Caroline. "*Specialities de la Maison*: California." *Gourmet*, 1974.

G. G. W. B. D. C.   February 22, 1908

DINNER   In Honor of the

at the GROVE HOTEL   LADIES' READING CLUB

Not by Special Request

Grove Hotel / Dinner in honor of the Ladies' Reading Club
1908

Beebe, Lucius. "Along the Boulevards." *Gourmet*, June 1948.

Bégué de Packman, Ana. *Early California Hospitality: The Cookery Customs of Spanish California*. Glendale: Arthur H. Clark, 1938.

Beyer, Richard O. "The Hot Bach." In *The Duke Ellington Reader*, edited by Mark Tucker and Duke Ellington. New York: Oxford University Press, 1993.

Bogle, Donald. *Bright Boulevards, Bold Dreams: The Story of Black Hollywood*. New York: Random House, 2009.

Bohemian Life magazine. Bohemian Distribution Company, 1939.

Broad, Garrett. "Food Is the Medium: Food Movements, Social Justice and the Communication Ecology Approach." Dissertation, University of Southern California Annenberg School for Communication and Journalism, Los Angeles, 2013.

Bryant, Clora, et al., eds. *Central Avenue Sounds: Jazz in Los Angeles*. Berkeley: University of California Press, 1999.

Cain, James M. *Mildred Pierce*. New York: Knopf, 1941.

_____. "Paradise." *The American Mercury*, March 1933.

Chandler, Raymond. *The Little Sister*. New York: Random House, 1988.

Choi Roy, with Tien Nguyen and Natasha Phan. *L.A. Son: My Life, My City, My Food*. New York: Ecco, 2013.

Choi, Roy. "A Gateway to Feed Hunger: The Promise of Street Food," MAD3 Symposium, August 2013, available at Madfeed. co (http://vimeo.com/75204171).

Christy, George. *The Los Angeles Underground Gourmet*. New York: Simon & Schuster, 1970.

Cobb, Sally Wright. *The Brown Derby Restaurant: A Hollywood Legend*. New York: Rizzoli, 1996.

Coe, Andrew. *Chop Suey: A Cultural History of Chinese Food in the United States*. New York: Oxford University Press, 2009.

Cordova, Jeanne. *When We Were Outlaws: A Memoir of Love & Revolution*. Midway, Florida: Spinsters Ink, 2011.

Counihan, Carole. *Food in the USA: A Reader*. New York: Routledge, 2002.

Curtis, Erin M. "Cambodian Doughnut Shops and the Negotiation of Identity in Los Angeles." In *Eating Asian America: A Food Studies Reader*, edited by Robert Ji-Song Ku, Martin F Manalansan, Anita Mannur. New York: York University Press, 2013.

Dolan, Don. "Food a la Concentrate in Los Angeles." In *Food of a Younger Land*, edited by Mark Kurlansky. New York: Riverhead Books, 2009.

_____. "A Los Angeles Sandwich Called a Taco." In *Food of a Younger Land*, edited by Mark Kurlansky. New York: Riverhead Books, 2009.

Dosti, Rose. *Dear S.O.S.: Favorite Restaurant Recipes from the Los Angeles Times*. Los Angeles: Los Angeles Times, 2001.

Dunning, Glenna. "China City—The Busy Little Village North of the Plaza." *The Branding Iron*, #274 Spring 2014. Los Angeles: The Westerners, Los Angeles Corral.

Dwan, Lois. "Foreword." In *Super Los Angeles Restaurant Guide*. Western Periodicals, 1968.

_____. "L.A.'s Creative Chefs—The Main Ingredient," *Los Angeles Times*, September 17, 1978.

Ellington, Duke. *Music is My Mistress*. New York: Da Capo Press, 1976.

Estrada, William David. *The Los Angeles Plaza: Sacred and Contested Space*. Austin, Texas: University of Texas Press, 2009.

"Feeding America" (http://www.feedingamerica.org/). Chicago: Feeding America.

Ferguson, Priscilla Parkhurst. *Word of Mouth: What We Talk About When We Talk About Food*. Berkeley: University of California Press, 2014.

Fine, Gary Alan. *Kitchens: The Culture of Restaurant Work*. Berkeley: University of California Press, 1966.

Finkelstein, Joanne. *Fashioning Appetite: Restaurants and the Making of Modern Identity*. New York: Columbia University Press, 2014.

Fisher, M.F.K. *The Art of Eating*. New York: Collier Books, 1990.

Flammang, Janet A. *The Taste for Civilization: Food, Politics, and Civil Society*. Urbana: University of Illinois Press, 2009.

Fogelson, Robert M. *The Fragmented Metropolis: Los Angeles, 1850-1930*. Berkeley: University of California Press, 1993.

Fort Street Methodist Episcopal Church Ladies' Aid Society. *Los Angeles Cookery*. Los Angeles: Mirror Print and Binding House, 1881.

Gabaccia, Donna. *We Are What We Eat: Ethnic Food and the Making of Americans*. Cambridge: Harvard University Press, 1998.

Gelakoska, Veronica. *Pig 'n' Whistle*. Charleston: Arcadia, 2010.

Gesner, C.W. "Concerning Restaurants." *Harper's New Monthly Magazine*, April 1866, 591–594.

Gleason, Agnes. "Tea Room Management from the Manager's Point of View," *Journal of Home Economics* (7:4) April 1920.

Glozer, Liselotte F. and William K Glozer. *California in the Kitchen: An essay upon, and a Checklist of, California Imprints in the Field of Gastronomy from 1870-1932. Gathered from many sources*. Berkeley: privately published, 1960.

Gold, Jonathan. *Counter Intelligence: Where to Eat in the Real Los Angeles*. New York: L.A. Weekly Books, 2000.

Goldstein, Joyce. *Inside the California Food Revolution: Thirty Years that Changed Our Culinary Consciousness*. Berkeley: University of California Press, 2013.

Goodwin, Betty. *Hollywood du Jour: Lost Recipes of Legendary Hollywood Haunts*. Santa Monica: Angel City Press, 1993.

Gottlieb, Robert. *Reinventing Los Angeles: Nature and Community in the Global City*. Cambridge: MIT Press, 2007.

Grace, Roger M. "Old Menus Tell the History of Hamburgers in L.A." *Metropolitan News-Enterprise*, January 15, 2004.

Grimes, William. *Appetite City: A Culinary History of New York*. New York: North Point Press, 2009.

Haffner-Ginger, Bertha. *California Mexican-Spanish Cookbook*. Los Angeles: Citizen Print Shop, 1914.

Haley, Andrew P. *Turning the Tables: Restaurants and the Rise of the American Middle Class, 1880-1920*. Chapel Hill: University of North Carolina Press, 2011.

Heimann, Jim. *May I Take Your Order?: American Menu Design, 1920-1960*. San Francisco: Chronicle Books, 1998.

_____. *Out with the Stars: Hollywood Nightlife in the Golden Era*. New York: Abbeville Press, 1985.

Heimann, Jim and Rip Georges, eds. *California Crazy: Roadside Vernacular Architecture*. San Francisco: Chronicle Books, 1985.

Heimann, Jim and Steven Heller. *Menu Design in America: A Visual and Culinary History of Graphic Styles and Design, 1850-1985*. Los Angeles: Taschen, 2011.

Henstell, Bruce. *Sunshine and Wealth: Los Angeles in the Twenties and Thirties*. San Francisco: Chronicle Books, 1984.

Herrick, Elisabeth Webb. *Curious California Customs*. Los Angeles: Pacific Carbon & Print, 1935.

Hines, Duncan. *Adventures in Good Eating: Good Eating Places along the Highways and in Cities of America*. Ithaca: Duncan Hines Institute, 1959.

Houck, Bertha Anne. "Gastronomic Adventures," *Los Angeles Times*, May 13, 1928.

Hsu, Hua. "Wokking the Suburbs." *Lucky Peach*, May 2013.

Huxley, Aldous. *After Many a Summer Dies The Swan*. New York: Harper, 1939.

Jencks, Charles. *Heteropolis: Los Angeles, the Riots and the Strange Beauty of Hetero-Architecture*. London: Academy Editions, 1993.

Johnson, Sharon. "In Los Angeles Saloon, Women Get the Red Carpet," *Lakeland Ledger*, June 1976.

Kleiman, Evan, et al. "How Angelenos Eat Now." Los Angeles: Zocalo Public Square talk November 19, 2013 (http://www.zocalopublicsquare.org/category/events/video-archive/?postId=51713).

Ku, Robert Ji-Song, Martin F. Manalansan, and Anita Mannur, eds. *Eating Asian America: A Food Studies Reader*. New York: New York University Press, 2013.

Kuh, Patric, *The Last Days of Haute Cuisine: The Coming of Age in American Restaurants*. New York: Viking, 2001.

Kurlansky, Mark. *The Food of a Younger Land: A Portrait of American Food before the National Highway System, before Chain Restaurants, and before Frozen Food, When the Nation's Food was Seasonal, Regional, and Traditional, from the Lost WPA Files*. New York: Riverhead Books, 2009.

Lakoff, Robin T. "Identity a la Carte: You Are What You Eat." In *Discourse and Identity*, edited by De Fina, Sciffrin, and Bamberg. Cambridge: Cambridge University Press, 2006.

MacConnell, Scott. "Jean-Louis Vignes: California's Forgotten Winemaker." *Gastronomica: The Journal of Food and Culture* (11:1) 2011.

Markarian, Yervand. *Kavkaz: A Biography of Yervand Markarian*. Palm Springs: self-published, 1996.

McMillan, Tracie. *The American Way of Eating: Undercover at WalMart, Applebee's, Farm Fields, and the Dinner Table*. New York: Scribner, 2012.

McWilliams, Carey. *Southern California: An Island on the Land*. New York: Duell, Sloan & Pearce,1946.

Meehan, Peter, Chris Ying, and David Chang, eds. *Lucky Peach Issue 5: The Chinatown Issue*, Fall 2012. San Francisco: McSweeney's, 2012.

"Menus and Their Manufacture." *Caterer and Household Magazine*, March 1885.

Mintz, Sidney W. *Tasting Food, Tasting Freedom: Excursions into Eating, Culture, and the Past*. Boston: Beacon Press, 1966.

Mortimer, Charles C. and Robert C. Mortimer. *The Menu Guide of Los Angeles*. San Francisco: Corm Enterprises, 1975.

Moste, John. "Iowa Picnic in Los Angeles." In *The Food of a Younger Land*, edited by Mark Kurlansky. New York: Riverhead Books, 2009.

Murphy, Jean. "She's Gung Ho for Oriental Cookery." *Los Angeles Times*, August 31, 1967.

Myers, Betsy. "L.A. Nouvelle Cuisine." *Los Angeles Times*, August 12, 1980.

Nagahara, Shoson. *Lament in the Night*. Translated by Andrew Leong. New York: Kaya Press, 2012.

The Negro Motorist Green Book: International Travel Guide. New York: Victor H. Green, 1949.

Newmark, Harris. *Sixty Years in Southern California, 1853–1913*. New York: Knickerbocker Press, 1916.

O'Neill, Molly, ed. *American Food Writing: An Anthology With Classic Recipes*. New York: Library of America, 2007.

"American Restaurant Publisher Pays Tribute to L.A. Caterers." *Pacific Coast Record*, August 1923.

"Passing of the Kitchen." *Pacific Coast Record*, July 1923.

Pearlman, Alison. *Smart Casual: The Transformation of Gourmet Restaurant Style in America*. Chicago: University of Chicago Press, 2013.

Perelman, S.J. "Avocado, or the Future of Eating." *New Yorker*, May 1, 1937.

Perry, Charles. "Dinner in the Exploding City: Los Angeles 1830–1930." Recorded lecture, September 10th, 2011. Culinary Historians of Southern California (http://vimeo.com/55343240).

_____. "From Chop Suey to Chiu Chow." *Los Angeles Times*, February 21, 2007.

_____. "Go West, Jean-Francois." *Los Angeles Times*, July 14, 2004.

_____. "Piedad Yorba." *Gastronomica: The Journal of Food and Culture*, Summer 2010.

_____. "The Cafeteria: An L.A. Original." *Los Angeles Times*, November 5, 2003.

_____. "The Vita-Veg Days." *Los Angeles Times*, March 8, 2000.

Pilcher, Jeffrey M. *Oxford Handbook of Food History*. New York: Oxford University Press, 2012.

_____. "Was the Taco Invented in Southern California?" *Gastronomica: The Journal of Food and Culture* (8:1) 2008.

Pillsbury, Richard. *From Boarding House to Bistro: The American Restaurant Then and Now*. Boston: Unwin Hyman, 1990.

_____. *No Foreign Food: the American Diet in Time and Place*. Boulder, Colorado: Westview Press, 1998.

Reichl, Ruth. "Dinosaur Under Glass." *Los Angeles Times*, January 4, 1987.

"Menu Profit-Maker." *Restaurant Management*, October 1936.

"The Woman Executive." *Restaurant Management*, May 1936.

Ruiz, Vicki L. "Citizen Restaurant: American Imaginaries, American Communities." *American Quarterly* (60:1) March 2008.

Rymer, Russ. "The Cafeteria of the Golden Rule." *Los Angeles magazine*, November 1, 2003.

Schlesinger, Arthur M. *Paths to the Present*. New York: Macmillan, 1949.

Schulberg, Budd. *Some Faces in the Crowd: Short Stories*. New York: Random House, 1953.

Schwartz, Arthur. "Mangled Menus." *Gastronomica: The Journal of Food and Culture* (1:2) 2001.

Shippey, Lee. "The Lee Side o' L.A." *Los Angeles Times*, November 7, 1932.

Sides, Josh. *L.A. City Limits: African American Los Angeles from the Great Depression to the Present*. Berkeley: University of California Press, 2003.

Simmel, Georg. *Simmel on Culture: Selected Writings*. Edited by David Frisby and Mike Featherstone. London: Sage Publications, 1997.

Smith, Sarah Bixby. *Adobe Days: The Truthful Narrative of the Events in the Life of a California Girl on a Sheep Ranch and in El Pueblo de Nuestra Señora de Los Angeles While It Was Yet a Small and Humble Town*. Lincoln: University of Nebraska Press, 1987.

Soja, Edward. *My Los Angeles: From Urban Restructuring to Regional Urbanization*. Berkeley: University of California Press, 2014.

Spang, Rebecca L. *The Invention of the Restaurant: Paris and Modern Gastronomic Culture*. Cambridge, Massachusetts: Harvard University Press, 2000.

Starr, Kevin. *Material Dreams: Southern California through the 1920s*. New York: Oxford University Press, 1990.

_____. *The Dream Endures: California Enters the 1940s*. New York: Oxford University Press, 1997.

Steinberg, Ellen F. and Jack H. Prost. "A Menu and a Mystery: The Case of the 1834 Delmonico Bill of Fare." *Gastronomica: The Journal of Food and Culture* (8:2) 2008.

Strauss, David. *Setting the Table for Julia Child: Gourmet Dining in America, 1934-1961*. Baltimore: Johns Hopkins University Press, 2011.

The Super Los Angeles Restaurant Guide. Special Libraries Association. Western Periodicals, 1968.

Terrail, Patrick. *A Taste of Hollywood: The Story of Ma Maison*. New York: Lebhar-Friedman Books, 1999.

Tower, Jeremiah. *California Dish: What I Saw (and Cooked) at the American Culinary Revolution*. New York: Free Press, 2003.

Trillin, Calvin. "The Traveling Man's Burden." In *American Food Writing: An Anthology with Classic Recipes*, edited by Molly O'Neill. New York: Library of America, 2009.

Turner, Katherine Leonard. *How the Other Half Ate: A History of Working Class Meals at the Turn of the Century*. Berkeley: University of California Press, 2014.

Vallianatos, Mark. "Food Justice and Food Retail in Los Angeles." *Ecology Law Currents*, 36 (June 25, 2009): 186–194. (http://elq.typepad.com/currents/2009/06/currents36-05-vallianatos-2009-0625.html)

Voltz, Jeanne and Burks Hamner. *The L.A. Gourmet: Favorite Recipes from Famous Los Angeles Restaurants*. Garden City: Doubleday, 1971.

"Let's Dine Abroad in Los Angeles Metropolitan Area." *The Weekly Publishing Service of Los Angeles*, January 17–23, 1937.

Weiss, Milton. *Star Grazing in Hollywood: Reminiscence of a Beverly Hills Restaurateur*. San Jose: Writers Club Press, 2001.

Whitaker, Jan. "Domesticating the Restaurant: Marketing the Anglo-American Home." In *From Betty Crocker to Feminist Food Studies: Critical Perspectives on Women and Food*, edited by Arlene Avakian. Amherst: University of Massachusetts Press, 2005.

Wiles, Otis M. "All Nations Food Served Here." *Los Angeles Times*, January 15, 1922.

Williams-Forson, Psyche A. *Building Houses out of Chicken Legs: Black Women, Food, and Power*. Chapel Hill: University of North Carolina Press, 2006.

Wood, Ruth Kedzie. *The Tourist's California*. New York: Dodd, Mead, 1914.

WPA Writers' Program of the Work Projects Administration in Southern California. *Los Angeles: A Guide to the City and Its Environs*. New York: Hastings House, 1951.

Wright, Willard Huntington. "Los Angeles—The Chemically Pure." *Smart Set*, March 1913.

Zwicky, Ann D. and Arnold M. Zwicky. "America's National Dish: The Style of Restaurant Menus." *American Speech* (55:2) 1980.

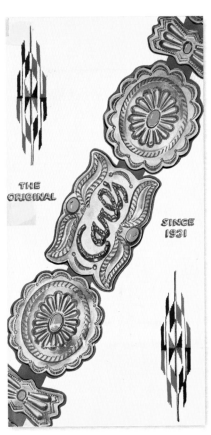

Carl's • (various locations) • 1930s

INDEX

ACKNOWLEDGMENTS

This book would not have been possible without the unflinching support, belief, and vision of City Librarian John F. Szabo and Library Foundation President Ken Brecher. The Foundation's Rebecca Shehee is the reason that projects like To Live and Dine in L.A. actually see the light of day. I am grateful to them all.

Among the hundreds of incredible librarians who make the Los Angeles Public Library such a special and invaluable resource, I am especially indebted to those who shepherd and steer the menu collection that we mined for this book. Thank you to Research and Special Collections Manager Ani Boyadjian and her dedicated team for being our guides. Librarian and Digitization Coordinator Kim Creighton was invaluable to the reproduction of the menus on these pages (and incredibly patient!), and Librarian Emma Roberts was a major archival treasure for both me and my students. Librarian Jacquie Welsh joined us as we neared the finish line, but was an immediate lifesaver.

Big thanks go to Chef Roy Choi for sharing his passions with us and teaching us how to think about menus, to Natasha Phan for keeping the dots connected, to Rakaa Iriscience for the friendship and matchmaking, and to the 3 Worlds Café team for always welcoming us with open hearts.

Midway through the project, Paul Abram made a very generous donation to the Library's collection of his family archive of Lord Printing Company materials. We are honored to be able to share parts of it with you in this book. Public thanks is also due to a generous private collector who prefers to remain anonymous, but graciously loaned some rare menus to this project; each menu is noted in its caption as "Anonymous Donor."

My USC doctoral students Perry Johnson and Inna Arzumanova tirelessly kept the whole research project afloat with patience and dedication. My USC research team included the sharp investigative eyes of Becca Johnson, Andrea Wenzel, Bianca Nasser, Jelena Grozdanich, Ashley Warner, Samantha Helou, and Sarah McAllister (on loan to us from Harvard-Westlake School). They did all of the primary source research that allowed me to write this book, scouring the archives of the *Los Angeles Times*, the *Los Angeles Herald*, the *Los Angeles Star*, *La Opinion*, the *California Eagle*, and the *Pacific Coast Record*, among many other sources.

Thank you, also, to Nathan Masters, Victoria Bernal, David Ulin, Chris Nichols, Aubrey Adams, Jim Heimann, Ryan Mungia, Oliver Wang, Charles Perry, Bill Deverell, Laura Shapiro, and Dana Polan, who all provided invaluable tips and feedback.

As always, Amy Inouye of Future Studio was an author's dream designer, and Paddy Calistro and Scott McAuley of Angel City Press were dream editors and publishers.

My gratitude goes to my USC colleague and friend Sarah Banet-Weiser for believing in the project, to the USC Annenberg School for helping me find extra time to work on it, and to the Annenberg Micro Seminar Fellowship for its funding support of an early brainstorm session.

My two graces, Ceci and Yamila, are the secret co-authors of this book. There will never be enough space to thank them for what they do for me.

ABOUT THE AUTHOR

Josh Kun is an Associate Professor in the Annenberg School for Communication and Journalism at the University of Southern California. His previous collaboration with the Library was the award-winning *Songs in the Key of Los Angeles*. He has written for the *New York Times, Los Angeles Times,* and many other publications. He is the author and an editor of several books, including *Audiotopia: Music, Race, and America, Tijuana Dreaming: Life and Art at the Global Border,* and *Black and Brown Los Angeles: Beyond Conflict and Coalition.* As a curator he has worked with the Grammy Museum in Los Angeles, the Contemporary Jewish Museum in San Francisco, Santa Monica Museum of Art, and the National Museum of Jewish History in Philadelphia. He also curated *Songs in the Key of L.A.* in 2013 and *To Live and Dine in L.A.* in 2015, exhibitions that originated at Los Angeles Central Library.

The Bagel • 1052 S. Fairfax, Los Angeles • 1960s

To Live and Dine in L.A.
Menus And The Making of the Modern City
From the Collection of the Los Angeles Public Library

By Josh Kun
Foreword by Roy Choi

Design by Amy Inouye, Future Studio

Copyright © 2015 The Library Foundation of Los Angeles

ISBN-13 978-1-62640-028-3

Kun, Josh.
  To live and dine in L.A. : menus and the making of the modern city / by Josh Kun ; foreword by Roy Choi ; from the Collection of the Los Angeles Public Library.
    pages cm
  Includes bibliographical references and index.
  Summary: "To Live and Dine in L.A. is a project of the Library Foundation of Los Angeles, based On The Menu Collection of The Los Angeles Public Library. This lavish pictorial work celebrates the rich — and untold — history of restaurants and food in the City of Angels"—Provided by publisher.
  ISBN 978-1-62640-028-3 (hardcover : alk. paper)
  1. To live and dine in LA 2. Restaurants--California--Los Angeles. I. Los Angeles Public Library. II. Title. III. Title: To live and dine in Los Angeles.
  TX909.2.C22L678 2015
  647.95794'94—dc23
                2015014005

Published by Angel City Press

    2118 Wilshire Blvd. #880
    Santa Monica, California 90403
    +1.310.395.9982
    www.angelcitypress.com

Printed in Canada

LOS ANGELES PUBLIC LIBRARY

Richlor's Attains High Rating

Fine service recognized during nine years of operation

A<small>FTER</small> nine years of service to the public, Richlor's looks back with pride to a continuous record of satisfaction delivered to a patronage that rates well above the average in its appreciation of fine food. Those qualified to make comparisons place Richlor's alongside Lawry's and Stear's for Steaks in quality, a position we prize. To sustain and augment this record has been the constant aim of the management and the entire organization which is imbued with the desire to make your every visit here thoroughly enjoyable. To accomplish this end, food is the primary consideration—piping hot when it is supposed to be served hot, and cold as cold can be when the dish calls for it. Richlor's are keenly aware of their responsibilities to their guests, for no success is ever attained in the operation of a restaurant unless the food is excellent and unless it is served in a manner and in surroundings that are conducive to comfort and enjoyment. From the time you drive up to an off-the-street entry under a large motor canopy, and until you have your car delivered to you again by anxious-to-please attendants, your every desire is considered important. The lobby is commodious and comfortable if you must wait, there is a marvelous seafood bar for those who like an appetizer before dinner, the cocktail bar is roomy and modern, and the general atmosphere of the dining room is relaxing and pleasing. But the greatest emphasis is placed upon the food which includes purchasing the finest and preparing it under ideal conditions by those who have had long training in their various specialties. We at Richlor's are happy to be your hosts and we all hope you will visit us again and again.

Historic Old Main Street and the Good Fellows Grotto

When Dad and Ma used to ride the street cars to the theatre they had their supper and after theatre parties at the Good Fellows Grotto. Then, there were five theatres on Main Street from First Street to Sixth. No movies, mind you, but the real old drammer—(drah-ma to you!)

Way back in 1905

Yes sir-ee, what a time. We boys in our derby hats, white "belmont" collars and high button shoes used to cut quite a swath down the old street of a Saturday night. When we were really on the loose we smoked a box of sweet caporal cigarettes in an evening with intermittent doses of sen-sen. Then to swagger into the Good Fellows like men-of-the-world and order a feast from your regular waiter who called you by name—oh heavens, what bliss!

Will you believe me when I say that this self-same restaurant is still in the same place under the same family management and serving the same high quality foods right now? It has all the intrigue we find in things of the gay nineties; all the soft whispering excitement of being out after ten of an evening in the early 1900's. There is no other music than the hum of conversation and the laughter of well-fed, contented human beings.

A Look into the Past

Why don't you and your friends visit us some evening; have your supper and then stroll up and down dear old Main Street. See the Pacific Electric Building built by Henry E. Huntington in 1906; see the old Burbank Theatre where Mme. Modjeska, T. Daniel Frawley, Phosa McAllister and H. S. Duffield were wont to "trod the boards" around 1899; where Fay Bainter played little girl roles in support of William Desmond about 1906. See the old Westminster hotel in all the glory of 1891— grand staircase and all. Then, there's the old Belasco Theatre—now the Follies showing nearly naked girls to the adenoidal young. But around 1910 you could see Lewis Stone, Charlie Ruggles, Hobart Bosworth and others in a variety of plays from "Julius Ceasar" to "Charlie's Aunt"—you bet your bottom dollar! And don't miss Holmes Book store right next door. Boy, if you love books, that smell will get you!

Main Street Today

You'll have fun watching the various amusements offered the Main Street regulars. Medicine men; fortune tellers; "scientific" museums; honest pawn shops and girls. Girls in shows; girls in shooting galleries; girls in hock shops; girls in beer joints; girls in and out of everything. Interesting ... well, you just take a stroll as I have suggested and you'll agree with one of our best writers when he said: "Main Street in Los Angeles is the most interesting street in the world."

Main Dining Room

One of Many Private Booths

Don't forget to see the City Hall and the Civic Center; the old Plaza and Olvera Street; Old Chinatown and New—all easily reached on foot from the Good Fellows.

We have specialized in Sea Foods, Steaks and Chops since 1905 and sincerely believe our dishes cannot be equalled anywhere at any price. Many of our customers have been dining with us for over thirty years. As one man of twenty-eight years standing said, "I have not had one inferior dish served me here at the Good Fellows."

Our soups and sauces have delighted epicurean men and women for years—an added zest that is the Grotto's very own style.

Wines and liquors have always played a dignified part in the rounding out of a fine meal. The Grotto is proud of its list and to the knowing, it speaks for itself. Thirty-six Fine Wines to choose from.

When Good Fellows get together at ...... *the Good Fellows it's a perfect meeting.*

Famous Quotations

Let us have wine and women,
mirth and laughter . . .
Sermons and soda water the
day after.
                    BYRON

One sip of this will bathe the droop-
ing spirits in delight beyond the bliss
of dreams.
                    MILTON

Let us eat and drink, for
tomorrow we die.
                    ISAIAH XXII - 13

I drink when I have occasion and
sometimes when I have no occasion.
—Don Quixote.
                    CERVANTES

A jug of wine . . .
                    OMAR KHAYYAM

All human history attests that happiness for man, the hungry sinner,
since Eve ate apples much
depends on dinner.
                    BYRON

Oh hour, of all hours, the most
bless'd upon earth,
The blessed hour of our dinner.
                    LORD LYTTON

The discovery of a new dish does
more for the happiness of man than the
discovery of a new star.
                    BROLLOT SAVARIN

History of Paris Inn

Established first in old Los Angeles,
 'Twas just twelve years ago.
A unique idea in restaurants,
 Paris Inn began to grow.

A clever chef, Pedroli,
 Of international fame,
And an operatic singer,
 Bert Rovere by name.

As partners, made their restaurant
 An artistic rendez-vous.
For all who work at Paris Inn
 Are artists through and through.

Entertainers, waiters, bus-boys,
 All know how to dance and sing.
This feature in itself
 Is a very novel thing.

In Bohemian surroundings,
 In a spot of unique zest,
The partners wished the public
 To have nothing but the best.

The best of food and music
 Soon made this cafe known,
And on its merits only
 Paris Inn has grown and grown.

To enjoy its atmosphere
 Patrons by the thousands came;
Though often moved and changed,
 Its ideal is still the same.

They give the public what it wants,
 That's why success they win;
This in brief's the history
 Of the famous Paris Inn.

ALOHA

You have just crossed the gangplank into another world—into a segment of Paradise—or such is the illusion that we of THE LUAU hope to create. And truly it is more than an illusion for there is authenticity in the adventure you are about to experience. What befalls you now is made of more than dream stuff.

The repast that will be served you, the feast, is the LUAU of the South Seas recreated for you. The cuisine is in every respect PA-KE and replete with every delicate nuance of flavor that characterizes the superb cookery of The Islands.

Both food and drink are prepared under the matchless guidance of one of our associates. The feast that he has prepared for you at the Luau will speak for itself.

Our drink specialties, Island Symphonies of rare and distinguished rums, irresistibly claim your fullest respect which is best shown by drinking slowly and reverently.

Yes, the comestibles and potables themselves will fluently convey their own merits and meaningfulness, but the surroundings may warrant some explanation.

When the Luau was in the planning we dispatched none other than "Stefooma" himself to The South Seas and The Orient to gather much of the decor for our restaurant. The chairs were found in Hong Kong. The table tops other than those in the Bar which are authentic hatch covers, are slabs cut from giant Monkey-Pod trees, Koa, Ear-Pod and Tamarind, the trunks of which were brought laboriously out of the Hawaiian hills on the backs of natives and milled in Papaaloa.

The structural bamboo in the building has been installed and hand-wrapped by Philippine craftsmen. Of special interest is the square bamboo obtained by forcing the trees to grow through square iron collars.

The tiles you see are of Chinese soapstone. The globular lanterns are actually glass floats from Japanese fish nets. The decorative rocks on the back bar are mainly volcanic, some being not rock at all but wood . . . petrified wood. The large shells back of the bar are (or were) man eating clams from the Indian Ocean. Some weighed 650 pounds alive. Your ash tray is of the same species. Presumably the smaller ones eat smaller men.

The dried and hollow fishes hung from the ceilings are blow fish and the hanging objects which look like bananas are—well, they're bananas. The mattings on the walls and ceilings are mainly NEPA, NIIU and PANDANA, all of which are hand-woven of cocoanut palm and are from Samoa and Tahiti.

The Tapas (figured panels on our walls) are from Fugi, Tonga-Tabu, Tahiti, Samoa and Hawaii. These Tapas are made from mulberry bark and hand-blocked with native vegetable dyes.

You will readily identify the tropical plants by their common names: Elephant Ears, Lobster Claws, Violins, Birds of Paradise, Orchids and Torches, the latter being of the genue ginger.

Of great interest are the TIKIS, the large and delightfully unlovely carvings about you. A TIKI is a pagan god, an idol. While today a majority of our South Seas neighbors are of the Christian faith, respect and deference is still extended to the gods of the elders, and we have with us here at THE LUAU such TIKIS as the god of rain, the god of sun, the god of war and others.

The especially large-mouthed TIKI is the god of drink, The Loud-Mouthed One. The TIKI with the most ample tummy is our favorite, perhaps, because he is the god of good food.

Now, the feast — The Luau — is about to begin.

Aloha! Komo Mai No Ka Ha-le. The words mean, simply: "Welcome! Come in, my house is yours."

                    [Signed] STEFOOMA,
                    High-Talking Chief
                    of The Luau.

Free Souvenir Menus Available at Our Gift Shop

Confrerie de la Chaine des Rotisseurs

In the year 1248 under St. Louis IX, King of France, the Guild "Des Ayeurs" was founded. This Guild expanded during the centuries and in 1610 by Royal Consecration was granted the Coat of Arms of Maîtres des Rotisseurs. In 1950 gastronomists and professionals took the oath to revive the Society and the Coat of Arms of the Rotisseurs were again raised to its full and just rights. The Brotherhood Chain of the Rotisseurs has for its purpose to unite gastronomes and professionals fervent of good living and the Cuisine of "De la Broche" in particular.